Writing Grant Proposals That Win

~

THIRD EDITION

Edited by
Deborah Ward, MA, CFRE
President
Ward and Associates
Lancaster, Pennsylvania

JONES AND BARTLETT PUBLISHERS
Sudbury, Massachusetts
BOSTON   TORONTO   LONDON   SINGAPORE

World Headquarters
Jones and Bartlett Publishers
40 Tall Pine Drive
Sudbury, MA 01776
978-443-5000
info@jbpub.com
www.jbpub.com

Jones and Bartlett Publishers International
Barb House, Barb Mews
London W6 7PA
UK

Jones and Bartlett Publishers Canada
6339 Ormindale Way
Mississauga, Ontario
L5V 1J2

Jones and Bartlett's books and products are available through most bookstores and online booksellers. To contact Jones and Bartlett Publishers directly, call 800-832-0034, fax 978-443-8000, or visit our website www.jbpub.com.

Substantial discounts on bulk quantities of Jones and Bartlett's publications are available to corporations, professional associations, and other qualified organizations. For details and specific discount information, contact the special sales department at Jones and Bartlett via the above contact information or send an email to specialsales@jbpub.com.

Library of Congress Cataloging-in-Publication Data

Hale, Phale D.
   Writing grant proposals that win / by Phale D. Hale, Jr. ; edited by Deborah Ward.—3rd ed.
      p. cm.
   Previous ed.: Alexandria, VA : Capitol Publications, © 1992.
   ISBN 0-7637-2930-2
   1. Proposal writing for grants. 2. Fund raising. I. Ward, Deborah L., 1957–   II. Title.
   HG177.H35 2006

                                    2005017206

Production Credits

Chief Executive Officer: Clayton Jones
Chief Operating Officer: Don W. Jones, Jr.
President, Higher Education and Professional Publishing: Robert W. Holland, Jr.
V.P., Sales and Marketing: William J. Kane
V.P., Design and Production: Anne Spencer
V.P., Manufacturing and Inventory Control: Therese Connell
Acquisition Editor: Kevin Sullivan
Associate Editor: Amy Sibley
Production Director: Amy Rose
Production Editor: Renée Sekerak
Production Assistant: Rachel Rossi
Marketing Director: Alisha Weisman
Marketing Manager: Emily Ekle
Manufacturing Buyer: Amy Bacus
Composition: Publishers' Design & Production Services, Inc.
Cover Design: Timothy Dziewit
Printing and Binding: Malloy Incorporated
Cover Printing: Malloy Incorporated

Printed in the United States of America
09 08 07 06 05   10 9 8 7 6 5 4 3 2 1

Contents

CHAPTER ONE

The Conceptual Framework   1

CHAPTER TWO

Other Important Features   21

CHAPTER THREE

Using Technology   29

❀

CHAPTER FOUR

Understanding Federal RFPs   39

❀

CHAPTER FIVE

The Review Process   53

❀

CHAPTER SIX

Private-Sector Funding   57

❀

CHAPTER SEVEN

The Politics of Grantsmanship   69

❀

CHAPTER EIGHT

Never Accept Failure   75

CHAPTER NINE

Sample Proposals 77

APPENDIX A

Federal and Private Websites 211

APPENDIX B

Resources 215

APPENDIX C

State Single Points of Contact 223

APPENDIX D

Sample Budget Form and Narratives and Federal Application Forms 229

~

Acknowledgments

There are several people I need to thank who contributed to this edition. First, thanks to Phale Hale, for providing the original text and the *Second Edition*, and to Kevin Sullivan, the Jones and Bartlett Acquisitions Editor who gave me the opportunity to update it and create the *Third Edition*. Renée Sekerak, the Production Editor, did a wonderful job guiding me through the publishing process. I appreciate all of your help!

Thanks also to the following people who played a critical role in helping me put the Sample Proposals chapter together: Ginny Lays, Joe Havellana III, C. Robert May, Barbara Ashbrook, Dr. Elizabeth Riorden, Jeannie Floyd, David Makepeace, and the Florida Learn and Serve Program. I also wish to acknowledge the staff members at various foundations who helped me secure permission to use their Websites as samples.

And last, special thanks to Megan Weagley and Chris Lewis for supporting me through the entire project.

~

Introduction

In Phale Hale's *Writing Grant Proposals That Win, Second Edition*, he states that writing grant proposals is "an art, not a science." I tend to take a slightly different view of proposal writing—that it is *both* an art and a science. I believe that everyone can learn the "science" of proposal writing. At times, it's the "art" part that seems a bit difficult.

This book is designed to provide you with the fundamental basics of proposal writing: how to understand a Request for Proposal (RFP), how reviewers function, and what reviewers look for in proposal sections, as well as tips to help you create winning sections, how technology can help you with a more "reader-friendly" proposal, and resources for you to use to find out about the vast number of funding opportunities that exist.

This edition goes through the most common proposal sections step-by-step, starting with the executive summary, followed by needs statement, goals and objectives, activities, personnel, and budget. Then, additional sections that are sometimes required are discussed. It is important to keep in mind that a standard grant form still does not exist. You will have to carefully read each and every RFP for public funders, and all giving guidelines for private funders, to make sure that your proposal responds appropriately. The sample grants in the last chapter illustrate the differences in several grant programs while providing you with genuine proposals that resulted in grant awards.

This edition has been updated to reflect the changes in the grant process since 1999. The grants process has become more sophisticated and now relies heavily on technology. An increasing number of both private and public funders are turning to online applications and eliminating paper proposals. The Internet is a tool that today's grantseeker cannot do without. Even the events of September 11, 2001, have had an impact on the proposal submission process for federal grants. All of these topics are covered in this new edition.

In the appendices you will find a number of helpful grantseeking resources—Websites and information about books, guides, directories, newsletters, and online databases. Also, I've included an updated list of Single Points of Contact, current federal forms, and some sample budgets and budget narratives for you to use as templates if the funder you are applying to does not provide a sample format to use.

My hope is that this book will provide you with the tools that you need to make the "science" part of the grants process easier. Combine this with your own "art", or creativity, and you will craft proposals that win!

Deborah Ward, MA, CFRE

CHAPTER ONE

The Conceptual Framework

Writing a grant proposal is an exercise in logic. Similar to a lawyer pleading a case or a debater making a point, the proposal writer must build a logical argument that justifies funding. The proposal's points must be well thought out, and the argument must flow rationally through all of the proposal's various sections, building the impression that funding of the proposed project is reasonable, sensible, and desirable.

The main reason proposals fail is that they don't make sense. They are poorly conceived, are not supported by documented needs, and do not have sound logic backing the request.

In this chapter, we will examine the general structure of a grant proposal and learn to build a conceptual framework that flows rationally from point to point and makes a logical case for funding. This framework can be adapted to meet the requirements of various funding sources, including federal agencies, foundations, and corporations. (*See Chapters Four and Five for guidance on applying to federal funders and Chapter Six for lessons in dealing with private-sector funders.*)

The basic concept is very simple. A proposal:

✔ Identifies a problem (Need Statement);

✔ Explains the project's intent to resolve the problem and sets measurable markers of success (Objectives);

✔ Describes steps that will be taken to reach the objectives (Activities);

✔ Introduces the individuals who will carry out the activities (Personnel);

✔ Outlines procedures for measuring the project's success in meeting its objectives (Evaluation); and

✔ Estimates the funding needed to carry out the project (Budget).

The key to success is in creating a proposal that pulls all these elements together and organizes them around a strong, logical plan. We'll take it step by step, illustrating all points with examples from a fictional proposal to the Substance Abuse and Mental Health Services Administration's Youth Drug Prevention Program.

NEED STATEMENT

The need statement is the most important part of any proposal. Unfortunately, it also is often the most poorly written section.

The need statement has two purposes:

1. To explain how your needs meet the funder's interests and priorities; and

2. To establish the specific problem the proposed project will address.

A public funder usually gives some indication of the types of projects it funds, either through a specific Request for Proposal (RFP) or a Notice of Funding Availability (NOFA). In the case of private-sector funders, the information is provided through general giving guidelines or an annual report.

No matter in what form the funder explains its interests, it is seeking proposals that specifically address them. The first thing a proposal should do is prove that it does address those interests.

This seems simple but frequently is neglected. For example, the U.S. Department of Education (ED) has a Magnet Schools Assistance Program, which helps school districts establish magnet schools as part of a federally approved desegregation plan. Unfortunately, many districts neglect to establish their eligibility for funding by describing their desegregation plans and the role that the magnet schools will play in the plan. ED rejects many applications for this basic flaw.

Base your need statement on the funder's RFP or guidelines, establishing your eligibility to apply and identifying which of the funder's interests you are attempting to address.

Be specific. If you are applying for a youth drug prevention grant, say you are requesting funds to reduce drug use among teenagers in your high schools. Don't make proposal reviewers guess what the project is about, tell them!

Example:

There is a need for the Sun Flower School District to reduce marijuana use among its students. This application focuses on the priority of developing and disseminating knowledge at the services delivery level by creating an on-site drug treatment clinic within the Sun Flower School District. This clinic will provide counseling and treatment for the 300 students in the Sun Flower School District who have been identified for using marijuana.

Once you have started your specific need, the second function of the need statement is to prove that need. Proof of need can take a number of forms. You can present numerical data, such as police records showing 200 recent arrests in the district for using or selling drugs. You can compare the records for the current year with those for previous years to show the problem is increasing.

An effective method for presenting this comparison is a simple bar graph that shows arrests for drug use or sales over the past five years (see Figure 1.1). It should be accompanied by a narrative explanation.

Example

According to the Police Department Drug Prevention Unit, the number of arrests for drug-related activities has increased over the past five years, rising from no drug activity in 1999 to 200 arrests in 2002. The unit shows the number of persons engaged in drug use in 2003 at 300. Figure 1.1 illustrates the dramatic growth in drug use.

You also can show how marijuana use has increased at a greater rate than other drug use by comparing the specific and general statistics in a line graph (see Figure 1.2) with an explanation.

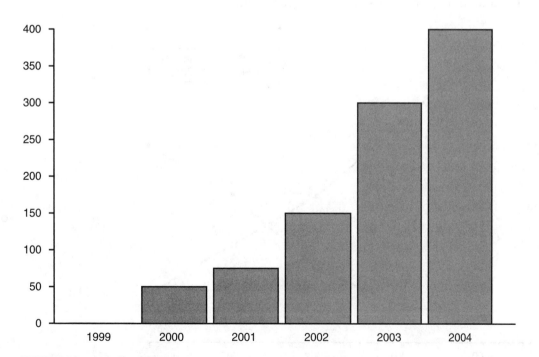

FIGURE 1.1   Number of Youth Engaged in Drug Use, 1999–2004*

*The statistics in this figure are fictitious.

Example:

This is in contrast to a general leveling off of usage of drugs other than marijuana. In fact, the number of users of drugs other than marijuana has decreased. Figure 1.2 contrasts marijuana use to that of other drug use.

Once we prove the district has a serious problem concerning drugs, particularly marijuana use, we must establish that it is a particular problem among high school students. Let's assume the police department does not keep records that would allow us to determine how many of the arrests were for high school students in the district, or that indicate the number of persons tested positive for drug use. Where can we obtain accurate data?

We can generate our own data tailored for the application by surveying high school students' opinions of the problem's severity. By going directly to the students, we obtain data that is specific to the funder's goal—to reduce the negative effects of drug use on students—and directly relates to the problem we are addressing. We may find that 60 percent of students in the target school have experimented with drugs.

But even if there is not enough relevant data to establish need, or time to develop project-tailored data, we still can find useful evidence. We can quote newspaper articles on drug problems. Or we can interview prominent members of the community and key public officials, such as the police chief, counselors, or teachers. We can go to our local Council on Drug and Alcohol Abuse and ask them about the incidence of drug use in our community. Even if we can't find sufficient data to prove need, such local reporting and expert testimony helps support our analysis of the severity and impact of the problem on the community.

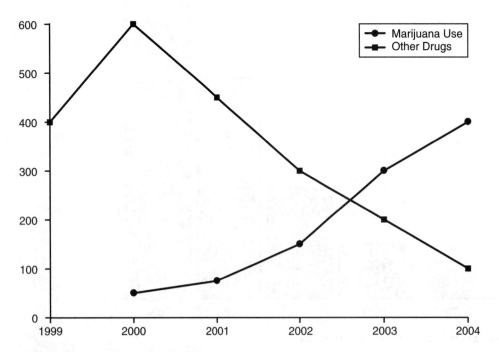

FIGURE 1.2 Marijunana Use v. Other Drug Use*

*The statistics in this figure are fictitious.

We also can use the Internet to search for information that supports our claims by conducting a simple search of the Internet on the topic of youth and drugs and collecting a list of articles on the subject and issues associated with them. Such articles can help document the extent of the problem with youth drug use and ways of combating the problem. An Internet search can give you enough information on almost any topic to make your need statement authoritative. See Figure 1.3 for the results of a search on youth and drugs.

Although it is appropriate to cite national statistics and indicate how the results of your project may help develop national solutions, your proposal must give a clear picture of an urgent need in the community in which the program will operate. Acknowledging a strong national need does not relieve you of the burden of proving there is as severe a need in your own community.

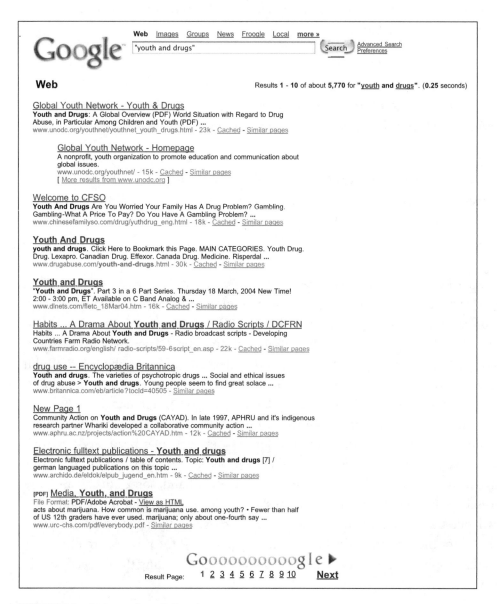

FIGURE 1.3 Internet Search Results

OBJECTIVES

Objectives are simply the intent of the project. They indicate what it will achieve and the time it will need to reach its goals. Objectives should be concise, specific, measurable, and relate directly to the need. In fact, the objectives should be an extension of the need statement. In the need statement, we described the current situation. Now, in the objectives statement, we must describe what the situation will be after we implement our project.

In our proposal, if the need is to reduce drug use among students in the high school, the objective should indicate how much the project will reduce drug use in the school, in what time frame, and how it will measure results.

Measurement should be in terms of the data we used to establish the need. Since we established the need using arrest records and student surveys, we should set objectives that show the project influenced those same measures.

Examples:

1. *By the end of the project, according to official police records, the number of incidents involving drug use will have decreased by 10 percent as compared to data for the base year, 1999.*

2. *By the end of the project, the number of surveyed students at the target school who respond that they have experimented with drugs will decrease by 50 percent from the results of the comparable survey conducted in May of the year prior to project implementation.*

The relationship between need and objectives seems like simple common sense, but unfortunately, many proposal writers fail to make the connection. An example would be a hazardous materials training project for emergency medical services (EMS) staff whose objectives relate exclusively to the general public and does not mention EMS staff training. Of course, the applicant could argue that the public needs this type of training in the aftermath of September 11, 2001, but the reviewer will only wonder why they were hesitant to set goals for their own staff if none have participated in this type of training. Needs and the objectives must go hand in hand.

The whole point of setting objectives is to show the funder—whose purpose in awarding grants is to help resolve problems—how the project will meet your particular needs and improve your situation if you have the funds to carry it out. In many proposals, authors seem timid about making any commitment to substantial improvement. On the other hand, some authors propose unrealistic improvements that could never be accomplished in a twelve-month time period. Again, reviewers will question how much the authors really understand the needs and whether they have a logical plan for meeting them during the funding period. If the proposal makes no such commitment, the proposal reviewer probably will conclude that funding the project would be a waste of money.

ACTIVITIES

The section outlining project activities (commonly called the methodology section) is simply an explanation of how the project will reach its objectives. The description of activities should focus on those aspects of the project that will resolve or prevent the problems identified in the need statement by obtaining the results promised in the objectives.

A project should undertake only activities that will move it toward its objectives. Too many proposal writers ramble on about activities that are nice things to do but have no relation to meeting their objectives. The rule of thumb for activities is, if it isn't necessary for reaching your objectives, leave it out of the proposal.

Activities that are necessary to the success of the project (success being the ability to reach all of its objectives) should be fully described in the proposal. The funder wants to know exactly how you plan to meet your objectives, so give an exact description. Be specific and give enough detail to justify each activity.

Example:

Drug users will participate in a special counseling program in which rehabilitated drug users and counselors in the community will provide them with personal support, letting them know the dangers of drug use, and shadowing the opportunities, social activities, and career possibilities that they have. Project staff will attempt to recruit mentors from the community. Street counselors will spend 15 percent of their time recruiting and coordinating the counseling program.

Often, a funder will want very specific information in this section. You can break the activities down into the following elements.

Program Description

This is the explanation of what the project will do and should describe and justify the approach you will use to attack the problem. You should cite any relevant research on the approach and discuss other situations in which it has worked. You must convince the funder of the validity of your methods.

Example:

The strategy proposed by the Sun Flower School District is a variation on one used successfully by the El Camino, Florida, Consortium of Social Agencies in reducing drug use. The consortium's project has been in operation for six years and has been cited as a model project. The project was the basis of the doctoral dissertation of Dr. Joanna Gray, who validated its benefits to the young adults and the community. Dr. Gray helped develop the model featured in this application.

The program description also should identify the human resources used in the project and explain the importance of each staff position to its success. In this section, you must justify each personnel position that will show up in the budget section of the proposal, showing how that staff member will help the project meet its objectives. This is critical. If there is no relation (or only peripheral relation) between the position and project success, delete it from the proposal.

Example:

A street counselor will be assigned to each student. Counselors will serve as advocates for drug users with social service agencies and schools and will work with them and their families to improve interpersonal relations and problem-solving skills. To effectively serve youths and their families, counselors will work afternoons, evenings, and weekends.

The amount of time staff will spend on project activities also should be consistent with the amount of time for which you request support in the budget. For example, a full-time position should have responsibilities that require full-time attention. If positions are only seasonal rather than year-round, describe the responsibilities that will occupy the staff for the balance of the funding period.

Management Plan

The proposal should explain how the applicant will manage the project, including outlining the project director's role. It should show what authority the director will have, what staff members he or she will supervise, and who will supervise the director.

To illustrate the direct lines of authority and communication for our project on reducing drug use in the schools, we can use an organization chart like the one in Figure 1.4.

As with all graphics, we need a narrative statement that explains the procedures and protocols that will allow the project to efficiently and effectively pursue its objectives.

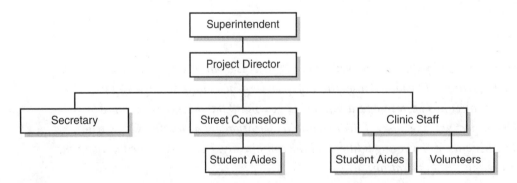

FIGURE 1.4   Eliminating Drug Use Project Organization Chart, Sun Flower School District

Example:

The operation of the project will be the responsibility of the project director. The director will report to the superintendent of the Sun Flower School District. The director will direct and supervise project implementation; coordinate and monitor project operation with the participating districts; supervise and monitor the project budget; prepare program reports; supervise the development of the information system; and give oral and written reports to the superintendent.

The project director will supervise the secretary, street counselors, and staff of the clinics. Student aides will report to the counselors and the clinic staff. Volunteers will work in the clinic.

The organization chart illustrates the project's management system (see Figure 1.4).

It's important to keep such organization charts simple and understandable. Many proposal writers working in large organizations hurt their funding chances by offering an organization chart that shows a huge bureaucracy with the proposed project as the bottom. This makes it hard to see how the project will operate within the overall structure and casts doubt that it will actually accomplish anything. If you have a large organization, draw a chart that shows only those segments of the organization that are relevant to the project.

The management plan also should include a timeline for implementing the project. The timeline should identify major milestones, target dates for meeting those milestones, and the person responsible for ensuring that each milestone is met.

Milestone	Person Responsible	Deadline (End Date)
Hire Director	Superintendent	First Quarter
Hire Staff	Director	First Quarter
Solicit Volunteers	Director	First Quarter
Staff Training	Director	First Quarter
Volunteer Training	Staff	First Quarter
Open Centers	Director	First Quarter
Recruit Gang Members	Staff	Ongoing
Hire Student Aides	Director	Second Quarter
Winter Program	Staff	Third Quarter
Interim Evaluation	Evaluator	Third Quarter
Program Revisions	Director	Third Quarter
Spring Program	Staff	Fourth Quarter
Summer Program	Staff	Fourth Quarter
Closeout	Director	Fourth Quarter

FIGURE 1.5   Eliminating Drug Use Project Timeline

You can construct a simple table like the one in Figure 1.5 that lists the project's major milestones in chronological order. Target dates for reaching each milestone and information on staff members responsible for each task complete the timeline. Once you have received the grant, you can convert this table into a simple checklist that can be a valuable tool in monitoring project performance.

As with all charts, the proposal should include narrative explanations for those readers who do not know how to interpret them or do not like charts.

Use of Resources

The activities section of the proposal also should give a clear idea of what nonpersonnel resources are necessary and how the project will use them. A useful rule of thumb is that any item noted in the proposal budget should be described in this section. The description should focus on the resource's relevance to achieving project goals. Items that cannot be shown as important to project success should not appear in the proposal.

Example:

The clinic will have two closed-circuit televisions displaying antidrug television specials. Students will be able to view these specials on a regular basis. The clinic will also have five desktop computers so that students will be able to use word processing software, access the Internet, design spreadsheets, and do their homework on the computers. Students will be attracted to the clinic because of the friendly environment. While at the clinic, they will be encouraged to watch the specials to learn what impact drugs have on their life, and use the computers so that they will be interested in learning and doing their homework.

When requesting support for computers, don't forget that they don't work without software. Identify the specific software the project will use, how it will use the software, and how often. In the example above, we obviously would buy word processing and spreadsheet software programs. But if our budget requests funds for math tutorial drill and practice software, the funder is likely to reject that expense because we haven't shown that the project will use such software.

Training

Often, implementing a project requires new techniques, procedures, equipment, and protocols in which project and nonproject staff need training. The proposal should detail any training necessary for the implementation of the project.

This description should include:

✔ Who will conduct the training;

✔ The content of the training;

✔ Who will be trained; and

✔ The training schedule.

Example:

Training will be provided by Dr. George Hipple of the College of Social Work at Sun Flower State University. Project staff will participate in two weeks of intensive training that will include the latest research on drug use, specific information on teenagers, sensitivity awareness to the various groups represented in the district, counseling techniques, and simulations of street work. Training will take place at the beginning of the project, prior to opening the clinic.

Facilities

The activities section should include a description of the facilities the project will use, including any changes or modifications needed. If new facilities must be rented or purchased, they should be described and justified.

Example:

The project will use the old Sun Flower Recreation building. The clinic must have living quarters, counseling rooms, an eating facility, and a recreation room. The clinic will designate a room for each of the activities to take place. The rooms, which have been assessed and found appropriate for project activities, are at least 800 square feet. The only need is for additional electrical connections to accommodate the computers and the closed-circuit televisions. The city is donating and renovating the building as an in-kind contribution to the project, and the district will upgrade the electrical system as part of its in-kind contribution.

PERSONNEL

The personnel section of a proposal should show that the persons who will be assigned or hired to implement project activities have the skills and experiences necessary for a successful program.

Obviously, the most important person to be described is the project director. The proposal should summarize the director's qualifications for leadership, focusing on experiences and skills pertinent to the project. It should cite other projects the director has run successfully, and any specific training he or she has had that is relevant to the project's goals.

Example:

Ben Arnold will direct the project. Mr. Arnold received his B.A. in Psychology from Arizona State University and an M.S. in Social Work from the University of Michigan. He is also a Certified Addictions Counselor.

He has taught for 16 years in the Sun Flower School District and has coached several sports. For the past four years, he has been a counselor at the Richard Nixon High School and worked closely with students who have used drugs. For the past six years, he has directed successful counseling programs, pilot-testing many of the techniques to be used in this project. During last year's winter break, Mr. Arnold directed a two-week residential camp for past drug users.

The proposal also should profile other project staff members, offering brief sketches of their experience relevant to the project. This profile should be shorter than that of the project director and highlight only the education and experience that qualifies each candidate for the project.

If staff have not been designated, the proposal should describe the process for hiring personnel. The goal is to convince the reader that the project will recruit and hire highly qualified persons to staff the project. To do so, the proposal should:

1. Briefly describe positions, including the job qualifications, roles and responsibilities, and the level of education required (i.e., high school, college, graduate level). Full job descriptions can be placed in the appendix.

2. Outline plans for advertising positions. This should specify publications, letters, and other postings for the jobs.

3. If applicable, identify two or three recruitment strategies such as interagency advertisements, conferences, or personnel recruiters.

4. Identify the team that will conduct the interview process. The interview team should be composed of individuals with expertise in the area addressed by the project.

5. Explain how the final hiring decision will be made and by whom.

EVALUATION

Since the late 1990s, evaluation has become increasingly important to funders. They want to know if their money was well spent, who benefited from the project, and to what extent. Evaluation should, by the same token, be important to grantseekers as a means of showing funders they are capable, reliable, and can be trusted with future grants. Unfortunately, proposal writers too often treat evaluation casually and give funders very little information about their plans.

This can be avoided by asking the evaluator to be a part of a project development process and asking them to provide the information that is needed for this proposal section. (Often, the evaluator must be identified and his or her qualifications must also be included in this section.)

Evaluation asks: Did the project meet its objectives, and if so, how do you know? If it did not, what were the reasons why? If you have written clear, measurable objectives, your evaluation design should be apparent. For example, if your objective is to raise test scores of the target group as compared to a control group, the evaluation design section of your proposal should describe the selection procedures for the control group, the testing instruments and procedures, and the process for establishing validity of the test.

Your evaluation design should clearly indicate the criteria for success of the project. This criteria should be specific and ambitious enough to show that the impact of the project is substantial. For example, a criterion for success of the test score project described above could be that the average test score for the target group exceeds that of the control group by 15 out of 100 points.

The proposal also should describe how data will be collected and analyzed, and explain all evaluation instruments, such as tests and questionnaires. It should discuss how the instruments were chosen or developed and why they are appropriate for the project.

You may choose either to evaluate the project at its end to judge its ultimate result (summative evaluation) and/or conduct continuous assessments as the project proceeds to keep an eye on progress and make any necessary adjustments (formative evaluation).

In the following example of a summative evaluation plan, note how the evaluation measures accomplishment of the objectives we stated earlier in this chapter:

Example:

A summative (statistical) evaluation will be conducted for the project objectives relating to reducing drug use. This data will be collected and analyzed annually.

The evaluator will use official police records to ascertain the extent to which incidents involving students who have tried or sold drugs have decreased and whether that reduction is at least 10 percent as compared to the base year.

The evaluator will evaluate student perception of using drugs by conducting a survey that duplicates the survey administered prior to project implementation (see need statement). This survey will be administered to a stratified random sample of students in the target school. The survey will seek to gather data on the extent to which students are opposed to drugs. The evaluator will determine if 50 percent fewer students have never tried drugs at the end of the project compared to the beginning of the project.

In most cases, a summative evaluation meets the funder's evaluation requirements. But formative evaluation is a very valuable tool for managing projects because it provides information on the quality of project implementation in time to make changes and improve quality. However, formative evaluation is more expensive than summative because it requires a great deal of time to interview staff and participants and observe activities. Check the budget guidelines to see if the costs of an outside evaluator are an allowable expense—this will often allow you to include the cost of a formative evaluation.

The information gained through formative evaluation can be very important for multiyear grants. In most cases, summative evaluations are not complete in time to apply for continued funding. Formative evaluation, on the other hand, provides periodic reports you can use to convince a funder to renew your grant.

Because projects usually use formative evaluation to help with implementation, the proposal should describe how the evaluation report will be used. The project must publish the report in a timely manner, present it to the proper authorities, share it with project staff, and provide a plan to use the information to modify the project.

Discuss the costs of conducting a formative and summative evaluation with the evaluator before submitting the proposal. If it is not too costly, conduct both types of evaluation. This can enhance the credibility of your project and your proposal.

Example:

The evaluator will perform on-site evaluations at the clinic three times a year for each of the four project years. The evaluator will obtain qualitative and quantitative data through observation, record analysis, interviews with counselors, parents, youth staff, law enforcement personnel, and students. This information will be used to:

Identify problems encountered in project implementation, thereby identifying situations that need immediate attention and that may explain project outcomes;

Generate recommendations that may be useful in making necessary changes to improve the program;

Determine the adequacy of project services for the entire range of participants. Special emphasis will be placed on the project's impact on minority, female, and disabled students; and

Provide information that will be useful in informing the public about the project's progress.

The evaluation will use six criteria in the on-site evaluations:

1. *The philosophy, policies, and practices are developed and disseminated to project participants and the public;*

2. *The clinic provides sound, basic programs that use new technologies and methods;*

3. *The staff and leadership are energetic, creative, and supportive of project goals;*

4. *The activities and support services are appropriate for the project participants;*

5. *Community involvement, especially by parents, is significant; and*

6. *Staff members have high expectations for the youths, and the youths and their parents are aware of the expectations.*

The evaluator will provide oral and written reports. The project director and staff will receive copies of the written report. The evaluator will be available to meet with project staff. The evaluator will meet with the director and help develop recommendations based on the report.

Because of the tendency for organizations to put evaluations on the shelf and continue with business as usual, it often helps to make the evaluation report public and present it to some type of advisory committee. This committee can work with the project director to develop plans for improving implementation of the program. Another option you can take is to post the evaluation report (or an executive summary of the report) on your organization's website. These approaches guarantee that a plan will have to be developed and gives some outside credibility to that plan.

Who should conduct the evaluation? Rather than using the project director, the evaluation should be conducted by someone who is independent and impartial, someone who does not have a vested interest in the outcome. The most credible evaluation would come from an outside evaluator associated with a professional organization that is interested in maintaining its reputation. An evaluation by such an individual is likely to be honest and objective. You can often find such organizations at colleges and universities. You can also contact current grantees and ask them for the name of their evaluator.

Many organizations, however, have their own internal evaluation units that are partially supported by grant funds. In such a situation, the proposal writer is obligated to use internal staff for the evaluation. If this is the case, the proposal must prove that the internal evaluator can give a fair and unbiased assessment of the program. This can be done by showing:

1. The evaluation department is under a different administrative structure that is isolated from pressure from the project management;

2. The staff of the evaluation department have unimpeachable credentials in terms of training and experience; and

3. The evaluation department has conducted and published evaluation and research reports that have been highly regarded.

If the evaluator is not selected prior to proposal submission, tell how one will be selected, outlining selection criteria and the process for obtaining bids. In addition, state who will make the final selection and on what basis.

As stated earlier, you should involve the evaluator early in the project development process so he or she will understand the goals and be able to help formulate objectives. Further, the evaluator should understand the approach and techniques that will be used in the project so he or she can use the appropriate evaluation instruments to assess what the program is actually doing.

BUDGET

The budget should reflect the costs of the items and activities described in the project narrative portion of the proposal. If an item is not described and justified in the narrative, it should not appear in the budget. The converse also is true: If an item is listed in the narrative, it should show up in the budget. The relationship between the budget and the project description should be so tight that a reader can determine what the project is by simply reading the budget.

Referencing budget items to the project narrative pages in which they are explained makes that relationship clear. If you can't find a reference page for a particular item, you should either develop a justification for it in the narrative or drop it from the budget.

The budget itself should include brief explanations of each item, including the basis for the cost listed. The cost can be based on a salary schedule, catalog, estimate by a vendor, a state contract, average costs, or previous experience. The budget should indicate the cost per item and the quantity to be purchased. (*See **Appendix D** for a Federal Sample Form 424 and a sample Project Budget sheet from the Humanities-in-the-Arts Mini-Project Grant Application of the Pennsylvania Humanities Council.*)

If the budget does not need to meet page limit requirements, the proposal should also include a budget narrative, a full explanation of the items included in the budget listing. A budget narrative supplements the project narrative by putting all cost information in one place, which makes reviewing the proposal easier. However, it should not be a substitute for a complete and thorough project narrative. (*See **Appendix D** for a budget narrative sample from the U.S. Department of Education and the U.S. Department of Justice.*)

Example:

The city will renovate the building structure as a gift to the program. The Sun District Hospital will donate any medical supplies needed. The equipment expenses are for the purchase of the televisions, at $800 each, and the desktop computers at $1,800 per station. This system was selected through public bidding from careful specifications and has proven successful in a number of similar settings. The district's office of technology will provide installation, training, maintenance, demonstration, and trouble-shooting services. The equipment expense on a per-participant basis is $35.33.

There may be items in your project narrative for which you are not requesting monetary support from the funder, such as people or resources that already exist in your organization, or items to be supported by other funding sources or contributed by the organization. Such items may qualify as in-kind or cash contributions to the project; they are necessary to the project (and so should be included) but do not require extra expenditure by the organization and/or support from the funder. For example, the organization may assign a staff member duties in the project but use a source other than the grant to pay for that person's time.

Many funders require applicants to match their grant funds. Financially strapped organizations often use in-kind contributions to meet those requirements.

Example:

The district's local contribution, which exceeds the required 10 percent of project costs, includes the in-kind contribution of the site coordinators, who will spend 15 percent of their time on the project (worth $117,585), the renovation of the building ($300,000) and the city's lease. The lease is valued at $1,800 a month, for a total of $21,600. Total local contribution is $439,185.

Don't confuse in-kind contribution with indirect cost. The indirect cost is a percentage of the direct costs of a grant assigned to help cover the organization's overhead costs. These overhead costs include utilities, personnel offices, accounting, payroll, and so forth: anything that is necessary to operate the project but cannot be directly charged to the project. Items used to calculate the indirect cost figure may not be cited as in-kind contributions.

The funder usually negotiates with the grantee the maximum percentage it will allow for indirect costs. Some funders have a set indirect cost rate, whereas others do not allow them at all. Most allow a rate of between 5 percent and 15 percent. In most cases, the funder wants the bulk of the funds to go to program-related expenses. If the funder's RFP or guidelines do not specify, be sure to ask.

The budget as a whole must be precise and specific, detailing all of the costs you expect the funder to pay. There should be no miscellaneous categories or unexplained contingency accounts. You can break it down into several categories.

Personnel

List each staff title separately, explaining salaries based on the percentage of time each person is assigned to the project.

Example:

Project Director: 100 percent of time at $58,600 for 12 months (based on average salary in the field with 12 to 14 years of experience)   *$58,600*

Figure and explain fringe benefits separately from salaries.

Example:

Retirement benefits at 13.8 percent of annual salary	*$8,086*
Medical/life insurance	*$2,800*
Medicare at 1.45 percent of annual salary	*$850*
Unemployment insurance at 0.12 percent of annual salary	*$70*
Subtotal	*$11,806*

Travel

Requesting support for travel can be problematic if the funder does not require it to be included in the budget, and if reasonable cost estimates are not used. In some cases, staff will be required to attend specific training or conferences in specific locations, so be sure to get estimated costs for these items and include them in your budget request. Explain the purpose of the travel in the project narrative and the benefit you expect to receive.

Example:

Four staff members to travel to the American Social Workers Association annual meeting in Washington, DC, to disseminate project results

Estimated air fare at $600 each	*$2,400*
Hotel (three nights) at $360 each	*$1,440*
Meals at $90 each	*$360*
Ground transportation for the group	*$80*
Subtotal	*$4,280*

Local travel is less controversial than out-of-town travel. The project should reimburse staff members if they are required to use their cars for project business, and funders usually accept this. The organization should have rules and procedures for mileage reimbursement that can be used to justify local travel expenses. The budget should identify specific staff members who will travel and estimate the amount of travel required.

Example:

Local Travel (Mileage)

Estimated mileage of 200 miles per month at $0.36/mile for 12 months for the Project Director to visit three project sites in the Sun Flower School District   *$864*

Equipment

As with the other expense categories, equipment must be justified in the project narrative. Unfortunately, in many proposals, equipment such as copiers, computers, or a van can appear out of thin air in the budget section. If you cannot use a copier or a computer that is already at your organization, or rent a van from a local transportation provider, you must justify the purchase of these (and all other equipment items) in your narrative.

Example:

Five Pentium MMX computers with color monitors, CD-ROM drives, modems, 3 gigabyte hard drives, 64 megabytes of memory, running Windows 2003, for the clinic at $1,800 for each configuration	*$9,000*
Two closed-circuit televisions at $800 each	*$1,600*

Supplies

Give enough budget detail to justify the dollar figures for supplies but do not try to account for every pencil and sheet of paper. Consider itemizing large expenditures and group small items together.

> ### *Example:*
>
> | | |
> |---|---|
> | *200 T-shirts at $10 each* | *$2,000* |
> | *Books and magazines* | *$500* |
> | *Videotapes and compact discs* | *$2,500* |
> | *Paper, pencils, art supplies, games, computer supplies, and calculators at a total of $2,000 for each of the three centers* | *$6,000* |
> | *Subtotal* | *$11,000* |

Contractual Services

Contractual services should be detailed in the project narrative. For example, if you plan to contract with a university to conduct the evaluation, explain the contract arrangement as part of the evaluation plan. Include names, resumes, and profiles of individuals or firms to be hired in the appendix. The budget should list the length and rate for the service.

> ### *Example:*
>
> | | |
> |---|---|
> | *Evaluation provided by the University of Oklahoma's College of Education* | |
> | *Estimate quoted by university* | *$15,000* |

Pulling together all of the expense details and doing all of the calculations illustrated above seems a daunting task. Work closely with your business office to develop a project budget and if possible, automate the task. You can use a spreadsheet program, setting up a format and programming formulas to do the math calculations for you.

A very important point to make here is NEVER use a "miscellaneous" category in a grant budget. You must list items in the correct categories. Every expense should be listed. Grouping them into a "miscellaneous" category will send up immediate red flags to reviewers as they study your budget.

Making It All Work Together

There you have it: the core of any grant proposal. You have seen the logical progression from stating the problem to developing a plan for resolving that problem through relevant activities, conducted by experienced personnel, using appropriate resources. The basic logic of the idea flows throughout the proposal.

Just one word of warning before we go on to discuss features we can add to this framework to give the proposal even more impact: Writing proposals by committee negates the whole concept of "flow."

Proposal sections written by different people and "pasted" together appear disjointed. Their various sections show different writing styles, and in some cases, conflicting logic. Each proposal section should move smoothly into the next with consistency—in other words, "flow." The various sections must support and reinforce each other.

Someone should be responsible for maintaining the consistency, or flow. You can farm out various research and proposal development tasks to different people and should do so in order to speed up the process and create a greater sense of involvement in the project. However, if you do this, make sure one person takes all of the information and creates a proposal that has flow and speaks to the reader with one voice.

Helpful Hint

A good proposal contains:

Need statement

Objectives → Activities

Personnel → Evaluation

Budget

Remember to maintain the flow.

~

CHAPTER TWO

Other Important Features

~

In Chapter One, we dealt with the core of a grant proposal, the conceptual base, and how to develop a logical case that holds the whole document together. We built a framework that can be used in virtually any grant-seeking situation.

In this chapter, we will look at features we can add to that framework to enhance the proposal, make it even clearer, easier to read and, as a result, stronger. These sections—the abstract, introduction, appendices, table of contents, and dissemination and continuation plans—grow out of the conceptual base we have built for our proposal and support it.

ABSTRACT (OR EXECUTIVE SUMMARY)

The abstract is usually at most a one-page (or less) summary of the core concepts presented in the proposal. It appears before the narrative and gives the reader a clear idea of what is coming. An abstract must be clear and concise, while also being compelling. It identifies the applicant organization and gives a sense of its ability to implement the project.

The abstract should explain the needs the project will address and the objectives it will work to meet. (You can copy need and objectives statements directly from the body of the proposal.) It also should offer a summary of the project's proposed activities. Finally, it should state the cost of the project, including the amount requested from the funder, and briefly explain how funds will be used. Here is the abstract from an actual proposal developed by the Boston Public Schools and funded by the U.S. Education Department's Drug-Free Schools and Communities Program.

Example:

Beyond Curriculum: Intensive Intervention Program

According to the final report of the National Commission on Drug-Free Schools, local public schools are responsible for keeping students drug free. Comprehensive drug prevention programs should, the report states, provide a prevention curriculum supported by policies, programs, and services that consider needs for prevention both in and out of school.[1]

The Boston Public Schools accepted this responsibility several years ago. The public schools in Boston have a comprehensive drug and alcohol prevention program with the elements recommended by the U.S. Department of Education: means of assessment and monitoring; clear, specific rules against use and strong corrective actions; consistent enforcement; a K-12 curriculum that teaches that drugs are wrong and harmful; a program that involves uniformed police in classrooms (DARE and SPECDA), that trains teachers to identify and refer students for treatment, and a network of 85 community health and social agencies linked to our 116 schools for treatment and that makes extensive use of peer mentoring and tutoring related to this critical issue.[2]

Nevertheless, there is a significant need for additional assistance in order to combat drug and alcohol abuse. The school system is large and the poverty rates are high.[3] Many students are drawn in by the lure of big money in the drug trade; others are pulled in by chemically dependent family members or peers or pushed in by hopelessness, ignorance or apparent lack of better alternatives. Rising levels of crime and violence in the city spill over into the schools. This proposal seeks $1.1 million dollars to underwrite two parts of our comprehensive program: an expansion of an intensive intervention for most at-risk middle schoolers and startup for an innovative birth to 18 program which provides for intensive services for the most at risk.

---

[1]*Part III RESPONSIBILITIES, of the Final Report of the National Commission on Drug Free Schools.*

[2]*See Appendix for Code of Discipline; Curriculum Outline; Procedures relating to the control of drugs and alcohol use/abuse in and around schools.*

[3]*Boston, Massachusetts, with a population of about 459,500 overall and 387,700 excluding college students, is the inner city for a metropolitan area of 2.5 million. Fewer than 20% of Boston's households include children under 18 years of age, and almost one third of those households send their children to parochial or private schools or out of the inner city to suburban public schools. The result of these patterns is that the public schools serve a predominantly low income, predominantly minority group of students and families. The single largest group of students is African American (48%); Hispanic students, at 21% of the system, will soon outnumber white students (22%). The rest of the students are Asian (9%) and Native American (1%). As of December, 1990, a total of 116 public schools served 56,414 students. The Boston Public Schools have all the demographics and most of the problems characteristic of large, inner city school districts.*

TABLE OF CONTENTS

The proposal should include a brief (no more than one page) table of contents, following the abstract, that outlines its sections and cites page numbers for each.

Remember to number each page of the proposal, starting with the introduction and running sequentially through the appendices, unless you are given other instructions regarding page numbers in the RFP. (In that case, be sure to follow those instructions!) It is impossible for multiple reviewers to discuss a proposal without having page numbers to refer to. Also, if your proposal is unbound and pages fall out, it may be impossible to put your document back together in the proper order.

INTRODUCTION

The introduction should provide background information the reader needs to understand the proposal and lead directly into the need statement, taking the reader from the general to the specific.

The introduction serves to acquaint the reader with the applicant. Some proposal writers make the assumption that readers "know" the circumstances of an inner city agency in New York City, or of a school in a rural area in North Dakota, and do not provide detail. Make no assumptions about the readers, and use the introduction to "paint a picture" for them, including history and current status.

The introduction should outline the applicant's goals, service area, and major accomplishments. This information should be supported by data and references, such as endorsements of the organization and awards and citations that verify its accomplishments. This is the point at which you must establish a rapport with the reader, putting him or her in a sympathetic frame of mind before presenting the actual proposal.

To be most effective, the introduction should be brief so it doesn't wear the reader out too early; to the point so it doesn't lose the reader in miscellaneous, unnecessary facts; and interesting so it captures the reader's imagination.

Here is part of the introduction to an actual proposal developed by the Cleveland, MS, School District for submission to several funders. It attempts to give the reader an understanding of the culture and economic status of the area in which the project will be conducted.

Example:

Bolivar County (population 45,965) lies at the geographic center of the Mississippi Delta, approximately 110 miles south of Memphis, Tennessee. Bolivar County is a microcosm of the entire Delta. We are a people who, by virtue of place, are surrounded by thousands of square miles of some of the country's richest natural resources and physical assets. We have used this sense of place to develop a cultural and historical heritage that is both rich and unique. And yet, we are the people who by statistics are the poorest in the United States.

Ours is a region where jobs are scarce and job training is almost unknown; where infant mortality rates rival those of the Third World; where dropping out of school and teenage pregnancy are commonplace; where illiteracy reigns as a supreme piece of irony: the Delta has produced some of the best writers and the worst readers in America.

However, it is a region whose people prefer hope to despair. Given the right tools and knowledge, it can become a full partner in the American Dream and can help the nation as a whole strike a new balance of competitiveness in a global economy. Being in the vanguard of change need not be a distinction limited to the freedom-hungry citizens of Eastern Europe or the aggressive business people of Asia. The people in the Delta belong in that vanguard. This is a land where the right actions can spell a new day.

Bolivar County has historically been regarded as an agricultural area. As in any typical Delta county, the principal crop was cotton for many years. Soybeans and rice have now become major crops, with additional diversification into catfish farming. Manufacturing plants employ over 3,300 people in the county. Principal products include:

- *ceramic wall tile*
- *stapled aluminum automotive trim*
- *nails and staples*
- *intravenous solutions*
- *sterile disposable hospital devices*
- *metal kitchen and sink cabinets*
- *marine construction*
- *aluminum die castings*

Recently, Brandywine Corporation moved into the area to process Chicken Nuggets. Think of us the next time you go to McDonalds!!

APPENDIX

If the RFP allows an appendix, keep it brief and remember that it should support the rationale and logic of the entire proposal. Keep in mind that readers have limited time to review and score proposals and do not have time to read every item that is included in the appendix.

Read every piece of paper to be included in the appendix. If it doesn't support your proposal's statements, do not include it! The appendix should also contain any additional documents or information requested in the RFP. Appendices could include the following:

Job Descriptions

In the appendix, you can list the specific duties and responsibilities of each position involved in the project.

Resumes

The proposal narrative should highlight the qualifications and experience of key personnel, but the appendix should offer their full resumes. Update and rewrite all resumes so they are appropriate for the project. In other words, highlight all education and experience relevant to the project and eliminate any information that is not. Retype the resumes so they all have the same format and match the style of the rest of the proposal. Try to keep them to one page in length.

Letters of Commitment

Any letters included with your proposal should actually commit collaborators to some specific action in support of the project. Include only letters from those who will provide funds, staff, equipment, or expertise to help achieve project objectives.

For the most part, **letters of support**—in which officials, experts, or others pay only lip service to the project—are not helpful. But sometimes it's necessary to include such letters for political reasons. Letters of support might not impress a funder, but having documentation from individuals or organizations who are important to reaching consensus about the problem and the proposed solution can help ease the process when you implement the project.

In some situations, you might want to include letters of support as a courtesy. For instance, requesting such letters from your congressional representatives for federal applications keeps them up to date on what's going on in their districts.

Newspaper Articles

An appendix of newspaper articles that support the proposal's case can be very valuable. Articles can show the need for the program, back up the project's proposed methods and activities, and strengthen the applicant's credibility. But read each article carefully to be sure it is accurate and supports the proposal. Try to steer clear of general articles that are not specific to the proposed project. Remember that readers have limited time to score proposals and even less time to read articles!

Advisory Committee Information

If the RFP does not ask for detailed advisory committee information in the narrative, you can list its members and affiliations in an appendix. You also can provide minutes of meetings and formal resolutions and reports that support the proposal.

If not asked for in specific sections of the narrative, an appendix can include research results relevant to the project; an annotated bibliography that surveys the relevant research in the field;

your complete, detailed evaluation design, including instruments; copies of contracts and/or agreements described in the narrative and budget; and any other documents specifically required in the RFP.

DISSEMINATION PLAN

Occasionally, funders require their grantees to develop plans for disseminating project results so the project can be replicated in other locations. There are many ways to disseminate the results of your project, including: (1) create a website, (2) create a CD-ROM, (3) develop and distribute brochures, (4) publish articles in professional publications, (5) present workshops at conferences, and (6) send information via email and/or U.S. mail to interested people. Whichever dissemination method you use, make sure you present all of the details in your preposal. Check the budget section of the RFP to see what, if any, dissemination costs are allowable.

SUSTAINABILITY

Often, funders want to know how a grantee will continue its project after the grant runs out. They aren't interested in your best intentions and dreams for the future; they want a specific, credible plan that shows where funding and resources will come from after they're out of the picture.

Your sustainability plan can cite other grants you will seek if you can identify grant programs that fund your type of project. However, do not rely solely on grants as your planned source of ongoing support! Because you have no guarantees that you will secure future grant awards, using only grants weakens your sustainability plan. In addition to grants, explain the fundraising process you will use in the future.

Consider adding staff to the agency budget at the end of the grant award period, making grant-funded training an ongoing part of staff development, or turning services provided during the grant period into a sliding scale or fee-for-service arrangement.

Example:

It will require $75,000 a year to maintain the project after the three years of grant funding. The agency will have an annual banquet to raise $25,000 and will apply for an additional $25,000 to the Hawkins Community Fund, a local community foundation that supports successful projects after they have been pilot-tested. The remaining $25,000 will come from local and national foundation grants. The agency employs a talented grantseeker who has an outstanding record in securing funds. In the final year of the original grant, the agency will research foundation sources and prepare grant proposals for three new funders. The Anytown Chamber of Commerce has agreed to provide clerical support after the grant funding end. The Speedy Printing Company will print materials free of charge.

Another way to continue the project is to use it to re-place other, less efficient activities currently conducted by the organization. Whatever method you choose, be specific and show your commitment to it. Funding sources are justifiably skeptical about sustainability plans because too many applicants throw them together just to get the grant and never intend to carry them out. Remember, the funder doesn't want to support you forever.

Helpful Hint

Other features a strong proposal can have:

- ✔ Abstract
- ✔ Table of Contents
- ✔ Introduction
- ✔ Appendix
- ✔ Dissemination Plan
- ✔ Sustainability

CHAPTER THREE

Using Technology

So far, we have seen that a proposal is a presentation. And, as in any other form of presentation, the proposal writer's aim is to bring the audience around to his or her point of view and convince it to take a particular course of action. To succeed, the presentation must have substance and logic. But it also must have style.

That's where technology comes in. Proposal writers who use computers and the wide variety of software available today turn out documents that are well researched, easy to read, easy to understand, and, most of all, easy to fund. Now, we can add and delete material at the touch of a key, produce charts and bar graphs to illustrate complicated statistics, add digital photographs, and use a variety of graphic elements to attract the reader's attention.

HARDWARE

The technological tools needed are relatively common. You should have a personal computer with as much memory (RAM) and hard disk storage space as you can get. A large memory will help protect against computer crashes, and a sizable amount of storage space will allow you to keep old proposals on your hard disk so you can cut and paste pieces needed in future proposals.

It is also a good idea to have a zip drive, which will allow you to store 100, 250, or 750 megabytes of information on a zip disk. If you can put a large and complex proposal on a single zip disk, it will be much easier to transport that proposal to different work locations, such as another computer station, or your home computer.

You should have a good printer so you can produce a high-quality final document. A number of inkjet and laser printers on the market today are reasonably priced and produce good quality copy—a must for today's proposal writers. You should also purchase high quality paper and use it for your final copies that are submitted.

On the software side, you will need word processing, spreadsheet, and graphics software packages.

WORD PROCESSING

Word processing software allows you to make the most professional presentation, varying type faces and sizes to set apart the different sections and highlight important points, creating columns for comparing sets of information and justifying margins so the proposal look like it has been typeset. Word processing software has progressed to the point that it can do most of the things that used to be done with desktop publishing software. Plus, it comes with the invaluable spellcheck feature. Although spellcheck is not foolproof, it can help you eliminate many obvious and embarrassing errors. Always ask at least one person who is not familiar with your project or field to proofread your proposal before it is submitted.

You may want to supplement your word processing software with one of the many packages available that assist with proposal writing. *Grantslam* is a software package that can be used to prepare National Institute of Health applications. Other proposal writing software is generic and guides you through the common sections of proposals (discussed in Chapters One and Two), asking specific questions that will assist you with writing your responses. These software programs often allow you to keep the sections that you have written in the past in file folders. When you start a new proposal, you can use some of the "boilerplate" information, such as agency information, client data and community statistics, and cut and paste pertinent parts into your new proposal, saving time and energy for writing new text that is needed. (For more information about *Grantslam,* see **Appendix B**.)

SPREADSHEETS

Spreadsheet software takes a lot of the tedium out of developing project budgets. Using a simple spreadsheet program, you can set up a budget file that, with some basic input, automatically calculates expenses. And if you need to change a figure—which you often will—you don't have to recalculate. The program does it for you.

You can set up a standardized spreadsheet format for all of your budgets. One word of caution, however. Be sure that your format matches the funder's format if one is provided in the RFP. The readers will be looking for the specified budget and may penalize you if you include your own customized budget.

GRAPHICS

Graphics programs make it possible to incorporate professional-looking charts, graphs, and images into your proposals. After some initial set up, all it takes is the click of a mouse. Even easier is clip art: images on a disk or on the Internet that you can copy and paste into your document. You just find the picture that best illustrates your point and place it in your proposal. Software packages that create organizational charts speed up what often is an extremely tedious task. Some packages even allow you to add photos to your charts.

Another way to include graphics in your proposal is to use a scanner, which copies whatever you put onto its screen and translates it into a computerized image that can be inserted into another computer file. For example, you can scan in a headline and opening paragraph from a local newspaper article that discusses an urgent need and emphasizes the importance of your proposed project in your community.

Digital cameras, which take photographs that can be translated into computer format, also help you add graphics to your proposal. With a digital camera, you can easily place a picture of a deteriorating building in a request for historic preservation funds, a picture of the facility where a project will be housed, or photos that show examples of the problems cited in your needs assessment. Documenting your points with photos can make your argument more compelling. If you have questions about using photographs in your proposal, look at funded copies or check with the program officer. Ask the officer for a candid opinion regarding whether or not photographs will be viewed favorably by reviewers and follow his or her advice.

Effective use of graphics definitely can give a proposal a boost. You can use a graphic to present large amounts of data that would be tedious for a reviewer to read. People usually prefer looking at pictures to reading text. As a result, you can get your point across quickly, effectively, and efficiently. Graphics can be particularly valuable when applying to a funder that limits the number of proposal pages. A simple graphic can present information in less space than long tables or extensive text.

Be careful, though: graphics sometimes can obscure data. To make sure your graphics are clear, present the data in several different formats and ask people not associated with the project which one communicates the information most effectively.

Last but not least, don't forget to explain your graphics. Some people don't like to read charts, and many may read them in a different way than intended. Avoid both problems by providing an explanatory paragraph for each graphic (*see Chapter One*).

COLOR

Just as graphics can improve your proposal, color can improve your graphics. Color can make your graphics more vivid and alive. A color chart is more likely to catch the reader's attention and set your proposal apart.

Many software packages—word processing, spreadsheets, and graphics—allow you to add color as you work, and reasonably priced inkjet printers allow you to make color originals. (Unless you provide copies of your proposal with the color included, funders will be making black and white copies for the readers and will not even see the colors you've included!) Remember to use color for emphasis or clarity, not just to make your proposal stand out from the others.

RESEARCH AIDS

Today, we find ourselves using a combination of directories, file folders, and the computer searching through commercial and nonprofit databases in order to research funders. (You'll find information on these and other research aids in *Appendix B.*) An invaluable resource for grantseekers is the Cooperating Collections of the Foundation Center. Located throughout the United States, these free funding information centers are in libraries, community foundations, and nonprofit resource centers. You will find a variety of Foundation Center materials (including the CD-ROM discussed below), directories, and other print resources that deal with fundraising. To locate the closest Cooperating Collection, go to the Foundation Center website (http://www. fdncenter.org/collections). Here is an example of funder research software that you may find helpful: The Foundation Center offers its database, *FC Search Version 8.0*, on CD-ROM. This listing of more than 76,000 foundations, corporate givers, and grantmaking public charities provides in-depth program descriptions and application guidelines, and links to grantmaker and corporate websites.

The Taft Group publishes an annual *Corporate Giving Directory*, which provides complete profiles of the 1,000 largest corporate foundations and direct-giving programs in the United States. The directory is arranged alphabetically by company name and provides Top 10 lists of givers to arts and humanities, civic and public affairs, education, environment, international, social services, health, and science.

The Taft Group's *Foundation Reporter* is a comprehensive resource that covers the top 1,000 private foundations in the United States that have at least $10 million in assets or have given away $500,000 or more in charitable gifts.

There are a variety of commercial databases available, for purchase or via monthly or yearly subscription. iWave Information Systems offers *Foundation Finder*, a research tool that contains 990-PF returns of over 67,000 private foundations in the United States. The database can be searched by keyword or specific field. The Foundation Center database on CD-ROM (described above) and Guidestar's *Grant Explorer*, an online database of over 42,000 of the nation's largest foundations and more than a million grants of $5,000 or greater, are both available via monthly or annual subscription.

THE INTERNET

The Internet offers a host of research opportunities for grantseekers. (It is hard to understand how we ever got along without it!) Almost all major funding sources—federal, state, and private—have established websites. (For a list for funding-related websites, *see Appendix A.*)

The U.S. Department of Education, for example, has developed a forecast of upcoming funding opportunities for discretionary grant programs (http://www.ed.gov/fund/grant/find/ edlite-forecast.html). This document lists virtually all of the programs and competitions that the Department expects to hold in a given fiscal year (see Figure 3.1). The forecast is in the form of

FORECAST OF FUNDING OPPORTUNITIES UNDER THE DEPARTMENT OF EDUCATION DISCRETIONARY GRANT PROGRAMS FOR FISCAL YEAR (FY) 2005 and FY 2006

(As of June 16, 2005)

This document lists virtually all programs and competitions under which the Department (we) has invited or expects to invite applications for new awards and provides actual or estimated deadline dates for the transmittal of applications under these programs. The lists are in the form of charts -- organized according to the Department's principal program offices -- and include programs and competitions we have previously announced, as well as those we plan to announce at a later date.

Note: This document is advisory only and is not an official application notice of the Department of Education. We expect to provide updates to this document starting in the first week of November in a fiscal year and continuing through the following July.

Note on printing: For best results, print this document in landscape orientation.

ORGANIZATION OF THIS DOCUMENT

We have assigned to each principal office a separate chart as follows:

Chart 1 - Office of English Language Acquisition, Language Enhancement, and Academic Achievement for Limited English Proficient Students.

FIGURE 3.1   Sample Page from the U.S. Department of Education Forecast of Funding

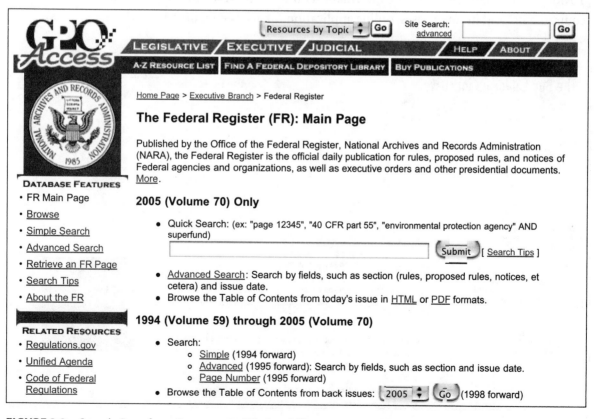

FIGURE 3.2   Sample Page from Government Printing Office

charts, organized according to the Department's principal program offices, and lists past as well as future programs and competitions.

Grantseekers can find federal grant competition announcements, program rules, and proposed rules on the Government Printing Office's Federal Register website (http://www.gpoaccess.gov/fr/index.html) (see Figure 3.2).

States and their departments also have websites that contain grant information. Go to your state's general website and check for listings of grant programs. Many state's websites are in one of the following address formats:

- http://www.(state abbreviation).gov, such as California's website, www.ca.gov

- http://www.state.(state abbreviation).us, such as Pennsylvania's website, www.state.pa.us

You can also do a Google search and type in the phrase "(name of state) website." At the state's general website, look for the state agency index and go to the state agency whose grant programs you are interested in. At the state agency page, look for a "grants" or "funding" link, or type these words into a search.

Figure 3.3 shows the Web page that came up after typing in the phrase "grants" on the California Department of Food and Agriculture Web page.

On the private side, many foundations and corporate givers have sites on the Internet that provide grantseekers with valuable information on their interests, funding eligibility requirements, and in some cases, online application forms. See Figures 3.4 and 3.5.

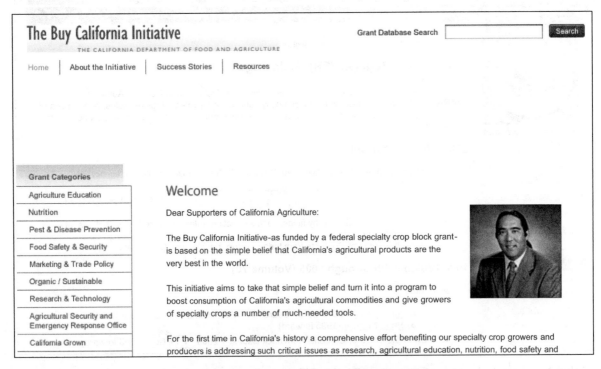

FIGURE 3.3   Sample Page from the California Department of Food and Agriculture

| HOME | GRANTEES | GRANT SEEKERS | SCHOLARSHIPS | ABOUT US | LINKS | REGISTER |

GUIDELINES FOR UNRESTRICTED GRANTMAKING

The Lancaster County Community Foundation is a non-profit foundation whose primary mission is to build a charitable reserve for the current and future needs of Lancaster County.

The Community Foundation uses grant resources to support responses to emerging community needs, empower programs that have a positive, broad affect on existing community needs, and to strengthen the capabilities of non-profit applicants to operate effectively.

In a competitive consideration of proposals, preference may be given to:

- The program that meets the greater community need or assists the larger number of individuals.
- The program that stresses prevention over treatment

FIGURE 3.4 Lancaster County Community Foundation Website. Reprinted with permission.

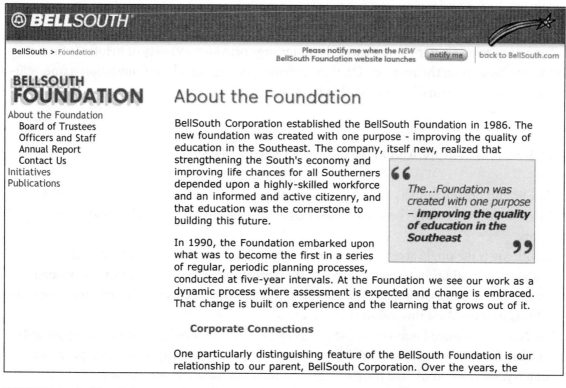

FIGURE 3.5 BellSouth Corporate Foundation Website. Reproduced with permission of BellSouth Intellectual Poperty Marketing Corporation.

FIGURE 3.6   The Foundation Center Website. Reprinted with permission.

The Foundation Center (http://www.fdncenter.org) provides a variety of helpful information to locate funders on the Internet. On their website, you can search by foundation name, 990-PF tax returns, and grantmaker type (see Figure 3.6).

ONLINE SUBMISSION AND GRANTS MANAGEMENT

Many public and private funders have applications that can be downloaded, completed, and submitted electronically, as well as online systems that enable grantees to use technology to manage their grants.

Grants.gov is the single access point for over 900 grant programs offered by 26 federal grantmaking agencies. In addition to searching for grant opportunities, an applicant can download grant application packages, complete and submit applications, and check the status of an application that was submitted via this website (see Figure 3.7).

The National Science Foundation (NSF) has one of the oldest online systems for applicants and grantees. Their system, called Fastlane, includes electronic proposal submission, proposal status inquiry, submission of final progress reports, and cash transaction requests.

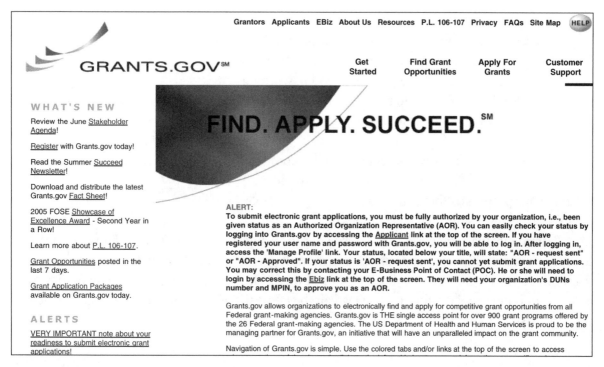

FIGURE 3.7   Sample Page from Grants.gov

The U.S. Department of Education, another public funder, has its own electronic grants, or e-Grants, system, which includes online applications for specially selected grant programs. The system also has three additional components related to grants management:

- e-Payments, which allows grantees to view payment requests and available balances, draw down award payments, and submit requests for refunds.

- e-Reports, which allows grantees to complete and submit annual performance reports online.

- e-Administration, which gives Project Directors the ability to submit administrative changes (i.e., address changes, personnel changes) to their grant awards.

OTHER TECHNOLOGY

Facsimile machines, modems, and laptop computers all help to make your life easier. In addition to electronic mail, facsimile machines enable you to get information that you need quickly. This is vital when you have no other means of accessing the information. You will find that if you ask them to, many program officers will be willing to fax you information.

Laptop computers enable you to carry your office with you wherever you go. You can store all of your proposal information on your laptop and work at home, on an airplane, or in a hotel. This is especially helpful when you're working under tight deadlines and need to be out of the office! A modem enables you to connect to both your office and the Internet.

Many funding sources will accept electronic submission of grant applications. This may allow you to add sound and video to your proposals. Someday, you may actually be able to talk your reviewers through your proposal!

Technology makes a world of difference in producing attractive and professional proposals. It is also changing the way that proposals are submitted and reviewed, and the way that grants are managed. In the future, as technology grows and we rely less and less on paper, many funders will only accept online applications. It is well worth the effort to spend some time now learning new technology skills to prepare for this change.

Helpful Hint

Technical aides con boost your proposal. Spend time trying variations of your proposal until you find the right fit.

CHAPTER FOUR

Understanding Federal RFPs

The federal government is the largest single source of grants. It also has the most intricate and complicated application process. If you can master the skills needed to write a federal proposal, other funders will seem easy.

In this chapter, we will examine an actual Request for Proposals (RFP) From the U.S. Education Department's (ED) Fund for the Improvement of Postsecondary Education. (*See Figure 4.1 pages 44–48 for a copy of the RFP published in the September 13, 2004 Federal Register. See Appendix D for samples of general forms including the federal application standard form, SF-424.*) Other federal agencies' RFPs may take a slightly different form but include the same basic types of information. In addition, changes to the federal grants landscape, since 2000, that impact potential applicants are discussed.

CFDA Number

This is the number assigned the program by the Catalog of Federal Domestic Assistance (CFDA), the government's annual directory of funding programs. It identifies the program and indicates where the program description is located in the CFDA.

ED requires applicants to list this number on the first page of their proposals so that its Application Control Center can direct them to the appropriate office.

Purpose of the Program

This section is critical. Before applying, you should consider whether your project is consistent with the program's purpose. If it is not, stop right here.

Eligible Applicants

This explains what types of agencies, institutions, organizations, individuals, or government units are eligible to apply. Your type of applicant must be listed or the agency will not accept your application. If you are uncertain about your eligibility, call the program office.

Applications Available

This is the date that the application is made available to the public and is typically the same date it is published in the Federal Register.

Deadline for Transmittal

This is the date by which you must mail the proposal. If it is not postmarked by this date, the agency will not review it. In the case of this RFP, the agency is requesting preapplications to check the merit of applicants' proposals before requesting final applications from those that qualify.

Deadline for Intergovernmental Review

This is the deadline for your state to review your proposal. This is a standard federal requirement and generally is not a big deal. You should submit your proposal to the state at the same time you mail it to the agency.

Most states have an office, called the single point of contact, designated to review proposals submitted to federal agencies from that state (*see **Appendix C** for a list of state single points of contact*). The office keeps the state apprised of federal activities within its border. If you do not see your state on this list, you only need to submit your proposal to the funding agency.

The state single point of contact may comment to the funder on proposals submitted from the state but doesn't often do so. If the state chooses not to comment or misses the deadline for intergovernmental review, it does not affect the agency's evaluation of your proposal.

Estimates

Agencies estimate the amount of money and number and size of grants they will award based on program history and funding levels set by Congress. But don't take these numbers literally; agencies retain the right to deviate from their estimates.

Project Period

This specifies the duration of the grant and often tells when projects may begin.

Applicable Regulations

This lists the various rules that govern grantees under the program. The RFP usually does not contain the text of the regulations, it just cites them by name and number.

When agencies do not offer complete application packages in their *Federal Register* or other RFP notices, they usually provide separate packages that include the text of the applicable rules. In most cases, program offices also can provide you with copies of these documents.

Priorities

Priorities express an agency's interest in funding a particular type or types of projects or activities under that year's competitions. In this RFP, ED establishes four "invitational priorities" indicating the Secretary is "particularly interested" in funding the types of projects cited. Responding to these priorities will not give the applicant any official extra points but will make the application more interesting to ED.

An RFP also may set out one or more "absolute," "relative," or "competitive" priorities as well. Absolute priorities limit the competition to a particular type of project; the agency will not fund anything else. Relative or competitive priorities offer applicants additional points for proposing a particular type of project but do not disqualify applications that don't.

Selection Criteria

These are the guidelines reviewers use to evaluate proposals. Agencies always publish their selection criteria and usually set a number of points a proposal can score for meeting each criterion successfully. Your job is to develop a proposal that meets all the specific criteria so it will win the highest possible score.

When deciding how much effort and detail to put into the various sections of the proposal, look at the number of points the agency has assigned the corresponding selection criteria. Obviously, the more points assigned, the greater the importance to the agency. For this program, under methods for Application Review Information, it states that the Secretary gives equal weight to each of the selection criteria and to each factor within each criteria.

It's best to organize your proposal to follow the criteria as they are listed in the RFP. The agency will give reviewers a rating sheet that lists them in the same order. Your proposal will be easier to rate if it follows the order the reviewer expects. And the easier a proposal is to rate, the more likely it is to get a high score. Don't make reviewers work any harder than they have to.

Using our conceptual framework in Chapter One and following the selection criteria established in this RFP, we would first discuss the severity of the problem we are proposing to address, the severity of the need for a solution, and the significance our proposed project would have in terms of: increasing understanding of the problem addressed; developing new strategies for dealing with the problem; the importance of the project's outcomes; and its ability to be replicated in other communities experiencing the same problem (*see page 2, Need Statement*).

Next, we would set out our plan of operation (*see page 5, Objectives and page 6, Activities*), discussing how the project design will address the needs of the target population; outlining goals and objectives in specific, measurable terms; and illustrating how the project's implementation and evaluation will contribute to efforts to replicate it.

Then, we would outline our evaluation plan and show how it relates to our objectives and will help guide future replications (*see page 12, Evaluation*); discuss our management plan and the qualifications of key project personnel (*see page 11, Personnel*); and explain and justify all expenses in the project budget (*see page 15, Budget*); including a discussion of how the project will continue after federal support ends.

Electronic Submission

This program is participating in the electronic submission pilot project of ED (*see **Chapter Three***). For this program, you have a choice between electronic and paper submission. This section provided you with important information and instructions for electronic submission, including how to secure an extension if you cannot access the e-Application system on the closing date.

For Further Information Contact

This section lists the name, address, and phone number of the person in the program office who can answer questions about the program or the application process.

One of the most frequent questions I hear from people who are new to writing federal proposals is, "What is a program officer and how do I find out how to reach one?" The program officer is a member of the staff of the department or office responsible for managing the grant program. The program officer supervises the grant competition and monitors the implementation of the funded projects. Program officers also are responsible for assisting applicants.

It is a good idea to call the program officer listed in the RFP for information that doesn't appear in the RFP and clarification of details that do. Often, the program officer can give you the following additional information:

- The number of applicants expected;

- Types of projects usually funded;

- Recent interpretations of aspects of the regulations or statute;

- Dates and locations of any meetings in which government officials will offer technical assistance to potential applicants;

- The availability of individual technical assistance, including program officers' ability to review draft applications and offer suggestions for improving them before submission;

- A list of previous grantees;

- Agency publications relevant to the grant program;

- Projected timelines for reviewing applications and awarding grants; and

- Copies of successful proposals from previous competitions.

This section also provides instructions for individuals with disabilities who may need to obtain the document in an alternative format.

You can also access this document electronically by visiting the ED website. The official document, however, is the one that is located in the Federal Register and at the website listed. You should be sure to read the official document and use it to write your proposal.

Program Authority

This line tells you what federal statute governs the program. It cites the United States Code, which you usually can find in any law office or library. And agencies' program offices usually can provide you with copies of the relevant sections if they aren't already included in the application package.

DEPARTMENT OF EDUCATION
Office of Postsecondary Education;
Overview Information; Fund for the
Improvement of Postsecondary
Education—The Comprehensive
Program; Notice Inviting Applications
for New Awards for Fiscal Year (FY)
2005

Catalog of Federal Domestic Assistance (CDFA) Number: 84.116A (pre-applications) and 84.116B (Final application).

Dates: Applications Available: September 13, 2004.

Deadline for Transmittal of Pre-Applications: November 3, 2004.

Deadline for Transmittal of Final Applications: March 22, 2005.

Deadline for Intergovernmental Review: May 21, 2005.

Eligible Applicants: Institutions of higher education or combinations of those institutions and other public and private nonprofit institutions and agencies.

Estimated Available Funds: $12,700,000 for new awards.

The Administration has requested $32 million for this program for FY 2005 (approximately $12.7 million of which will be available for new Comprehensive Program awards). The actual level of funding, if any, depends on final congressional action. However, we are inviting applications to allow enough time to complete the grant process if Congress appropriates funds for this program.

Estimated Range of Awards: $50,000–$600,000 per year.

Estimated Average Size of Awards: $212,000 per year.

Estimated Number of Awards: 60.

Note: The department is not bound by any estimates in this notice.

Project Period: Up to 36 months.

Full Text of Announcement

I. Funding Opportunity Description

Purpose of Program: The Comprehensive Program supports grants and cooperative agreements to improve postsecondary education opportunities. It encourages reforms, innovations, and improvements of postsecondary education that respond to problems of national significance and provide access to quality education for all.

Invitational Priorities: For FY 2005 these priorities are invitational priorities. Under 34 CFR 75.105(c)(1) we do not give an application that meets those invitational priorities a competitive or absolute preference over other applications.

These priorities are:

Projects to support new ways to ensure equal access to postsecondary education and to improve rates of retention and program completion, especially for underrepresented students whose retention and completion rates continue to lag behind those of other groups, and especially to encourage wider adoption of proven approaches to this problem.

Projects to promote innovative reforms in the curriculum and instruction of various subjects at the college preparation, undergraduate, and graduate/professional levels, especially through student-centered or technology-mediated strategies, and including the subject area of civic education.

Projects designing more cost-effective ways of improving postsecondary instruction and operations, i.e., to promote more student learning relative to institutional resources expended.

Projects to improve the quality of K–12 teaching through new models of teacher preparation and through new kinds of partnerships between schools and colleges and universities that enhance students' preparation for, access to, and success in college.

Program Authority: 20 U.S.C. 1138–1138d.

Applicable Regulations: (a) The Education Department General Administrative Regulations (EDGAR) in 34 CFR parts 74, 75, 77, 79, 80, 82, 84, 85, 86, 97, 98, and 99.

Note: The regulations in 34 CFR part 86 apply to institutions of higher education only.

II. Award Information

Type of Award: Discretionary grants or cooperative awards.

Estimated Available Funds: $12,700,000 for new awards.

The administration has requested $32 million for this program for FY 2005 (approximately $12.7 million of which will be available for new Comprehensive Program awards). The actual level of funding, if any, depends on final congressional action. However, we are inviting applications to allow enough time to complete the grant process if Congress appropriates funds for this program.

Estimated Range of Awards: $50,000–$600,000 per year.

Estimated Average Size of Awards: $212,000 per year.

Estimated Number of Awards: 60.

Note: The Department is not bound by any estimates in this notice.

Project Period: Up to 36 months.

III. Eligibility Information

1. *Eligible Applicants:* Institutions of higher education or combinations of those institutions and other public and private nonprofit institutions and agencies.

2. *Cost Sharing or Matching:* This program does not involve cost sharing or matching.

3. *Other:* All applicants must submit a pre-application to be eligible to submit a final application.

IV. Application and Submission Information

1. *Address to Request Application Package:* Education Publications Center (ED Pubs), P.O. Box 1398, Jessup, MD 20794-1398. Telephone (toll free): 1-877-433-7827. FAX: (301) 470-1244. If you use a telecommunications device for the deaf (TDD), you may call (toll free): 1-877-576-7734.

You may also contact ED Pubs at its Web site:

http://www.ed.gov/pubs/edpubs.html or you may contact ED Pubs at its e-mail address: *edpubs@inet.ed.gov*

If you request an application from ED Pubs, be sure to identify this competition as follows: CFDA number 84.116A.

Individuals with disabilities may obtain a copy of the application package in an alternative format (e.g., Braille, large print, audiotape, or computer diskette) by contacting the program contact person listed in this section.

FIGURE 4.1 Federal Register

FOR FURTHER INFORMATION CONTACT:

Fund for the Improvement of Postsecondary Education (FIPSE), U.S. Department of Education, 1990 K Street, NW., 6th Floor, Washington, DC 20006-8544. Telephone: (202) 502-7500. The application text and forms may be obtained from the Internet address: *http://www.ed.gov/FIPSE*

2. *Content and Form of Application Submission:* Requirements concerning the content of an application, together with the forms you must submit, are in the application package for this competition.

Pre-Application: Letters of support, references, and other appendices and attachments are discouraged for the pre-application.

Page Limit: The application narrative is where the applicant addresses the selection criteria that reviewers use to evaluate the application. You must limit the pre-application narrative to the equivalent or no more than 5 pages or approximately 1,250 words and the final application narrative to the equivalent of no more than 25 pages or approximately 6,250 words, using the following standards:

• A "page" is 8.5″ × 11″, on one side only, with 1″ margins at the top, bottom, and both sides.

• Double space (no more than three lines per vertical inch) all text in the application narrative, except footnotes, quotations, references, and text in charts, tables, figures, and graphs.

• Use a font size that is 11 point or larger and no smaller than 10 pitch (characters per inch).

The page limits for the pre-application and final application do not apply to the title page; the assurances and certifications; the budget section, including the narrative budget justification for the final application; or the one-page abstract, resumes, letters of support, or bibliography for the final application.

3. *Submission Dates and Times:*

Applications Available: September 13, 2004.

Deadline for Transmittal of Pre-Applications: November 3, 2004.

Deadline for Transmittal of Final Applications: March 22, 2005.

We do not consider an application that does not comply with the deadline requirements.

Applications for grants under this program may be submitted electronically using the Electronic Grant Application System (e-Application) accessible through the Department's e-Grants system, or in paper format by mail or hand delivery. For information (including dates and times) about how to submit your application electronically, or by mail or hand delivery, please refer to *Section IV. 6. Other Submission Requirements in this notice.*

Deadline for Intergovernmental Review: May 21, 2005.

4. *Intergovernmental Review:* This competition is subject to Executive Order 12372 and the regulations in 34 CFR part 79. Information about Intergovernmental Review of Federal Programs under Executive Order 12372 is in the application package for this competition.

5. *Funding Restrictions:* We reference regulations outlining funding restrictions in the Applicable Regulations section of this notice.

6. *Other Submission Requirements:* Applications for grants under this Comprehensive Program may be submitted electronically or in paper format by mail or hand delivery.

a. *Electronic Submission of Applications.*

If you submit your application to us electronically, you must use e-Application available through the Department's e-Grants system, accessible through the e-Grants portal page at: *http://e-grants.ed.gov.*

While completing your electronic application, you will be entering data online that will be saved into a database. You may not e-mail an electronic copy of a grant application to us.

Please note the following:

• Your participation in e-Application is voluntary.

• You must complete the electronic submission of your grant application by 4:30 p.m., Washington, DC time, on the application deadline date. The e-Application system will not accept an application for this program

[competition] after 4:30 p.m., Washington, DC time, on the application deadline date. Therefore, we strongly recommend that you do not wait until the application deadline date to begin the application process.

• The regular hours of operation of the e-Grants Web site are 6 a.m. Monday until 7 p.m. Wednesday; and 6 a.m. Thursday until midnight Saturday, Washington, DC time. Please note that the system is unavailable on Sundays, and between 7 p.m. on Wednesdays and 6 a.m. on Thursdays, Washington, DC time, for maintenance. Any modifications to these hours are posted on the e-Grants Web site.

• You will not receive additional point value because you submit your application in electronic format, nor will we penalize you if you submit your application in paper format.

• You must submit all documents electronically, including the application for the Comprehensive Program (ED 40-514), the Comprehensive Program Budget Summary form, and all necessary assurances and certifications.

• Your electronic application must comply with any page limit requirements described in this notice.

• Prior to submitting your electronic application, you may wish to download it and print a copy of it for your records.

• After you electronically submit your application, you will receive an automatic acknowledgement that will include a PR/Award number (an identifying number unique to your application).

• Within three working days after submitting your electronic application, fax a signed copy of the Comprehensive Program Title Page (Form No. Ed 40-514) to the Application Control Center after following these steps:

1. Print ED 40-514 from e-Application.

2. The applicant's Authorizing Representative must sign this form.

3. Place the PR/Award number in the upper right hand corner (Item #1) of the hard-copy signature page of the ED 40-514.

4. Fax the signed ED 40-514 to the Application Control Center at (202) 245-6272.

FIGURE 4.1   *(continued)*

• We may request that you provide us original signatures on other forms at a later date.

Application Deadline Date Extension in Case of System Unavailability: If you are prevented from electronically submitting your application on the application deadline date because the e-Application system is unavailable, we will grant you an extension of one business day in order to transmit your application electronically, by mail, or by hand delivery. We will grant this extension if—

1. You are a registered user of e-Application and you have initiated an electronic application for this competition; and

2. (a) The e-Application system is unavailable for 60 minutes or more between the hours of 8:30 a.m. and 3:30 p.m., Washington, DC time, on the application deadline date; or

(b) The e-Application system is unavailable for any period of time between 3:30 p.m. and 4:30 p.m., Washington, DC time, on the application deadline date.

We must acknowledge and confirm these periods of unavailability before granting you an extension. To request this extension or to confirm our acknowledgement of any system unavailability, you may contact either (1) the person listed elsewhere in this notice under **FOR FURTHER INFORMATION CONTACT** (see VII. *Agency Contract*) or (2) the e-Grants help desk at 1-888-336-8930.

Extensions referred to in this section apply only to the unavailability of the Department's e-Application system. If the e-Application system is available, and, for any reason, you are unable to submit your application electronically or you do not receive an automatic acknowledgement of your submission, you may submit your application in paper format by mail or hand delivery in accordance with the instructions in this notice.

b. *Submission of Paper Applications by Mail.*

If you submit your application in paper format by mail (through the U.S. Postal Service or a commercial carrier), you must send the original and two copies of your application, on or before

the application deadline date, to the Department at the following address: U.S. Department of Education, Application Control Center, Attention: (CFDA Number 84.116A and 84.116B), 400 Maryland Avenue, SW., Washington, DC 20202-4260.

You must show proof of mailing consisting of one of the following:

1. A legibly dated U.S. Postal Service postmark;

2. A legible mail receipt with the date of mailing stamped by the U.S. Postal Service;

3. A dated shipping label, invoice, or receipt from a commercial carrier; or

4. Any other proof of mailing acceptable to the U.S. Secretary of Education.

If you mail your application through the U.S. Postal Service, we do not accept either of the following as proof of mailing:

1. A private metered postmark, or

2. A mail receipt that is not dated by the U.S. Postal Service.

If your application is postmarked after the application deadline date, we will not consider your application.

Note: Applicants should note that the U.S. Postal Service does not uniformly provide a dated postmark. Before relying on this method, you should check with your local post office.

c. *Submission of Paper Applications by Hand Delivery.*

If you submit your application in paper format by hand delivery, you (or a courier service) must hand deliver the original and two copies of your application, on or before the application deadline date, to the Department at the following address: U.S. Department of Education, Application Control Center, Attention: (CFDA Number 84.116A or 84.116B), 550 12th Street, SW., Room 7041, Potomac Center Plaza, Washington, DC 20202-4260.

The Application Control Center accepts hand deliveries daily between 8 a.m. and 4:30 p.m., Washington, DC time, except Saturdays, Sundays and Federal holidays. A person delivering an application must show photo identification to enter the building.

Note for Mail or Hand Delivery of Paper Applications: If you mail or hand deliver your application to the Department:

1. You must indicate on the envelope the CFDA number and suffix letter, if any, of the competition under which you are submitting your application.

2. The Application Control Center will mail a Grant Application Receipt Acknowledgment to you. If you do not receive the notification of application receipt within 15 days from the mailing of your application, you should call the U.S. Department of Education Application Control Center at (202) 245-6288.

V. Application Review Information

Selection Criteria: The selection criteria for this competition are as follows:

In evaluating pre-applications and final applications for grants under this competition, the Secretary uses the following selection criteria chosen from those listed in 34 CFR 75.210. The Secretary gives equal weight to each of the selection criteria, and within each of these criteria, the Secretary gives equal weight to each of the factors.

Pre-applications. In evaluating pre-applications, the Secretary uses the following four selection criteria:

(a) *Need for project.* The Secretary considers the need for the proposed project. In determining need, the Secretary considers each of the following factors:

(1) The magnitude or severity of the problem to be addressed by the proposed project.

(2) The magnitude of the need for the services to be provided or the activities to be carried out by the proposed project.

(b) *Significance.* The Secretary considers the significance of the proposed project. In determining significance, the Secretary considers each of the following factors:

(1) The potential contribution of the proposed project to increased knowledge or understanding of educational problems, issues, or effective strategies.

(2) The extent to which the proposed project involves the development or demonstration of promising new strategies that build on, or are alternatives to, existing strategies.

(3) The importance or magnitude of the results or outcomes likely to be attained by the proposed project.

FIGURE 4.1   *(continued)*

(4) The potential replicability of the proposed project or strategies, including, as appropriate, the potential for implementation in a variety of settings.

(c) *Quality of the project design.* The Secretary considers the quality of the design of the proposed project. In determining the quality of the design, the Secretary considers each of the following factors:

(1) The extent to which the design of the proposed project is appropriate to, and will successfully address, the needs of the target population or other identified needs.

(2) The extent to which the goals, objectives, and outcomes to be achieved by the proposed project are clearly specified and measurable.

(3) The extent to which the design for implementing and evaluating the proposed project will result in information to guide possible replication of project activities or strategies, including information about the effectiveness of the approach or strategies employed by the project.

(4) The extent to which the proposed project is designed to build capacity and yield results that will extend beyond the period of Federal financial assistance.

(d) *Quality of the project evaluation.* The Secretary considers the quality of the project evaluation to be conducted of the proposed project. In determining the quality of the evaluation, the Secretary considers each of the following factors:

(1) The extent to which the evaluation will provide guidance about effective strategies suitable for replication or testing in other settings.

(2) The extent to which the methods of evaluation are thorough, feasible, and appropriate to the goals, objectives, and outcomes of the proposed project.

(3) The extent to which the methods of evaluation include the use of objective performance measures that are clearly related to the intended outcomes of the project and will produce quantitative and qualitative data to the extent possible.

Final Applications. In evaluating final applications, the Secretary uses the following seven selection criteria:

(a) *Need for project.* The Secretary considers the need for the proposed project. In determining need, the Secretary considers each of the following factors:

(1) The magnitude or severity of the problem to be addressed by the proposed project.

(2) The magnitude of the need for the services to be provided or the activities to be carried out by the proposed project.

(b) *Significance.* The Secretary considers the significance of the proposed project. In determining significance, the Secretary considers each of the following factors:

(1) The potential contribution of the proposed project to increased knowledge or understanding of educational problems, issues, or effective strategies.

(2) The extent to which the proposed project involves the development or demonstration of promising new strategies that build on, or are alternatives to, existing strategies.

(3) The importance or magnitude of the results or outcomes likely to be attained by the proposed project.

(4) The potential replicability of the proposed project or strategies, including, as appropriate, the potential for implementation in a variety of settings.

(c) *Quality of the project design.* The Secretary considers the quality of the design of the proposed project. In determining the quality of the design, the Secretary considers each of the following factors:

(1) The extent to which the design of the proposed project is appropriate to, and will successfully address, the needs of the target population or other identified needs.

(2) The extent to which the goals, objectives, and outcomes to be achieved by the proposed project are clearly specified and measurable.

(3) The extent to which the design for implementing and evaluating the proposed project will result in information to guide possible replication of project activities or strategies, including information about the effectiveness of the approach or strategies employed by the project.

(4) The extent to which the proposed project is designed to build capacity and yield results that will extend beyond the period of Federal financial assistance.

(d) *Quality of the project evaluation.* The Secretary considers the quality of the evaluation to be conducted of the proposed project. In determining the quality of evaluation to be conducted, the Secretary considers each of the following factors:

(1) The extent to which the evaluation will provide guidance about effective strategies suitable for replication or testing in other settings.

(2) The extent to which the methods of evaluation are thorough, feasible, and appropriate to the goals, objectives, and outcomes of the proposed project.

(3) The extent to which the methods of evaluation include the use of objective performance measures that are clearly related to the intended outcomes of the project and will produce quantitative and qualitative data to the extent possible.

(e) *Quality of the management plan.* The Secretary considers the quality of the management plan for the proposed project. In determining the quality of the management plan, the Secretary considers the adequacy of the management plan to achieve the objectives of the proposed project on time and within budget, including clearly defined responsibilities, timelines, and milestones for accomplishing project tasks.

(f) *Quality of project personnel.* The Secretary considers the quality of the personnel who will carry out the proposed project. In determining the quality of project personnel the Secretary considers each of the following factors:

(1) The extent to which the applicant encourages applications for employment from persons who are members of groups that have traditionally been underrepresented based on race, color, national origin, gender, age, or disability.

(2) The qualifications, including relevant training and experience, of key project personnel.

(g) *Adequacy of resources.* The Secretary considers the adequacy of resources for the proposed project. In

FIGURE 4.1 (*continued*)

determining the adequacy of resources, the Secretary considers each of the following factors:

(1) The extent to which the costs are reasonable in relation to the objectives, design, and potential significance of the proposed project.

(2) The relevance and demonstrated commitment of each partner in the proposed project to the implementation and success of the project.

(3) The potential for continued support of the project after Federal funding ends, including, as appropriate, the demonstrated commitment of appropriate entities to such support.

VI. Award Administration Information

1. *Award Notices:* If your application is successful, we notify your U.S. Representative and U.S. Senators and send you a Grant Award Notification (GAN). We may also notify you informally.

If your application is not evaluated or not selected for funding, we notify you.

2. *Administrative and National Policy Requirements:* We identify administrative and national policy requirements in the application package and reference these and other requirements in the *Applicable Regulations* section of this notice.

We reference the regulations outlining the terms and conditions of an award in the *Applicable Regulations* section of this notice and include these and other specific conditions in the GAN. The GAN also incorporates your approved application as part of your binding commitments under the grant.

3. *Reporting:* At the end of your project period, you must submit a final performance report, including financial information, as directed by the Secretary. If you receive a multi-year award, you must submit an annual performance report that provides the most current performance and financial expenditure information as specified by the Secretary in 34 CFR 75.118.

4. *Performance Measures:* The success of FIPSE's Comprehensive Program depends upon (1) the extent to which funded projects are being replicated, *i.e.,* adopted or adapted by others; and (2) the manner in which projects are being institutionalized and continued after grant funding. These two results constitute FIPSE's indicators of the success of our program.

If funded, you will be asked to collect and report data in your project's annual performance report (EDGAR, 34 CFR 75.590) on steps taken toward these goals Consequently, applicants to FIPSE's Comprehensive Program are advised to include these two outcomes in conceptualizing the design, implementation and evaluation of the proposed project. Consideration of FIPSE's two performance outcomes is an important part of many of the review criteria discussed below. Thus, it is important to the success of your application that you include these objectives. Their measure should be a part of the project evaluation plan, along with measures of objectives specific to your project.

VII. Agency Contact

FOR FURTHER INFORMATION CONTACT: Levenia Ishmell, Fund for the Improvement of Postsecondary Education, U.S. Department of Education, 1990 K Street, NW., suite 6147, Washington, DC 20006-8544. Telephone: (202) 502-7668 or by e-mail *Levenia.Ishmel@ed.gov.*

If you use a telecommunications device for the deaf (TDD), you may call the Federal Information Relay Service (FIRS) at 1-800-877-8339.

Individuals with disabilities may obtain this document in an alternative format (*e.g.,* Braille, large print, audiotape, or computer diskette) on request to the program contact person listed in this section.

For additional program information call the FIPSE office (202-502-7500) between the hours of 8 a.m. and 5 p.m. Washington, DC time, Monday through Friday.

VIII. Other Information

Electronic Access to This Document: You may view this document, as well as all other documents of this Department published in the **Federal Register**, in text or Adobe Portable Document Format (PDF) on the Internet at the following site: *http://www.ed.gov/ news/fedregister.*

To use PDF you must have Adobe Acrobat Reader, which is available free at this site. If you have questions about using PDF, call the U.S. Government Printing Office (GPO), toll free, at 1-888-293-6498; or in the Washington, DC, area at (202) 512-1530.

Note: The official version of this document is the document published in the **Federal Register**, Free Internet access to the official edition of the **Federal Register** and the Code of Federal Regulations is available on GPO Access at: *http://www.gpoaccess.gov/nara/ index.html.*

Dated: September 8, 2004.
Sally L. Stroup,
Assistant Secretary for Postsecondary Education.

[FR Doc. E4-2165 Filed 9-10-04; 8:45 am]

BILLING CODE 4000-01-P

FIGURE 4.1   (*continued*)

GENERAL CHANGES IN THE FEDERAL LANDSCAPE

Federal agencies have been making changes in their grantmaking process in the areas of funding decisions, funding set-asides, and funding for multiyear projects. Now, some federal funders consider a grant applicant's prior performance when making a new award, they set aside funding for first-time applicants and those who have not won prior grants, and they negotiate the budget for the entire multiyear project period at the beginning of the grant award process.

The following is a list of more general changes in the federal government.

DUNS Number Requirement

In the fall of 2003, the federal government passed a ruling requiring all applicants for Federal grants and cooperative agreements, with the exception of individuals other than sole proprietors, to have a Data Universal Number System (DUNS) number. This number is a unique nine-digit identification number provided by Dun & Bradstreet.

You should verify that you have a DUNS number or take the necessary steps to obtain one if there is any possibility that you will be applying for future federal grants or cooperative agreements. If your business office does not know if you have one, you should call Dun & Bradstreet at the dedicated DUNS number request line, 1-866-705-5711, and ask if your organization already has a DUNS number.

If you do not have a DUNS number, call the same phone number and obtain one. Tell them you are a prospective applicant. The process will take about 5–10 minutes and you will be asked for information about your organization, including legal name, address, phone number, contact name and title, and number of employees. Obtaining a DUNS number is free for all entities doing business with the federal government.

New Mailing Instructions

The events of September 11, 2001 have had an impact on the submission of proposals to federal agencies. Applicants are now highly discouraged, or in some cases prohibited, from hand-delivering applications to the agencies in Washington, DC due to heightened security in the buildings. In addition, funders are selecting specific courier services and are urging applicants to use them.

Proof of timely submission may be required if there is a problem with the delivery of the proposal package. Some federal agencies stipulate that if a package is not received by the deadline date, then it will be considered for review ONLY if the applicant can show proof that the application was mailed by 12:00 midnight local time on the application deadline. Proof of timely submission includes: delivery service receipts from courier services; United States Postal Service Form 3817—Certificate of Mailing; or a receipt from the U.S. Postal Service, which must contain the post office name, location, date, and time of mailing. If you use a delivery service, try to have your application package picked up or delivered at least 24 hours before the deadline.

You should confirm the delivery of your proposal package by return receipt card (if you use certified mail via the U.S. Postal Service) or use an online tracking system. If you do not receive an application number within 10 days, call the program officer for further instructions. You might be advised to contact an Application Control Center to request the assigned number.

Remember to look carefully at the submission requirements and the mailing instructions described in the RFP. Some federal grants must be received *by* the deadline date and thus cannot be mailed *on* that date. You certainly do not want to disqualify your application for failing to comply with the submission and mailing requirements!

Federal-State Pass-Through Funds

During the last five years, many federal grants have been redirected from categorical (designated to serve only a specific category) to block grants (where the money to be spent is left to the discretion of state and local officials). This means that grantseekers apply to their state government for federal pass-through funds, in response to the grant competition designed by the state, but they are guided to varying degrees by federal regulations. For example, grantseekers who wish to apply for a 21st Century Community Learning Centers grant submit an application to their state Department of Education. Previously, they would have applied to the U.S. Department of Education and competed against proposals from across the country. Each state's 21st Century Community Learning Center RFP differs slightly and each has a different deadline; however, the basic requirements for the program are still guided by the federal enabling legislation.

Grantseekers can use the following strategies to pursue local and state funding:

1. Locate state and local funding sources. In addition to pass-through funds, states fund their own initiatives and grant programs using dollars from the state budget. Stay informed of state legislation and federal funds through websites, newsletters, conferences, workshops, public hearings, and committee reports.
2. Gather intelligence. Find out about state and local government agencies' budgets, funding plans, and priorities. Additionally, find out what types of programs are funded, the mechanisms for funding, the average funding level, and how planning is conducted and funding is determined.
3. Make contact with agency personnel. Meet the state and local program officers. Volunteer to be part of the planning and grantmaking process by working on an advisory board or committee, formulating the state or local plan that determines funding priorities, and reviewing grant applications.

4. Renewal Community/Empowerment Zone/Enterprise Community. Certain federal agencies, such as the U.S. Department of Housing and Urban Development (HUD), give priority to those applicants that are located in federally designated empowerment zones, enterprise communities, and renewal communities. These designated areas receive special federal funding for economic development, linking them with education and training. Check the HUD website (http://www.hud.gov/offices/cpd/economicdevelopment/programs/rc/tour/index.cfm) or contact your city or county government to see if your community has any of these designations.

Helpful Hint

Read the Federal Request for Proposals carefully.

Don't hesitate to call the program officer if you are unclear about an item in the RFP.

Submitting a proposal that does not correlate to the RFP is a waste of your—and the reviewer's—time.

CHAPTER FIVE

The Review Process

One of the best ways to hone your proposal-writing skills is to serve on a review panel. By serving as a reviewer, you will gain a new perspective and shift your emphasis from packing information into a proposal to presenting your information in a way that is easy for readers to digest.

In this chapter, we will learn how to present information in a user-friendly format by understanding who reviewers are, the conditions under which they work, and how they respond to proposals. We'll focus on the review process for public funders in this chapter. The review process for private funders is discussed in the next chapter.

UNDERSTANDING REVIEWERS

Most federal and state programs use review panels made up of nongovernment experts. Programs select reviewers on the basis of their expertise in designated program areas. Reviewers are expected to draw upon their own experiences and expertise when they evaluate applications according to the selection criteria.

Reviewers are expected to put aside their own biases while reviewing proposals. For example, if a reviewer has any personal feelings or knowledge about an applicant, he or she is expected to evaluate the application solely upon the contents and put their feelings or knowledge to the side. In some cases, this prior knowledge is considered a conflict of interest and the reviewer must notify program staff. In most cases, the proposal will be given to a different reviewer. Some funders will not allow reviewers to participate at all if their own organization has submitted a proposal for that particular competition.

In most cases, reviewers do receive a modest honorarium for their participation. However, this amount often barely covers travel expenses if there are any. Funders are relying more and more on technology to carry out the review process rather than requiring reviewers to travel to another city (often Washington, DC in the case of federal grants) and take a few days out of their work schedule.

Most reviewers are motivated because of the benefits gained from serving as one. You can gain valuable insight into the federal and state grant review process, and the strategies and methods the funders use to award grants. In addition, you will get a real sense of the level of competition when you apply, which will help you determine whether the caliber of your proposed projects meet the rest that are being submitted for funding.

THE REVIEW SETTING

Now that we know who the reviewers are, let's take a look at the conditions they must work under. Some funding programs convene panels in central locations to discuss proposals in person. An increasing number of funders are using technology for the review process. Reviewers are assigned to a panel and asked to read and score a specific group of applications. They score them based on the extent to which the applicant addresses the selection criteria, and are asked to make comments regarding the applicant's responses. Their scores and comments are then posted to a secure, online system. The reviewers are then asked to participate in several conference calls with their fellow panel members to share their scores and comments.

Often, reviewers must read and review several proposals in a short period of time. This can range anywhere from ten to over fifty proposals, depending on the competition and the number of reviewers being used. As you can imagine, reviewers appreciate proposals that are specific, concise, and formatted so that they are easy to read. Use graphics, bullet points, and headings to break up your narrative and make it interesting to read (*see Chapter Three for a discussion about graphics*).

Some writers feel proposals are judged by weight: the more pages, the better. In fact, the opposite is closer to the truth. Reviewers do not like long proposals. They want to read a document that gives sufficient information to address the selection criteria and stops. Your proposal should be sculpted so that every word is pertinent to the criteria and necessary for thoughtful evaluation of the project.

To make it easy on the readers, you should clearly label each section heading in the proposal, using the same section headings found in the RFP. (Also, always include a Table of Contents, with the section headings listed with their corresponding page numbers.) Don't be creative here; your section headings must be identical to those listed or you might lose points from reviewers.

One of the biggest complaints of reviewers is not being able to find the required information in the right section in a proposal. For all practical purposes, any information the reviewer cannot find after a cursory search does not exist. And if it doesn't exist, you will receive a low score, or in the worst case scenario, a "zero" for the section. (It is difficult, if not almost impossible, to earn enough points to be considered for funding if you earn a "zero" in a section.) Panelists do not memorize the proposals, nor do they know and understand them as well as their authors.

Easy to read also means easy to see. The rooms used for panel meetings frequently are poorly lighted, and reviewers have to read thousands of pages of print. You can save them from eye strain and negative reactions to your proposal by following a few basic production rules.

1. Use type that is large enough to be easily read. Many funders now stipulate a 12-point font in the RFP, which seems to be a generally accepted size for easy readability. Do not irritate reviewers by using small or compressed type; they may just stop reading your proposal altogether. Always follow the directions in the RFP if a specific font and size is required.

2. Double space the text. Again, most funders now require this in their format requirements. Also, check to see if the "double space" requirement applies to charts and tables.

3. Use only one side of the paper.

4. Be sure the proposal will lay flat. Follow the binding instructions in the RFP. If there aren't any instructions, use binder clips or ring binders.

REVIEW PROBLEMS

The panel review process does have some built-in problems. Reviewers have different standards and score proposals differently. Many programs use panels to read groups of proposals. As a result, there may be no common logic for scoring across groups.

To address this problem, program officials standardize the scores, putting all of them through a statistical formula to adjust them based on particular reviewers' tendency to score either high or low. They then rank proposals by the resulting standardized scores and award grants by rank. A proposal with a high raw score could come out with a low standardized score and a correspondingly poor chance of funding.

Officials can take other factors into consideration, though, when choosing which proposals to fund. For example, the program's authorizing law may require it to limit the amount of funding in any state or distribute grants evenly among states. These factors are detailed in the request for proposals. Read it carefully to understand the award procedures.

In spite of all the steps taken to ensure fairness, reviewers are people. They have their preferences and biases. It is impossible to predict all of the variables that will apply in a particular grant competition, which means luck will always play a role. In the end, you can only do your very best job of preparing a proposal and then cross your fingers.

Helpful Hint

Keep it simple. Make your proposal easy to read and avoid heavy text. Try to serve as a proposal reviewer. The experience will give you a better perspective when you write your proposals.

CHAPTER SIX

Private-Sector Funding

There are thousands of foundations and corporations that award grants, but the procedures and protocols they use are very different from government funders, and sometimes even from each other.

Perhaps the biggest difference is that, because they don't answer to taxpayers and legislative bodies as their government counterparts do, most foundations and corporations are far less conservative in their grant-making and often willing to fund innovative, experimental projects.

Private funders also may draw on resources not available to government agencies to provide applicants with much more than money. Corporations in particular often provide nongrant support, such as computer and other equipment, use of company facilities, supplies, and technical assistance. Many also conduct employee matching gift programs, in which the company makes contributions to organizations its employees personally support.

Often the application package for corporations and foundations is simpler than the ones for federal and state funders. Most private funders require a shorter narrative, usually between three and five pages. Because increasing numbers of private funders are using online applications, this may limit your responses for a section to a few hundred words!

Both corporations and foundations may award operating support grants to cover the day-to-day expenses of an organization or program; seed money to help a program get started; technical assistance; matching grants to add on to funds awarded by another source; or other types of assistance.

There are four basic types of private-sector funders, all of them legally chartered to provide for the public good and required to report their grant-making activities annually to the Internal

Revenue Service. Within the four general categories, funders can differ greatly in purpose, size, assets, geographical limitations, staff, and procedures.

Independent Foundations

Designated by the IRS as private, nonprofit funders, these organizations make up the largest group of foundations. They usually make grants from assets derived from individuals. Some may be family-created foundations. Independent foundations tend to have limited grant-making interests, and some may change their priority giving areas periodically to respond to societal needs. Most restrict their giving to specific geographic areas.

Company-Sponsored Foundations

These foundations are established and funded by assets from a profit-making company or corporation. They are separate entities from the founding corporation, and their grant-making is independent of contributions made directly by the corporation. Company-sponsored foundations are governed by a board of directors that usually includes corporate officials, and they may include employees in grant-making decisions. They usually give in the geographic areas in which the company has facilities. Grant-making priorities may be set by corporate officials, and often are in areas of interest to the company.

In addition to giving through their company-sponsored foundations, many corporations also fund projects directly out of their pretax earnings through direct corporate giving programs. Other corporations have only a direct corporate contributions program. Direct corporate giving may fluctuate as company profits fall and rise, but company-sponsored foundations tend to have more steady giving patterns because their grant-making is based on endowment earnings.

Community Foundations

Community foundations serve specific geographic areas, such as a city or state. They raise and administer funds from many sources and set grant-making priorities based on local needs. They are considered public charities by the IRS.

Operating Foundations

Operating foundations exist to conduct specific activities, such as research or charitable services or programs, and seldom award grants.

FINDING THE RIGHT FUNDER

In the private sector, there is much to do before you even get to the point of developing and submitting a proposal. The most extensive, and certainly the most important, part of the private grantseeking process is identifying funders whose interests match your institution's needs, and getting to know those funders inside and out. The research you do initially will help you target your grantseeking correctly and enable you to make a stronger case when you actually do apply for the grant.

There are several strategies you can use in the initial research stage:

- Ask members of your governing body, administration, and/or staff if they have any contacts in foundations or corporations. People who work in or represent your institution may know someone on a foundation or corporate board of directors or have contacted foundation or corporate officers for support in previous instances. Or they could just be neighbors of, attend church with, or belong to the same social organizations as potential funders. Never underestimate the value of personal contacts.

- Find out what foundations and corporations have given your organization grants in the past. If a source already has funded your organization, it knows and trusts your capabilities and will be more likely to take a chance on you again. Even funders to whom you have applied and been rejected can be a good prospect for a second try if you can figure out what you did wrong the first time. Also, check the recent grant listings from the funder. Even if a funder has never awarded money to your organization, they may have given to a similar organization for a similar project.

- Read publications and documents that can tell you about funders who give in your geographic area. Watch newspapers and trade publications for information on local foundations and corporations who are making grants in your community or region. Look up IRS Form 990 and 990PF tax returns in your local library to identify community donors.

- Subscribe to publications that track foundation and corporate grant activity. There are many directories and periodicals that report on private-sector philanthropy and can point you in the right direction. They include directories of local, state, and regional foundations, and independently published newsletters that report on foundation and corporate funding trends and opportunities. (*See **Appendix B** for a list of books, directories, databases, and other grantseeking resources.*)

- Use resources provided by the Foundation Center, a national service organization established by foundations to gather and disseminate information on private giving. You can purchase resource publications from the center or you can use its reference materials available in libraries across the country. The center also has comprehensive reference collections in New York City, Washington, DC, Cleveland, and San Francisco.

- To research corporations that make direct contributions, start in your own community. Businesses tend to give in their own backyards. Don't be discouraged if your community doesn't have any major corporate presence. Most cities and towns have a variety of potential business sources within their bounds. And they don't have to be large, multimillion-dollar operations. You could look into local utilities, including gas, water, power, and telephone; banks and other financial institutions; and communications companies, such as television and radio stations and cable services.

- Check the annual reports of organizations in your area, especially those that are similar to yours. Annual reports usually list foundation and corporate sponsors from the local community.

- For more ideas, keep your eye on local newspapers, business indexes for the community or region, and other guides available from the local chamber of commerce, business bureau, or library. Learn as much as you can about the business and financial activities and health of your community, and find out who the players are. Focus on areas of your local and state economy that currently are most profitable, such as automobile sales and financial services, so you request support only from those who can afford to give it.

When researching private funders, pay attention to their eligibility requirements. If your type of organization is not eligible, do not apply. Also, read carefully the other limitations foundations and corporations place on their grant-making, such as geographic area, program area, and grant type. Select those funders that give in your geographic area, have an interest in your subject, and fund your type of organization.

MAKING CONTACT

Once you've identified potential funders, you need to collect: (1) information about their mission, (2) their grant-making interests and activities, (3) a copy of their annual report, (4) an application (if one is available), and (5) their giving guidelines (the same as an RFP for public funders). First, check the Internet to see if this information is available online at the foundation or corporate website. If it is not, call or write and ask the funder for this information (see Figure 6.1).

Although it's usually easy to locate the appropriate contact for a corporate foundation by looking in the annual report, it can be more difficult to determine whom to approach in a company that gives directly. Remember, corporations may not have a specific grants or contributions office. Often, your best bet is to call the corporate public relations, community relations, or marketing department because businesses usually consider philanthropy a community service/advertising function. However, if a multisite company operates a facility in your area; it's usually best to contact the local manager rather than corporate headquarters, again, because corporate giving generally is locally focused.

When you receive the materials you have requested, search for the following critical information before starting to develop your proposal:

40 Tall Pine Drive   Sudbury   Massachusetts 01776   phone 978 443 5000   fax 978 443 8000

[Date]

[Name of foundation director or president]
[Name of foundation]
[Address]

Dear   ,

The [name of your organization] would like to propose a project for [brief project description]. This proposed project coincides with the interests of the foundation as shown by its previous grant-making. [Explain the link between your project and the funder's interests.]

Please send current information on your grant programs and policies, especially any information regarding your support of historic museums [or specific program area]. Specifically, we would like a copy of the following documents:

- Annual report;
- Application guidelines, including information on deadlines for submitting proposals;
- Any additional information on current grant priorities; and
- A list of previously funded grants.

Please add the [name of your organization] to your mailing list for future publications, such as newsletters, announcements or priorities, annual reports, etc.

Thank you for your assistance.

Sincerely,

[Name]
[Title]

[Telephone Number]

FIGURE 6.1   Information Request Letter

Purpose

Read carefully the description of the foundation's purpose and what it chooses to fund. You need to understand a funder's grant-making focus so you can link your project idea with its interests and avoid applying to funders whose giving patterns do not coincide with your needs and projects. When developing a proposal, state clearly the ways in which the funder's purpose would be furthered by your proposed project.

Areas of Giving

Review the specific areas in which the funder has chosen to give, including funding priorities. Know the types of grants the foundation will award.

Eligibility

Funders will state the types of organizations to which they give and often will list those to whom they will not give. Review this information carefully. If you have any questions or concerns about the eligibility of your organization, contact the funder. Usually, foundations and corporations give to organizations classified as tax-exempt under IRS Code Section 501(c)(3).

Limitations

Usually, funders state in their guidelines what they will *not* fund. Foundations and corporations often choose not to fund the following types of organizations: for-profit organizations, labor groups, political organizations, and religious organizations. Types of expenses and activities some funders will not support include routine operating costs, endowment-building, deficit reduction, fundraising, advertising, challenge grants, annual drives, trips or tours, lobbying efforts, and scholarships.

Each funder has its own rules for what it will and will not fund. Take these limitations literally and do not request funding for items or projects the guidelines expressly state will not be funded. And beware: Some foundations and corporations do not accept unsolicited proposals, a fact that sometimes is hard to discern from their annual reports.

Application Procedures

If the funder provides an application form, be sure to request and complete it. Many funders don't have forms or formal procedures for submitting a proposal but do provide general instructions for submitting an initial inquiry. Often, they request a brief summary of the proposed project, including its purpose, methods, personnel, financial support requested, and the way in which the project meets the funder's interests. You can contact the funder's staff to review the project summary in person or by telephone, or submit a copy through the mail.

If your project summary interests a funder, the funder will request a formal proposal. In addition, the funder may want to send a staff member or consultant to visit your institution and evaluate its activities.

Selection Criteria

Funders' guidelines may include a list of selection criteria or an explanation of review procedures. When developing your project and proposal, respond to each of these items fully to demonstrate that your project is worthy of funding.

Budget

Determine what project expenses the funder will support. Many will not allow you to charge indirect costs to the grant. Contact foundation or corporation staff and question them if the guidelines don't make this area clear.

Deadline

Foundations and corporations vary in their deadline policy. Many have no deadlines and review proposals as they receive them. Others will list the dates of monthly, quarterly, or annual board of directors meetings and will let you know how early they need to receive proposals for consideration at each meeting.

Contact

Funders usually list the name, title, address, and telephone number of the person in charge of the overall giving program or its different segments. This is the person to go to for more information or clarification of the annual report and guidelines.

When you've collected and read all the information about a particular funder, remember to ask yourself the following questions:

1. Does the project fit the purpose and priorities of the funder?

2. Does the funder give in this geographic area?

3. Does the funder give to this type of organization?

4. Does my organization have any links with the funder's trustees or staff?

If the answer to questions one through three is yes, then the light is green for seeking a grant from the funder. If the answer to question four also is yes, use those connections to help get your foot in the door.

DEVELOPING THE PROPOSAL

In general, foundation and corporate proposal requirements are less stringent and less extensive than for federal grants. Unlike the federal grants arena, in which organizations often develop the project and its proposal simultaneously, private-sector grantseeking usually involves informally questioning a funder about a fully developed project idea. The proposal often is just formal documentation for a funder that already has expressed interest.

Sometimes, a funder will ask that you submit a two-or three-page letter of inquiry or a slightly longer concept paper to introduce your idea. Often, the letter of inquiry provides a starting point for personal discussion and can even lead the funder's staff to suggest changes or improvements in the project to make it more fundable.

The letter should be on your organization's letterhead and signed by the chief administrator. You can send inquiry letters to several different funders at the same time, but be sure to tailor them to each funder's priorities and guidelines. All inquiry letters should contain the following elements:

Introduction

Refer to previous conversations and meetings. Thank the funding officer for sharing information about his or her foundation or corporation and for expressing interest in your organization and project.

Connection to Funder's Purpose

Briefly explain your project and how it meets the funder's interests and priorities.

Need and Solution

Describe the problem and need for the project as well as the solution it proposes.

Project Description

State the project's activities, methodology, timetable, and expected results.

Key Personnel

Give the names of the project director and key staff and briefly summarize their qualifications.

Funding Request

State the amount of funding requested and the proposed project period. Explain the financial support and resources provided to the project from your organization. Describe the means for continuing the project after the grant expires.

Eligibility

Explain how your organization meets the funder's giving criteria.

Closing

Provide a name and telephone number for further contact and request a follow-up meeting or conversation.

If you would like to submit more information than the few paragraphs the inquiry letter allows, write a brief concept paper. This two- to three-page document should outline the project and give the funder a clear picture of your proposed ideas. Otherwise, keep attachments to a minimum.

If the funder is interested in your project, it will request a formal proposal. By the time you start developing your actual proposal, you already are well on your way to a grant.

For the most part, you should be able to modify the conceptual framework described in Chapter One when you develop a private-sector proposal. Be sure, though, to follow the format and criteria the funder requires. If the funder does not provide any proposal guidance, use the framework format with an abstract, introduction, and complete appendix.

Usually, private-sector funders also require the following information:

✔ Proof of tax-exempt status under Internal Revenue Service Code Section 501(c)(3);

✔ Audited financial statements;

✔ Operating budgets;

✔ Names and affiliations of the applicant's directors; and

✔ Information on the activities of your agency.

THE NATURE OF CORPORATE GIVING

Grantseekers often look to foundations to fill in for shortfalls in government funding, but may overlook or misunderstand the world of corporate grant-making. When they do approach corporations, many grantseekers tend to use the same techniques they employ in foundation relations, despite the fact that businesses give for very different reasons and in more diverse ways. Successful corporate grantseeking requires its own set of research and development skills.

Corporations tend to award grants to nonprofits for several broad reasons:

- To strengthen the communities in which their employees live;

- To gain name recognition among potential consumers; and

- To solve social problems in health, education, and the environment.

Think of this kind of "enlightened self-interest" as a two-sided coin. On one side, corporations are interested in the real, human problems their communities face. They want to improve the quality of life in that community and gain the halo effect of being part of that improvement. On the other side, they are accountable to their owners and stockholders to maximize profit. So their philanthropic interests often are related directly to social issues that affect corporate services or products. Selective philanthropy is a way for corporations to bring the two sides together, resulting in enhanced community and public relations and, hopefully, an increase in profits.

Corporations also make donations and award grants to gain tax exemptions. Corporate foundations, which companies set up as nonprofit entities to handle their grant-making programs, must contribute at least 5 percent of the market value of the company's assets each year and file Internal Revenue Service Form 990-PF to account for their activity. In addition, corporations that give directly, rather than through a company foundation (or both), may deduct contributions of up to 10 percent of pretax income. The fluctuating nature of corporate profits, however, means that donations also rise and fall with a business's fortunes.

In tight times, corporate contributions managers may be under pressure to demonstrate to their management how the company's philanthropy can help it be more competitive and profitable. So it's important that you remember they will want to see how their donations will affect not only social problems but also company operations.

THE CORPORATE GRANT PROPOSAL

You will probably find that the proposal experience is different when dealing with a corporation that awards funds directly rather than through a corporate foundation.

Given the corporate world's focus on lean staffing structures, it's understandable that companies have fewer employees to deal with grant proposals than do government agencies and some private foundations. So it's not unusual for a corporation to settle with you on the terms of a grant before (or even instead of) asking for a formal proposal. The initial letter of inquiry—that brief, persuasive request for support—often is the only written documentation you will need.

Corporations tend to use a more informal, personal approach than other funders and generally prefer to work out details of their support in conversations and meetings rather than reading lengthy proposals. This can throw some grantseekers who are used to putting a lot of time and effort into writing impersonal proposals. Don't worry about asking a corporate executive face-to-face for support. Make the contact and get to know the people who will be deciding the fate of your proposal. Follow their lead in the request process. If they prefer to talk things through, oblige them. But if they want a written proposal—as some do—be sure to include the following points:

- Specific ways in which you will recognize the company's support, such as news releases, plaques or other awards, recognition at a banquet or luncheon, or a letter from your governing board;

- An invitation to corporate staff to an event that will demonstrate the effect of the company's support;

- Ways in which corporate employees are involved in providing services to your organization; and

- The effect of the company's contribution on the successful operation of your organization.

No matter what your approach to corporations, be sure to use your biggest guns. Although you, as the development officer, do all the research and lay the groundwork, it should be your chief executive officer and/or board members who present the request. Corporate executives expect to deal with their peers when they're giving away large amounts of money or goods.

PRIVATE FUNDER REVIEW PROCESS

The private-sector review process also differs from that of the federal government. While federal agencies use outside readers, foundations and corporations usually conduct internal reviews, generally by their board of directors or staff.

At most foundations, a program officer or staff member reviews all of the proposals to make sure that there is a match between the proposed project and the funder's interests. Based on their knowledge of the board members and their prior history regarding funding decisions, they select the proposals that are a "good fit" for the board to review. It is important, then, to develop a positive relationship with this person, since he or she makes this critical decision. This individual can also tell you if your proposed project even stands a chance of being considered for funding.

In most cases, foundation board members come from various backgrounds and are probably not experts in your field. Stay away from jargon and terms unfamiliar to the general public. If you do use them, be sure to define them in the narrative. Ask the funder about its review process so you will understand the type of reader for whom you are writing.

Because of the role boards of directors play in the funding process, meeting application deadlines is very important. Staff must process proposals in time for the next scheduled board meeting, which often is once every quarter, and sometimes annually. If you miss a deadline, you will have to wait until the next meeting, which unlike public funders, might only delay your project for a few months.

Helpful Hint

Try to find out as much as you can about the funder. Prematurely approaching a funding agency may hurt your proposal if you don't have your facts straight.

≈

CHAPTER SEVEN

The Politics of Grantsmanship

≈

If the task of writing proposals consisted simply of studying a solicitation, collecting the most recent research, and developing a project that meets a need, it would be a challenging one. Still, it would be much less challenging than the one most proposal writers actually face.

Most of us must write proposals for organizations, and those organizations often throw major roadblocks in our path. Some proposal writers are faced with the prospect of putting together a proposal that doesn't make sense, because that is "what they were told to do."

Too many times, you, as a proposal writer, will be directed to write proposals that don't make any sense. Your task will be to make a rational, logical case for basically absurd ideas. Creating reason from someone else's nonsense is as much a political exercise as an intellectual one.

The basic problem is that the process occurs in the midst of an organization filled with personalities, conflicting values, departmental jealousies, traditions and protocols. All of this affects the writing of proposals. Let's look at some of the major obstacles.

Educate Your Organization

Often, individuals in the organization who aren't normally involved in grantseeking feel the process is magic: you write a proposal and money appears.

This is the problem with the manager who calls you into his or her office and orders you to "get me a grant." The manager has no idea of what kind of grant is needed or even the type of project required to win one. The only thought is to get some money. Worse is the manager who wants something that is unlikely to get funded—like new secretaries because the current ones are overloaded. This is not a winning grant idea.

Education is the best way to deal with lack of knowledge. You must teach your organization's staff about the grant process. One way to do this is to establish and publish procedures for requesting assistance in seeking grants. These procedures should include filing a form with you that identifies:

- ✔ Funding source;

- ✔ Problem (client centered);

- ✔ Project idea;

- ✔ Estimated budget; and

- ✔ Resources available to assist in proposal preparation.

Make it clear that anyone who wants your help in pursuing a grant first must fill out the form, which, of course, forces them to think through the process and guarantees they will come to you with some solid, reasonable ideas. The form also gives you a starting point for discussing the project and focusing it on the needs of the people your organization serves. It also gives you an out: You can point out gaps in a person's plan and send him or her back to the drawing board. Never accept a plan that isn't well thought out. Encourage your staff to complete the form in the early stages of the proposal process to ensure ample time for proposal preparation.

Another method is to hold an annual workshop for staff members who are interested in seeking grants. At that workshop, you can teach them the elements of a fundable project and how to conceptualize a grant proposal. You can also provide brief information about funders and copies of funded proposals.

Sidestep Rivalries

Personal and departmental conflicts often hinder proposal development. People want to fight over the money, prestige, and power that accompanies a grant. Some projects have been effectively sabotaged by being directed to a unit or department whose only claim to the privilege is that "it never gets any grants." Usually, there is a reason it never gets any grants. It either is not eligible for most grant programs or its staff is unwilling to entertain any ideas or approaches a funder would support.

Having a capable, experienced project manager who can develop a consistent direction for the project helps ease the process. Such leadership can result in a stronger, more fundable proposal. But selecting a project manager often is a source of contention itself and may be deferred until after the grant is won. In such a situation, the task of directing proposal development often falls to the proposal writer.

The best way to keep everyone happy is to open up the grant development process. Establish a grant development team that includes the major factions and some neutrals. Have the team meet on a regular basis during the proposal-writing process so it can recommend answers to major problems. As the experienced grantseeker on the team, you should act as moderator and provide objective information for making decisions. To do this, you must remain neutral and able to communicate with all factions. Using the team method can help you develop compromises without destroying the proposal's viability.

Of course, opening up the process slows it down. The more people involved in developing the proposal, the longer it will take. Plan accordingly when looking at proposal deadlines!

WORKING WITH PROGRAM OFFICERS

At the heart of every funding source—public and private—is a person who is responsible for managing the grant program: the program officer. Program officers have varying degrees of authority and influence depending on the funder. Some make funding decisions, some only recommend projects for funding, and others simply process the applications according to established procedures.

Because program officers can be very powerful—or, at the very least, helpful—it is important to build good personal relationships with them. Program officers can save you valuable time by giving you a frank assessment of your project's chances for getting funded. They may also be able to suggest other funders that you could approach.

The best way to build a good relationship is to be polite and patient in all your dealings with a program officer. Program officers look forward to dealing with polite grantseekers, and your patience shows you respect the fact that the program officer is facing mountains of work and demands from numerous other applicants.

On the other side of the coin, pushiness, harassment, and threats can only damage your relationship. Program officers are irritated by aggressive, overbearing grantseekers, and they have every right to be! Putting pressure on program officers can backfire with disastrous results. This is something you should avoid at all costs.

You should stay in touch with your program officers, reminding them of you and your interests as often and in as many ways as possible. Routinely send them any publications you produce, any newspaper articles about your activities, and invite them to your agency events. They may not attend (they have limited time in their schedules) but they will appreciate your thinking of them.

Your communication should be a two-way street. Be responsive and reliable if your program officer asks for a favor. They may need some information for a report or a quote from a grantee for an article. Make sure your program officers are comfortable asking you for assistance and always respond promptly and appropriately. The favor you do this month may be returned next month.

FEDERAL POLITICS

People often ask how much politics has to do with getting proposals funded. The truth is, sometimes politics plays a major role in the decision. (If you have ever had a high scoring proposal that did not get funded, you understand perfectly!)

If you want to use politics to assist your federal grantseeking, you should understand the rules; i.e., what is allowable and what is not. There are some things you can do to help your proposal's chances with the federal government. It all depends on how much time and energy you want to invest in the political process. Playing the game requires a great deal of effort and years of building contacts and knowledge about the process.

Use Your Elected Officials

Begin with a relatively simple approach: Get to know your congressional representatives. Make sure they know about your application and are willing to help get it funded. This means communicating with them throughout the grant development process and providing a summary of the final proposal.

The benefits of building such relationships are not immediately apparent. Your congressperson or senator cannot influence agencies' grant decisions. But if you find yourself in a dispute with an agency—perhaps over compliance with one of the myriad rules governing federal grants—your representatives can help you through the process and make sure you get a fair shake. So it helps to plan ahead and make sure your friends in Washington are familiar with your federal activities.

Don't stop communicating when you win the grant. Continue to keep your representatives informed about the project and its successes. This will give them a good feeling about you and your organization and make them more helpful to you in the future.

Add Your Two Cents

If you're prepared to take the long view, you can take advantage of several opportunities to influence legislation that creates the rules that govern grant programs.

You can testify before congressional committees, write letters to your representatives, and attend professional organizations' strategy sessions to help shape legislation that meets your needs.

Once Congress passes a piece of legislation, it goes to the federal agency responsible for implementing it. The agency then must develop regulations to govern programs created by the law, which may give them considerable flexibility. This is the time to share your ideas with agency staff. You can meet with them and provide them with position papers that could convince them to slant the rules your way. Remember, the agency is responsible for making sure the program serves the field Congress intended it to serve. You can act as a representative of that field.

Agencies also offer another, more formal opportunity for you to offer input. When agencies draft rules, they must allow the public to comment on them before making them final. These proposed rules are published in the *Federal Register* along with a deadline for comments. Agency staff must read and consider every single response and explain why they do or do not choose to make the changes suggested.

Get Involved

If you want to get deeply involved in the political side of the grant process, you must participate actively in the professional and trade organizations that have an interest in the grant programs you want to influence. Such organizations often administer large-scale lobbying programs to convince Congress to pass legislation of interest to their constituents. To have serous political influence, you must rise to a decision-making position in one or more of these organizations.

If you decide to get involved in lobbying, check with your organization's legal staff. The federal government limits the extent to which many organizations may lobby and restricts any lobbying in connection with a grant proposal.

Avoid Tinkering with the Review Process

As you can see, there are several ways to influence the federal grant process, but there is one approach you should avoid. Don't try to influence the panel review process. The process trends to rely on networks of cronies that are well-known experts in a particular field. If you belong to such a network, you don't need to exert direct influence because your colleagues already know and respect your work. If you don't belong and try to sway reviewers anyway, you probably will only get yourself in trouble. Federal programs guard their review panels carefully to ensure fairness and objectivity.

You also can get into trouble by trying to persuade a program officer to influence a panel review. Program officers are career civil servants. They don't like to have their jobs endangered.

Helpful Hint

Do not be aggressive and overbearing. You will simply irritate the program officer and hurt your chances for funding.

CHAPTER EIGHT

Never Accept Failure

So now you know the basic concepts involved in writing an effective grant proposal, how to adapt them to suit different situations, and how to deal with various factors that affect grantseeking.

But keep this in mind: You could do everything right and still not win a grant. Most proposals do not win funding because of the tremendous competition. While the country's needs have grown explosively, the amount of money available to meet them has grown slowly. One failure doesn't have to mean the end of hope, though. It often takes several attempts to win a grant. If you don't make it the first time, you can use that proposal as a basis for the next try.

The first thing to do is to contact your federal or state program officer, or foundation or corporate funding officer, to find out why your proposal wasn't funded. Be professional and do not let your disappointment over being rejected get the better of you. Remember, you are asking for this information to reapply and need their cooperation in order to get useful information.

Ask public funders for a copy of the reviewers comments and ask foundation or corporate officers to point out specific weaknesses in your proposal. Take careful notes and be sure that you know where you need to make revisions for the next submission. If you feel it is necessary and the funder is open to doing so, ask for a meeting to discuss your proposal in person. Learn from all of their input and revise your proposal accordingly.

Be careful when revising a proposal for resubmission to a federal program. Agencies select new review panels for each round of competition, and next year's reviewers may not hold the same opinions as this year's. It's best to discuss reviewers' comments with the program officer, who has a good overview of panels' reactions, to determine which changes would be most effective in future proposals.

Reading copies of proposals that have won funding in previous years also helps. (Actually you should try to do this *before* you even sit down to write your proposal.) You can pick out common elements and approaches in the successful proposals and incorporate them into yours. Check the public or private funder website to see if there are samples of funded proposals. If you cannot find any, call the grantees listed and ask for a copy of their funded proposal. You will find that many grantees are willing to share their funded proposals and give you some tips about how to write your proposal! If they cannot send you an electronic copy, be prepared to pay a small copying fee if asked. (*See **Chapter Nine** for samples of funded proposals.*)

> ### Helpful Hint
>
> "No" is just an interim response. Don't give up. You can always revise an unsuccessful proposal and resubmit it to another competition.

CONCLUSION

These are just the tools of proposal writing—the painter's brushes, so to speak. Designing an effective, convincing grant proposal is an art. As with any art, you need to understand the technical aspects in order to produce a work that is coherent. The real challenge is in using them in your own creative way to produce a proposal that makes an impact, and receives public and/or private funding.

CHAPTER NINE

Sample Proposals

This chapter presents six actual proposals that successfully won federal, state, corporate, and foundation grants. The first proposal was submitted by the School of Architecture and Design, DAAP/University of Cincinnati to the Grants for Teaching and Learning Resources and Curriculum Development program administered by the National Endowment for the Humanities. The second was submitted by the Greencastle-Antrim School District in Pennsylvania to the Teaching American History Grant Program administered by the U.S. Department of Education. The third was submitted by the Guam Office of Homeland Security to the Federal Emergency Management Agency.

The fourth proposal was submitted by Coral Shores High School to the Florida Learn and Serve Program. The fifth was submitted by the Greencastle-Antrim Education Foundation to the Environmental Challenge Fund administered by NiSource, Incorporated. The last proposal was submitted to the Abigail L. Longenecker Memorial Foundation in Lancaster, PA, by the Lancaster Emergency Medical Services Association.

The RFPs for the federal and state grants are included. The online application for NiSource, Inc. is also included, as well as the giving guidelines for the Longnecker Foundation. You will note that the first four grants, all submitted to either a federal department, federal agency, or state program, tend to have longer narratives and are more complex than the other two grants. The NiSource application and Foundation application are relatively short and took far less time to write than did the first four.

These six examples were chosen to illustrate the vast differences between the formats of proposals and funder specifications. They are concrete, real examples of proposals that combine the art of proposal writing with the technical aspects of what the funders were looking for.

These proposals are not perfect—they never are! However, the reviewers felt that each applicant responded clearly to the RFP or guidelines and presented a project that they felt was worthy of being funded.

PROPOSAL #1

Grants Program Description

Grant for Teaching and Learning Resources and Curriculum Development support projects that improve specific areas of humanities education through the development of new or revised curricula and instructional and learning materials. Projects are intended to serve as national models of excellence in humanities education. They must draw upon scholarship in the humanities and use scholars and teachers as advisers. NEH is especially interested in projects that offer solutions to problems frequently encountered by teachers in a particular field of the humanities. Projects may:

- help schools, colleges, and universities develop (or revise) and implement significant humanities programs, curricula, courses, and materials for teaching and learning;
- develop and apply technologies to integrate outstanding humanities scholarship into teaching and learning at all levels of K–12 and higher education; or
- provide materials and tools to ensure that future teachers acquire advanced knowledge and understanding of the humanities.

Support is available for two types of projects, Curriculum Development and Materials Development.

Curriculum development projects typically unite faculty within individual institutions or from cooperating schools, colleges, and universities to prepare, implement, and evaluate new or revised curricula that can serve as models for humanities teachers nationwide. These projects often involve collaboration among schools and institutions of higher education or organizations such as libraries or museums and regional and national consortia. They also allow faculty to investigate humanities subjects as pathways to instructional reform.

Projects must produce specific materials and include plans for maintaining or expanding the results of the grant after the funding ends.

Materials development projects involve groups of teachers and scholars working collaboratively to create materials focused around a specific humanities topic. The development of the materials will have a significant impact on humanities instruction nationwide. Projects may include the preparation of sourcebooks, document collections, or teaching guides that suggest strategies for reading and interpreting specific humanities topics and texts. Such materials may use print or electronic formats, but preparation of traditional textbooks is ineligible for funding.

Applicants may design, produce, and test interactive educational software and other electronic technologies. Projects involving digital materials must run on multiple platforms and must include provisions for long-term access and maintenance.

Type of projects not supported:

- large-scale acquisition of computer equipment by schools or colleges;
- creative or performing arts;
- empirical social scientific research;
- specific policy studies;
- educational or technical impact assessments;
- work undertaken in the pursuit of an academic degree;
- preparation or publication of textbooks;
- projects that focus on cognitive psychology, pedagogical theory, research on educational methods, tests, or measurements;
- projects designed to persuade participants of a particular political, philosophical, religious, or ideological point of view;
- projects that advocate a particular program of social or political action; or
- projects whose principal purpose is professional development (applicants seeking such grants should consult the guidelines for Summer Seminars and Institutes and other NEH education grant programs).

We the People Grant Initiative

To help Americans make sense of their history and of the world around them, NEH has launched an initiative: *We the People*. NEH encourages applications that explore significant events and themes in our nation's history and culture and that advance knowledge of the principles that define America. To learn more about *We the People*, visit the initiative's website. Proposals will be evaluated through NEH's established review process and will not receive special consideration.

Award Information

Curriculum Development Projects can be funded to a maximum of $100,000 and may span a period of 12 to 18 months.

Materials Development Projects can be funded to a maximum of $200,000 and may span a period of up to three years.

NEH encourages applications in any amount up to the maximum. In every case, the budget must be appropriate to the activities proposed.

Cost Sharing

NEH support is limited to 80% of the total project costs. The balance must be met by cost sharing (i.e., cash contributions made to the project by the applicant and third parties as well as third-party in-kind contributions, such as donated goods and services) .

Eligibility

Any U.S., nonprofit, IRS tax-exempt organization or institution dedicated to improving humanities education is eligible. When two or more institutions or organizations collaborate on an application, one of them must serve as the lead applicant and administer the project on behalf of all the participating units. Grants are not awarded to individuals.

NEH generally does not award grants to other federal entities or to applicants whose projects are so closely intertwined with a federal entity that the project takes on characteristics of the federal entity's own authorized activities. This does not preclude applicants from using grant funds from, or sites and materials controlled by, other federal entities in their projects, as long as these resources are not used as gifts to release NEH matching funds.

How to Prepare and Submit an Application

Preliminary proposals

Prior to submitting a proposal, applicants are encouraged to contact program officers who can:

- offer advice about preparing the proposal;
- supply samples of narratives from successful applications as models; and
- review preliminary proposal drafts if they are submitted well before the relevant deadline (up to six weeks). Although this preliminary review is not part of the formal process and has no bearing on the final outcome of the proposal, previous applicants have found it helpful in strengthening their applications.

Preparing an application

Project titles should be brief, descriptive, and substantive. Appendices should be used to provide supplementary material. The font size should be no smaller than eleven point and all pages should have one-inch margins. The application should be collated and numbered consecutively throughout. Applicants should keep in mind the criteria listed below used to evaluate proposals. A complete application consists of the following:

1. **Application cover sheet**

   Complete the cover sheet. Project titles should be brief, descriptive, and substantive.

   The cover sheet should be signed by the official authorized to submit the application on behalf of the institution.

Beginning October 1, 2003, all institutions applying to federal grant programs are required to provide a DUNS number, which is issued by Dun & Bradstreet, as part of their application. Project directors should contact their institution's grant administrator or chief financial officer to obtain their institution's DUNS number. Federal grant applicants can obtain a DUNS number for free by calling 1-866-705-5711. More information about the new requirement is available.

2. **Table of contents**

Include all parts of the application, with page numbers.

3. **Summary**

Provide a one-page, single-spaced summary of the narrative.

4. **Narrative description**

The narrative description is an extended discussion of the project, its intellectual content, its activities, and its intended beneficiaries. Narrative descriptions must not exceed *fifteen* double-spaced pages. The narrative should refer to items included in the appendices. It must include the following:

- **Intellectual Rationale**
  Explain the intellectual rational for the project. Identify the central topic for the project. Identify the humanities themes and discuss why they are intellectually important.

- **Content and design of the project**
  Describe in detail the specific topic(s) and area(s) of the humanities that the project will address. Identify the specific humanities topics to be explored and explain their significance for the academic levels the project addresses. List the texts to be used and explain the rationale for their selection and order of study. Describe the nature of the project's activities. Use an appendix to provide a detailed schedule of activities and project reading list. Discuss how the project approaches particular issues of teaching and learning in a humanities area. Finally, identify the intended beneficiaries of the project. When appropriate, describe how the project helps teachers meet applicable frameworks and standards.

  If curriculum development is proposed, the applicant must demonstrate how the curriculum will affect teaching and learning in the humanities nationwide even if it may have an initial use in a single region or institution.

  If materials development is proposed, list and discuss any similar materials already available. Demonstrate why the proposed materials are needed, what they will add to existing materials, what their potential is for national impact on the humanities and how they will be made available to others. If a newer technology is to be used, explain why.

For interactive technology projects, describe the nature and structure of the interactivity and explain how it is appropriate to learning the subject. Outline the potential pathways that will guide the user through the project, and describe the audio and visual images, text, and interactivity. If a website is proposed, describe plans for regular site management and updates.

- **Institutional context**
Briefly describe how the resources (e.g., faculty, library, archival or museum holdings) of the participating institution(s) support the project. If applicable, discuss any previous efforts to address the issues and objectives of the project. If the proposal is related to a project previously funded by NEH, describe how the current effort builds on past work. Include in the appendices any evaluation of the initial project.

- **Staff and participants**
Using a brief paragraph for each person, identify project staff members, consultants, and visiting scholars. Define their roles and state their qualifications for their responsibilities in the project. In the appendices, provide a brief résumé (two pages) for the project director and brief résumés (two pages) and letters of commitment for other scholars. If the proposed project involves participation of teachers, administrators, or an advisory board, provide their names, pertinent information. In the appendices, include brief résumés (two pages) and letters of commitment for each participant.

- **Evaluation**
Describe the projects anticipated impact and the criteria by which it will be measured. Include a specific internal and external evaluation plan that is appropriate for the project's scope and objectives. Detail the benchmarks that will serve as the basis for interim reporting to NEH. The plan should include an evaluation of the project's effects on teaching and learning in the humanities, and when appropriate, its impact on student learning gains. Explain how and when any grant products will be completed and what arrangements will be made for their ongoing availability. Describe the qualifications of the external evaluators. Include in the appendices brief résumés (two pages) and a letter of commitment for each evaluator.

- **Follow-up and dissemination**
Describe follow-up activities (e.g., workshops with colleagues, dissemination of new curricula, and in-service presentations). Indicate how the results of the project will have a lasting impact after the grant funding ends.

When appropriate, include your plan for making materials produced by a project accessible nationwide. For example, indicate why the format or formats chosen for a final product (e.g., printed volume, CD-ROM, DVD, Internet distribution) represent the most effective means of dissemination for the intended audience. Describe how the electronic products will remain on accessible platforms after the end of the grant period. Indicate what publication arrangements have been made and whether an agreement to publish has been reached. Include in the appendices any pertinent correspondence. Provide the expected price of the product and the plans for publicity, including announcements in professional journals, electronic discussion groups, or newsletters; the preparation and distribution of demonstration versions; and participation in conferences or exhibits.

5. **Project budget**

   Complete the budget form. Review the following budget instructions in addition to those accompanying the budget form.

   - **Salaries and wages**

     Include all project personnel except participants and consultants who are not employees of the applicant institution. Calculations for faculty compensation should be based on a percentage of academic year or annual salary. The program does not support replacement teachers or compensate faculty members for performing their regular duties. Compensation for support staff may be calculated as a percentage of salary or based on an hourly rate.

     Salary compensation for employees of colleges and universities should be shown in the project budget as follows:

     - For project directors during the academic year, released time normally should not exceed one course per quarter or semester.
     - For protect directors during the summer, compensation is based on a percentage of the director's academic year salary. For example, one month of full-time work would equal one-ninth or 11.1 percent of a nine-month academic year salary.
     - For higher education and elementary and secondary school participants, stipends should be calculated on the basis of $150 per full day.

   - **Consultant fees**

     List those individuals who will contribute to the project as visiting lecturers and leaders of faculty study sessions. The honoraria for visiting faculty and other consultants range from $350 to $500 per person per day or $2,200 per person per week, not including travel and subsistence costs.

   - **Travel**

     Travel and subsistence costs, including consultant and participant travel, should be entered in budget section 4. Costs should be calculated in conformity with institutional policy. The lowest available commercial fares for coach or equivalent accommodations must be used. Room and board for participants in residential projects should be entered in budget section 7.

- **Other costs**
  Participant Stipends: Stipends for participants not employed by the applicant institution should be listed here. Stipends should be calculated on the basis of $150 per full day.

- **Inadmissible budget items**
  The following costs are not allowable and may not appear in project budgets:
  - Cost of substitute teachers or compensation for faculty members performing their regular duties.
  - Costs related to the regular activities of the institution.
  - Rental of recreational facilities and costs related to social events such as banquets, receptions, and entertainment.
  - Tuition fees for participants. Credit may be awarded to participants seeking compensation for tuition fees at the discretion of the applicant institution. If any filing fee or tuition is charged, it should be charged directly to those participants wishing to receive credit and should be fixed at the lowest possible rate. Such fees may not be deducted from the participant's stipend.
  - Travel associated with independent scholarly research.
  - Development of solely pedagogical education technologies or materials.

- **Budget notes (optional)**
  If needed, include a brief supplement to the narrative explaining projected expenses or other items in the financial information provided on NEH's budget form.

6. Appendices

Use appendices to provide only relevant supplementary materials, such as detailed agendas and workplans, reading lists, syllabi, brief résumés, and letters of commitment. Each appendix should be identified clearly and listed in the table of contents. Pages of the appendices should be numbered consecutively.

Applicants should also provide any evaluations, whether self-evaluations or external evaluations, of any project(s) previously funded by NEH.

Projects proposing an electronic component (e.g., website, CD-ROM, or DVD) should provide samples that demonstrate the proposed component and its relationship to the goals of the project. Applicants may provide a website address, or material on CD-ROM or a DVD (ten copies). Printed screen-shots of essential pages or components should also be provided. All samples must be clearly labeled with the name of the project director, the applicant institution, and the title of the project. Include operating instructions when applicable.

Application checklist

Include 9 copies, each arranged in this order:

- signed NEH application cover sheet
- table of contents
- one-page summary
- narrative
- project budget (budget form and budget narrative)
- appendices
    - work plans or schedules
    - reading lists or syllabi (if applicable)
    - brief résumés for all project personnel
    - documentation of the commitment of key project personnel, including those not affiliated with the applicant institution (for example, visiting lecturers or outside consultants)
    - criteria and procedures for selecting participants
    - evaluation of project previously funded by NEH (if applicable)
    - prototypes of digital materials, such as CD-ROMs or website addresses (if applicable)

In addition, place the following on top of 9 copies of the proposal:

- application cover sheet with an original signature
- 3 copies of the application cover sheet
- 3 copies of the one-page summary
- original completed budget form

Do not use covers, notebooks, or other methods of binding that add unnecessary weight to these documents. Please clip, rather than staple, application pages together.

Send applications to:

Grants for Teaching and Learning Resources and Curriculum Development
Division of Education Programs
National Endowment for the Humanities
Room 302
1100 Pennsylvania Avenue, NW
Washington, DC 20506
202-606-8380

NEH continues to experience lengthy delays in the delivery of mail by the U.S. Postal Service. To ensure that your application arrives by the receipt deadline, please consider using a commercial delivery service. NEH will acknowledge the receipt of your application by email. Although formal applications cannot be accepted by email or fax, we do recommend the use of such alternatives for other kinds of correspondence, including inquiries, preliminary drafts, recommendations, or reports.

To ensure that your application is processed in a timely fashion, the envelope or package used to send your application materials should prominently display your return address and should not be overwrapped with tape.

Deadline for Submissions

Applications must be received at NEH by **October 14, 2004** for projects beginning no earlier than April 1, 2005.

Application Review

Criteria

Applications for this program are subject to three general criteria for evaluation:

1. **Intellectual quality of the project**
   - The intellectual rationale is clear and persuasive with detailed exposition of the topic(s) in the humanities to be addressed.
   - The project draws on sound humanities scholarship.
   - The proposal explains in detail how the grant product will provide teaching and learning resources that are academically rigorous, thoughtful and stimulating.
   - The project addresses effectively the appropriate issues of teaching and learning in its subject area.

2. **Quality of the project design**
   - Activities are well planned and described in adequate detail.
   - Activities advance the project in thoughtful and creative ways.
   - Personnel are qualified to carry out their proposed responsibilities.
   - Plans for administration are sound.
   - The letters from scholars, other consultants, and participants demonstrate interest and commitment.
   - Evidence of commitment and support among the participating institutions is provided.
   - Plans include appropriate evaluation and the letters from external evaluators demonstrate interest and commitment.
   - The project budget is reasonable.

3. **Potential for significant impact**
   - The project will significantly enhance humanities teaching and learning.
   - The results will be disseminated and made available to all appropriate users.
   - The project's impact will extend beyond the period of the grant.

Review and Selection Process

Knowledgeable persons outside NEH who are asked for their judgments about the quality and significance of the proposed projects assess each application. Panelists represent diverse disciplinary, institutional, regional, and cultural backgrounds. The advice of evaluators is assembled by NEH's staff, who comment on matters of fact or on significant issues that would otherwise be missing from the review. These materials are then presented to the National Council on the Humanities, which meets throughout the year to advise the chairman. The chairman takes into account the advice provided by the process and, by law, makes the final decision about funding.

Award Administration Information

Award notices

Applicants will be notified by letter in March 2005.

Administrative requirements

Before submitting an application, applicants should review their responsibilities as a grantee and the certification requirements.

TROY ON THE INTERNET

> "The way to Troy! Surely there are few other names which evoke such feelings for so many of the inhabitants of the world? In all the stories told by mankind and recorded through its history, is there a more famous place?"

> —Michael Wood, In Search of the Trojan War

THE NATURE OF THE REQUEST AND THE RATIONALE

The Project and its Goals. Troy's fame is unquestionable, yet exceeds its legibility. Although it is perhaps the most famous archaeological site in the world, and so closely associated with histories, myths, and the origins of Western literature and civilization, its complexity and lack of grand intact architecture mean that it is one of the most under-interpreted. We request a $200,000 Teaching and Learning Resources grant to build and launch a website about Troy targeted to students K–12.

The Iliad is taught in some form to almost all students, yet few understand the relationship between the legends of Troy and the actual site and its context, especially as it is viewed by archaeologists working there in northwestern Turkey. Our goal is to elucidate the site of Troy in all its complexity including the historical connections between Troy legends and the place. The interaction of history and myth is part of the rich learning experience we will make possible by opening this new, multi-layered, interactive "window" on the past and the meanings of this famous site.

This project team is uniquely positioned to create the definitive educational resource on Troy. PI Riordan has been the site architect for most of the last eight years. Key advisors Korfmann and Rose have led the excavations since 1987. We have direct access to and control over all the necessary archival materials and computer generated reconstructions already created. CERHAS, at the University of Cincinnati, meanwhile, is an emerging world leader in multimedia presentations on historical and archaeological content. We will complete a set of three-dimensional computer visualizations on the site of ancient Troy, animate and package those models with pertinent multimedia material, and disseminate the result by launching a website. It will be created for a grade 6 comprehension level, but guides and suggestions for teachers will make much of it accessible to younger students; and the material will certainly intrigue older students and adults.

OUR APPROACH TO TROY

The site of Troy is undeniably complex. Archaeology shows that the real hey-day of the place was in the Early Bronze Age, almost a thousand years before the Mycenaeans (the real prehistoric settlers of mainland Greece) might have come into conflict with an obscure population in Northwest Anatolia (today's Turkey); and it was home to other societies for centuries afterward. All this is now piled and partially excavated on a hill that some describe as a layer cake, others as a "heap of stones". The core of our presentation, and our interface design, will be these "layers," reflected in computer models of all the levels, or "cities", of Troy. These visualizations, and the many types of data and information we will locate within them, will make legible and accessible the results of decades of research.

Many scholars, including the Primary Investigator of this project, have spent time explaining and illustrating interpretations of Troy. So far no one has attempted to find a way to package the vast amounts of data now available (see Appendix C, Bibliography) and disseminate that material to the widest possible audience. We propose here to combine the collaboration of the three primary current excavators of Troy and the PI's own intimate knowledge of the excavation via a ten year campaign as site architect with the expertise of CERHAS in multi-layered, multimedia visualizations based on computer reconstructions. With this convergence of a wealth of material, and all the key expertise on the site, we at the University of Cincinnati are uniquely qualified to present the Troy material to that audience. The project will include:

1. A Website, where visitors will be welcomed to "dig" down through the layers of Troy, then at most stages take a guided tour of a three-dimensional model of the city, exploring freely several buildings with virtual objects and features in them; seeing the chronological context; hearing and reading narrative descriptions of various related topics; cross-referencing the site with the legends; and finally being able to click on a series of user-friendly "Frequently Asked Questions" about Troy. Also included will be a Bibliography, Teachers' Guides, and Links.

2. Launching and Upkeep of the Website, will be hosted by OhioLINK. OhioLINK is the Ohio Library and Information Network, a state funded consortium of Ohio's college and university libraries and the State Library of Ohio serving more than 600,000 students, faculty, and staff at 84 institutions. The OhioLINK Digital Media Center (DMC) serves to archive and provide world-wide access to digital material created by member institutions. OhioLINK and the DMC are housed at the Ohio Supercomputing Center. The OSC is a fully scalable center with mid-range machines to match those found at the National Science Foundation centers and national labs. The website will be maintained by CERHAS. Upkeep will be on a semi-annual basis after the site goes live Spring 2007.

3. A Public Symposium on "Reading Troy" will occur at the assembly of the Board of Advisors in Fall 2005. This will complement the concurrent publication (already funded elsewhere) of the journal Practices 9/10, E. Riorden editor. The special topic of this issue of Practices will be "Culture and Technology", and will be based in part on a related conference to be held at the University of Cincinnati's College of Design, Architecture Art and Planning in the Spring of 2005.

The Funding Context. This request is for NEH support from May 2004 through April 2007. The pre-existing models, which we will be able to use and adapt, were created in Germany with support primarily from the German Ministry for Education and Research (approximately $250,000 in actual monies). For the development of the current project the University of Cincinnati (UC) has provided a small seed-grant. UC and other partners will provide cost sharing to support the successful completion of the work; CERHAS infrastructure and management effort from other sources will also be of benefit to the work. We anticipate funding from other sources for a documentary on the life of archaeologist Carl Blegen, whose archives are housed here, which will also have much overlap and direct benefit to this Website project.

BACKGROUND TO THE PROJECT

A Centuries-old Debate. When Heinrich Schliemann astounded the world with his publicized initial excavation at a place known as Hissarlik, near the Dardanelles city of Canakkale, claiming he had found Priam's Troy, he was the last of many seekers. Many of his predecessors were armchair essayists who had never set foot in that part of Turkey, yet, Homer in hand, they pored over maps and verses of the Iliad and published harsh critiques of their rivals' theories. Schliemann had the virtue of putting ideas into action, and indeed he had discovered something. His results of the 1870s predated the discoveries of Mycenae and Knossos by several years and therefore he lacked an essential archaeological tool: the comparative site. He himself worked at Mycenae, then returned to Troy. At the very end of his life, the Bronze-Age Aegean had finally come into focus, and Schliemann knew he was very wrong to call his "second from the bottom" city that of Priam—if there ever was a Priam, king of Troy who faced Agamemnon and Achilles, he would have existed many centuries later. Schliemann realized this shortly before he died in Naples in 1889. But by that time he had also uncovered impressive fortifications from the Late Bronze Age, the so-called Homeric period with clear parallels to Mycenae, the legendary home of Agamemnon, and so he died a vindicated man: most now believed this was Troy, and few have disputed that since Schliemann's death.

Troy is a Tell. A tell is a settlement which has been repeatedly destroyed and then built again; each time a new layer is added until eventually a man-made hill is the base for the last layer. Schliemann and the excavators who followed him, beginning with his architect, Wilhelm Dörpfeld, targeted certain levels of the Trojan tell at various points. The result is a confusing maze of trenches each revealing fragments of the level at its bottom. A scramble up three meters of scarp can take you two centuries forward in time, or almost two millennia, depending on where you are at the site. A knowledgeable guide and a timeline are both needed to understand Troy.

Dörpfeld's Brilliant Synthesis. It was Schliemann's architect who was able to put together a comprehensible picture of the whole tell of Troy. He recognized that there were 9 major phases, each a city in itself. Several of these cities had distinct sub-phases. Dörpfeld also established a working relative chronology, which has needed little adjustment in 100 years. His schematic section of Troy and its layers is conceptually the essence of the site, and therefore becomes the basis for our "Home Page".

The University of Cincinnati's Role. From 1932 to 1938 Carl Blegen led a team of prehistory scholars from Cincinnati to continue the excavations of Troy. Blegen's publications of his work at established the standard for the prehistoric excavation report. The chronology of Troy became a benchmark for the Aegean Bronze Age; archaeologists working even further afield made reference to Troy's material culture, known to all experts thanks to the Blegen publications. However, because of impending war in 1939, Blegen never produced a new comprehensive plan of Troy.

Continuing the Research. In 1987 the Universities of Tübingen and Cincinnati started working together at Troy. Tübingen Professor of Prehistory Dr. Manfred Korfmann holds the permit and his team continues the research agenda for Bronze Age Troy. Cincinnati Professor Dr. C. Brian Rose has established the Post-Bronze Age research agenda (much neglected by previous excavators) and is now writing up the results with his team. In 1993 architect Elizabeth Riorden completed the new comprehensive plan of Troy, published in 1994, and then commenced with the creation of a computer plan for each level of Troy, in addition to supervising teams doing surveying, documentation and conservation on site.

Troy goes Virtual. In 2001 the German Federal Ministry for Education and Research granted 7.2 million DM (+/− 3.6 million USD) to a group of archaeologists, including the Troy Project, for a "Virtual Archaeology" project. A company in Berlin, ART + COM was the Troia Projekt Tübingen's partner in Troia VR, which was scheduled for completion in July, 2003. As Troia VR did not have a general-public outcome the co-principals have graciously agreed to allow their models to be used by CERHAS, and further developed for this work. One of the reasons they openly agreed to this was that the models of Troy were based on the digitized plans of Troy produced by Elizabeth Riorden in 1994–1995.

Next Steps. The effort proposed here involves the leading experts and scholars of Troy, those who know Troy best. CERHAS is in a unique position with this project because we benefit from the direct participation of the current excavators of Troy (Professor Manfred Korfmann of the University of Tübingen, Professor C. Brian Rose of the University of Cincinnati, Dr. Peter

Jablonka of the University of Tübingen's Troia Projekt, and Dr. Billur Tekkök, independent scholar). Other scholars participating actively in the project will bring the overview expertise to this core group of Troy experts, always with a mind to a two-fold aspect of the project: (1) archaeological and historical content, and (2) rich, well-designed graphics and multi-media formatting and integration (see below, section on Participants, and Appendix D).

Primary Humanities Topics and Themes. Four main clusters of humanities content areas will be prominent in the project; and within each we will emphasize the themes described here:

1. History of cultures and civilization, emphasizing how cultures change over time; how we interpret the past; and how it affects who we are today.

2. Literature and mythology, emphasizing the relationship between what we call history and what we call imaginative literature, and how myth exercises power in real life.

3. Archaeology itself and its methodological practices, emphasizing how archaeologists gather information and combine it to reveal the life-ways as well as the physical artifacts of a vanished society;

4. Art history (including fine arts, architecture, and crafts), emphasizing how arts can "live" for generations through lasting beauty and shared human values; and how arts reveal and help shape the activities and priorities of people in any era.

In its statement of curricular standards, the National Council for the Social Studies has emphasized the need, in studying content areas such as these, not just to gain knowledge, but to develop skills. Students studying history for example should "Develop the habits of mind that historians and scholars in the humanities and social sciences employ to study the past and its relationship to the present in the United States and other societies." In the study of cultures, students should "explore and ask questions about the nature of culture and specific aspects of culture" and the influence of those aspects on human behavior. At CERHAS we encourage these questioning habits of mind and focus on this openness to discovery, featuring specific design and interactive approaches to "exploration" as well as the vivid portrayal of places and material culture.

CONTENT AND DESIGN OF THE PROJECT

(see sample CD, enclosed, and Appendix A)

General Description of the Organization of the Website. The homepage will present an image of the layers of Troy, corresponding to a timeline on the right edge of the screen. Selecting any one of the layers starts a multimedia narrative animation of the city. Following each such tour, users may select specific architectural features or other topics that are offered on that layer. Many topics will be presented in "story scenes" —short narrated videos on a particular topic, including interviews, site features, artifacts and cultural life ways. At many points there are links to the legends, opportunities to "pick up and examine" an artifact, enter a room, house, or temple, and link to FAQs, etc. Content is organized such that users mainly have the feeling of "exploring" the site, and "discovering" individual stories or knowledge segments located specifically in space and time.

Specific Educational Objectives. Learners of all ages can engage with the project materials at different levels of intensity and thoroughness. Some will spend only a few minutes casually exploring; others will study deeply and investigate every detail. Complete achievement of each goal will depend partly on how, and for how long, the individual is involved. We are envisioning materials that will fulfill the following objectives, but this list may change; the themes however will not.

In general, as a result of directed exposure to our materials, learners will be able to do the following in relation to one or more of the theme clusters identified above:

1. Gain a vivid, experiential understanding of a major location in the heritage of western civilization by immersion in multimedia recreations.

2. Identify some ways in which Troy represents one point of origin for our civilization's history, literature and sense of destiny.

3. Describe several different ways in which the people of Troy lived, in different eras.

4. Recognize that cities develop for many reasons, including fulfilling the myths of their builders; and that what we remember as history may not be the whole story.

5. Place the history of Troy in the context of world history by identifying contemporary events elsewhere around the globe.

6. Debate how much truth there is to legends of the Trojan War.

7. Explain why some myths about Troy may have served political or practical purposes, and how myths can still serve such purposes.

8. Appreciate the human effort and social inspiration that went into building palaces, temples, fortifications, workshops and dwellings.

9. Identify several questions asked by archaeologists at the Troy site, and name diverse methods of investigation used to answer them.

10. Trace paths of daily life through a cityscape of ancient Troy, and compare the use of space to that of modern Americans.

11. Identify several items from ancient Troy most people would consider beautiful today, and explain why.

12. Recognize that real places that are part of our heritage need protection from real destruction.

Specific Design and Content Approaches. Several key features of the Website's design and interactive methods will reinforce these learning objectives.

First, the concept of "layers" will be prominent, both in the interactive cross-section of the Troy site, and in the similarly color-coded timeline always present on the right edge of the screen. Reflecting the structure of both Troy and archaeological practice, these layers will be the key to orientation and the distribution of all content. Thus our Troy Homepage will graphically illustrate the concept that "digging down" will take you "back in time." The timeline has the same orientation (down = back in time), and will expand horizontally at a mouse-drag to show comparative timelines (Egypt, Northern Europe, the Americas, Asia, and Africa). The timeline will be a constant through the pages and always linked to the current view or activity. This will help users remain oriented in history.

Second, each layer of the city will be introduced in a 3D model, either rendered as a pictorial image or as an animated fly-through. This will orient the users to the urban and civic spaces, key structure, and locations and find-spots of key artifacts or sites associated with important stories and content. This will reinforce the way that cultural life and history are embedded in civic space.

Third, animated tours of more detailed buildings will lead, in turn, to objects and artifacts that can be manipulated freely (Quicktime VR) and "tell their stories" through the voice of a narrator. This will provide users with a direct, interactive engagement with the content, and the connection of interpretations with the material evidence obtained through archaeological excavations.

Fourth, narrative descriptions will accompany all of the "story scenes" delivering content in voice as well as text. Hearing a story has an immediate dramatic impact, and reinforces text.

Fifth, the legends vital to the Troy heritage will always be close by, in the form
of story summaries, imagery, and identification of important figures and gods. (Further weblinks will direct those interested to full versions of the legends.) These elements will be prominent at appropriate spots in the cityscapes of Troy, and will also be accessible independently as the "Legend Index."

And finally, a "Frequently Asked Questions" feature will serve as the "on-site tour guide," and will be developed from PI Riorden's years of experience explaining the site to tourists. This will allow the users to pause on their journey at any point and ask questions even very elementary ones.

Additional hypertext resources will include guides and activity suggestions for teachers at various grade levels, thematically tied to the key learning objectives and humanities themes, and associated with specific "routes" through the site, and a Bibliography/Webography with links. These will allow users to customize their inquiry for multiple purposes, suitable for anything from a grade school classroom to advanced research.

Differing User Types. In order to make the site appealing to a wide variety of user audiences, we will use a combination of very new features, such as web-based real-time navigation, and very familiar features, such as an FAQ section (Frequently Asked Questions). We want to establish an immediate comfort level with "browsers," including those with little experience, encouraging them to stay and explore; yet also allow ease of access for "seekers" and "informed seekers" who are after more advanced material. The middle range between these poles, and a large amount of the material, will be pre-arranged animations and multi-media scenes, arranged in clusters, but always with exploratory choices about where to go, and suggested links.

THE PLAN OF WORK

(see Appendix B for detailed plan)

The project is planned in stages: in the first 12 months the required models are edited or created, depending whether they are pre-existing or not. During phase one all scene scripts are written, edited and recorded. During the second 12-month period the scripted scenes are animated, and all the other material is written and edited. During the third 12-month phase all the web pages are encoded with all the desired links, and the "virtual" segments are compressed and encoded. The symposium will occur in the middle of the process, but after all the written material is ready for review.

The core of the project content is tied to the three-dimensional models, which are based on the excavation documentation. The "user interface" provides content interpretations, situated within the models, in the form of narrated animations, virtual interiors or artifacts, stories and interviews, and other content types. The models themselves will require some adjustment of detail and complexity to effect the visualization. This also depends, however, on other levels of manipulation. The rapid pace of industry development will enable significant improvements in technology over the period of the project which will favor our outcomes: beyond the animated views of the models, we will be able to provide real-time video compression and authoring. The design and assembly of resources and their copyrighting for Web use will take place during a 36-month period, in four phases.

> Phase 1 (months 1–12): 3D modeling, writing, recording.
> Phase 2 (months 13–18): multi-media assembly and writing, animating.
> Month 19: 2-day Advisory Board Meeting and Symposium "Reading Troy".
> Phase 3 (months 20–24): editing, evaluations, follow-up.
> Phase 4 (months 25–35): authoring, graphic design, classroom evaluation, marketing.
> End Phase (month 36): launch of website.

Pedagogical Approach and Comparable Websites We foresee the website providing material for teachers of western or world history courses who wish to see the curriculum enhanced by lively, illustrative, engaging and scholarly sound content. Some educators teaching literature will also find the website an exciting complement to teaching the Iliad, Odyssey and Greek mythology. Natural sciences teachers and history teachers alike will be able to use to website to introduce the methodology of archaeology, and as a forum for debate about the nature of history. The website will offer teacher guides in these key curricular areas, with classroom exercises and activities relating to the material on the web. To date, the information that has come out of the Troy site has barely been suggested on the Web. What little there is has been presented mostly in print. One very good resource along these lines is the Perseus project (HYPERLINK http://www.perseus.tufts.edu/cgi.bin/siteindex?entry=Troy; but while that digital library offers source readings and photos, they are not connected. Strictly literary sites on the subject of the mythic Troy include the excellent "The Trojan War: An Illustrated Companion" (HYPERLINK http://www.calliope-free-online.co.uk and HYPERLINK http://www.Trojanwar.net), both student oriented. Our website will include links to these and other sites. However no site coordinates the history, archaeology, and myths of Troy as this one will by anchoring it all in the actual site. And certainly there is no Website remotely comparable in terms of accurate lifelike navigable modeling, giving students the feel of this highly charged place.

Updating the Material. Troy is a vast topic, and we are in control of vast amounts of original, archival data. But for this project we will make very careful selections from the data available. We want to offer breadth and consistency with our website. The new results likely to emerge after launching Troy on the Internet will provide opportunities to incrementally expand the website. It is one of the characteristics of this medium that new information, new interpretations and new nuances, can be added during our semi-annual updates. The logical format proposed here will also lend itself easily for adaptation in the next phase (not part of this request) as a DVD-video and/or museum exhibition (which may well involve translation into Turkish and German).

Copyright. The existing models from the University of Tübingen and the Troia Projekt photo archive (over 8000 images) are both under copyright of the Troia Projekt in Tübingen. For the educational purposes of this project they are available at a small fee. The material produced by CERHAS would be copyrighted to CERHAS, but in a reciprocal arrangement, made available to the Troia Projekt for museum and educational purposes (translations would be the responsibility of the Troia Projekt). The Blegen film material is the property of the University of Cincinnati Department of Classics and is available for this project because of its educational and scholarly nature.

Interactive Media. CERHAS has learned through experience (see Appendix G) that "interactive" has a three-fold meaning. First, the various media themselves interact through design integration. Second, the users interact with the media (the usual sense). Third, interaction occurs when users and observers explore the media together. Our media create sensory excitement and entertainment value through large moving images and high quality sound. Transparent, intuitive controls enable even inexperienced users to become engaged interactively and be drawn into the content of the program. Because we are based in a top-rated art and design college, staffing for any CERHAS project is highly trained in design, and thus a hallmark of CERHAS products is very high visual and functional quality. Our experience with other projects confirms that design quality in interactive media corresponds directly with more effective engagement and learning outcomes for audiences of all ages.

Navigational Experience. Our principles of Web design involve, on the one hand, clear self-evident reference to the universal nature of web navigation, which makes it very easy for any user to move around who is familiar with a browser. Accordingly, we will use links across clearly and logically organized sectors of the site, and bright distinctive buttons for consistent movement. On the other hand, we also need to offer a sense of exploration and discovery, and enough complexity to spark curiosity. We will reinforce that by allowing real-time navigation of some spaces in the architectural models—usually buildings one can enter and examine at will, where modeled objects (actually found in situ) can be "picked up" and "examined".

Updating and Maintaining the Website. CERHAS will update and maintain the site. The actual hosting of the project will be through OhioLINK. CERHAS has past experience with Ohio-LINK, and we rely on their educational mission to ensure the proper maintenance of the hardware requirements of the Troy site, and can also call on their affiliated "Ohio Learning Network" of teachers and curriculum developers for classroom involvement and evaluation studies.

Innovation in Real-Time Navigation. One of the partners for the project in Germany, which modeled several levels of Troy, is a firm in Berlin, Art+Com that specializes in high-tech museum display and other similar applications. The Art+Com project manager was Steffen Kirchner, who also instigated the project with the Troia Projekt in Tübingen, and donated his own time to the project. He has generously agreed to be on our Board of Advisors, and has also mentioned that currently he is researching the compression of the Troy models so that they are ready for realistic real-time navigation, and would be willing to share this outcome. We feel that the full impact of the models, whether existing or still to be created, is not felt without this component of real-time navigation, normally not available via the Internet. The expertise offered by Mr. Kirchner could be supplemented by new "out-of-the box" products currently emerging, however we think that we will have higher quality, potentially, from Art+Com, which in return has a case study project it can add to its portfolio.

Impact and Significance. After over 130 years of excavation, accompanied by the enthusiasm of a public familiar with Homer, there is a mass of information about Troy. Our selection of content and materials will reflect two main ideas: First, we begin with the three-dimensional models of all the major levels of Troy, because this is a unique asset and provides the most vivid possible way to orient our users to the site and its data. (Topics that are too far removed from the site itself, such as the impact of the Iliad during the Middle Ages and early Modern periods, are not included.) Secondly, our project is unique because it will be created by the people who excavated Troy, assuring that the material will be more current and accurate than anyone else could provide. All of this material will be edited for consistency of language, level and internal logic. Archaeological material appears to be all about catalogs of "things", yet there is always the second part of the story: the interpretation of the meaning of those "things". Troy on the Internet will reflect a healthy balance of specific and theoretic forms of knowledge, and try to "tell a good story" based upon empirical truths.

Those of us active in the field at Troy over the years have a large amount of anecdotal evidence that Troy will always fascinate people of the world, because of the power of the legend and the power of Homer's poetry. However, we also discovered a growing interest in archaeology in general during the 1990s. An informal survey of visitors to Troy in 1996 showed that one of things visitors enjoyed most was seeing the archaeologists at work. Our website will be the only one designed for the general public and based on a direct involvement with the most recent investigations of Troy. We intend to use abundant images from the Troy/Troia archive showing archaeologists at work, to explain parts of the material, because people get excited about the material when they see this aspect. Because of its unique authority over the subject matter, and its compelling visual features, we expect our Website to become an important resource for many audiences, beyond providing informative material for K–12 use to complement core humanities learning. Moreover the fact that in 1998 Troy was selected as one of UNESCO's World Heritage sites creates yet another audience, and suggests our website may offer prototypical ways of presenting other sites all over the world.

THE INSTITUTIONAL CONTEXT, STAFF, AND PARTICIPANTS

Who is CERHAS? Founded in 1995, CERHAS is the Center for the Electronic Reconstruction of Historical and Archaeological Sites, located in the top rated College of Design, Architecture, Art, and Planning (DAAP) at the University of Cincinnati, a major research institution. It is an award-winning, interdisciplinary laboratory dedicated to research in advanced multimedia and digital imaging, particularly as applied in educational, museum, artistic, and architectural settings, and involving vanished or otherwise inaccessible cultural resources, sites, or landscapes. For more information on the projects and accomplishments of CERHAS (see Appendix G).

Project Team

(Staff CVs are supplied in Appendix D.)

Elizabeth H. Riorden, FAAR, MArch, Assistant Professor of Architecture. Principal Investigator and Project Director of Troy on the Internet. Her involvement as an architect seeking active links to archaeology began in the 1970s with the Psalmodi Project, the field project at the site of a mediaeval monastery near Nîmes, France. In 1989 she became a registered architect and was practicing in New York City, but in 1991 chose to move to Tübingen, Germany, at the invitation of Professor Manfred Korfmann, to work full-time on the Troy Project. During the 1990s she became Site Architect for the international Troy Project, appeared on European radio and television, presented a virtual model of Troy I (earliest Troy) at the 1995 Hannover computer exposition (CeBIT), initiated and completed a digital CAD plan of every level of Troy, and supervised site conservation activities. In 2001 she was awarded a Samuel H. Kress Foundation Rome Prize in Historic Preservation and Conservation, and spent six months as a Fellow of the American Academy in Rome. She has also participated as a team member in an award winning field project on Milos, Greece. She has published several articles on her work as an architect in archaeology, illustrated several books and has lectured in Rome, California and Massachusetts on her research.

Elizabeth Bartley, M. Litt, Co-Principal Investigator and Executive Director of CERHAS. With degrees in Interior Design and Medieval History and Archaeology, an extensive background in Web development, business training and consulting, and teaching in various areas of design, general education and technology, Ms Bartley will be the overall supervisor of the project and its administration and dissemination.

Cathryn J. Long, MA, Writer and Curriculum Developer. Author of many classroom materials for grades 4–12, including a recent history volume, Ancient America, and a standard secondary civics textbook. She has been the chief researcher and script writer on CERHAS's EarthWorks Project since 1996. Ms. Long brings a broad and general expertise in making material accessible to general audiences, in multimedia scripting and conceiving curriculum materials for various levels and subject areas.

John E. Hancock, RA, MArch. Co-founder of CERHAS, Senior Project Director of Earth-Work and Midea, Professor Hancock will continue in his role as general advisor to CERHAS projects, including Troy, and their overall artistic, scholarly, and management aspects. Professor Hancock has already dealt with material from the Aegean Bronze Age ("The Dirt on Midea") and the ancient Greek world (The Argive Heraion), and has lectured internationally on topics in architectural interpretation and multimedia, and won many awards and honors for his work. His CV is contained in Appendix D (see also Appendix G: About CERHAS).

College of DAAP Student Staff, Drawing from both graduate and undergraduate programs in Interior, Industrial, Graphic, Digital, and Architectural design, we will hire one or more students for the project. We will also incorporate specific project tasks of research and visualization into teaching curricula for one or more courses in these programs, as CERHAS has done in the past reflective of its optimal role in the academic life of the College.

Advisory board

There are 9 members of the Board of Advisors, described in Appendix D, followed by letters in Appendix E. A short list of the 9 members is below:

Prof. Jack Davis, Blegen Chair Professor of Greek Archaeology, Dept of Classics, UC

Dr. Peter Jablonka, Assistant Director of Troia Projekt in Tübingen and co-principal of Troia VR Projekt.

Steffen Kirchner, Project Manager at ART+COM, Berlin (media for art) and co-principal of Troia VR Projekt.

Prof. Dr. Manfred Korfmann, University of Țbingen and Director of Troia Projekt.

Prof. Marty Plumbo, School of Design, University of Cincinnati (UC), specialist in interactive multi-media.

Prof. Robert Probst, Head of the School of Design, UC, and award-winning graphic designer.

Prof. C. Brian Rose, Head of the Dept. of Classics, UC, and Director of Post-Bronze Age Troy Research.

Dr. Billur Tekkök, Independent Scholar, Ankara, Turkey, and Head of Post-Bronze Age Ceramics at Troy.

Prof. Gisela Walberg, the Marion Rawson Professor of Aegean Prehistory at UCs Dept. of Classics and CERHAS collaborator.

EVALUATION

(Evaluators are described in Appendix D, followed by letters in Appendix E.)

How will the Evaluation be done? We anticipate formative evaluations in two areas. First, educational evaluation will be carried out in collaboration with Dr. Janet Bohren, of the University of Cincinnati's School of Education, who has worked with CERHAS in the past. Dr. Bohren's network of local practicing teachers at all grade levels will be supplemented by help from teachers associated with the National Council for History Education. We will seek student and teacher responses and suggestions when we reach the fourth phase of the work, when the actual graphics and links can be tested.

Second, we will evaluate the material from a design standpoint, and do so early enough to be able to respond to valuable suggestions. Both evaluators for this aspect have a very special combination of expertise: in architecture (so that they understand part of our visual approach), in archaeology (so that the material is properly presented), and in computer applications. One of the two, Dr. Donald Sanders, has also dedicated his company, Learning Sites, to the educational presentation of material such as ours, and his evaluation will be very important.

FOLLOW-UP AND DISSEMINATION

Symposium. Taking advantage of the unique group assembled for our Board of Advisors meeting we will host a one-day symposium on the issues surrounding the virtual depictions of archaeological sites. There are many groups such as CAA (Computer Applications in Archaeology) or ACADIA that touch on our area, but it remains a small topic within a larger sea at those conferences. Therefore, a true depth of discussion never seems to happen. We intend to narrow the focus so that the neglected intellectual exchange will occur.

Dissemination. We plan on targeting a small, selective mailing list of about 1000 with an attractive postcard format print announcement of the new website. We will submit the website for award consideration; if winning, there will be much free publicity in high profile magazines such as Natural History or Archaeology; or on the media side, Wired or SIGGRAPH where CERHAS and College projects have appeared previously. From the pedagogical side, we will post notices in appropriate journals of K–12 education and mount displays at annual disciplinary meetings such as the NCSS.

Further Impact. We are already answering preliminary requests to allow the material to be used in museum didactic settings internationally; and we fully anticipate being involved in the design and production of these exhibits in the future. This is especially true because of the plans in Turkey and Germany for a Troy Museum (currently the material is housed in Istanbul and «anakkale). With more than enough material for a single Website, there is ample opportunity to develop deeper treatments in DVD or CD form.

from http://www.socialstudies.org/standards

Troy on the Internet/CERHAS/ University of Cincinnati/October 15, 2003

PROPOSAL #2

DEPARTMENT OF EDUCATION

[CFDA No. 84.215X]

Office of Innovation and Improvement—Teaching American History Grant Program; Notice Inviting Applications for New Awards for Fiscal Year (FY) 2003

Note to Applicants: This notice is a complete application package. Together with the statute authorizing this program and the Education Department General Administrative Regulations (EDGAR), this notice contains all of the information, application forms, and instructions needed to apply for a grant under this competition.

Purpose of Program: Teaching American History grants support projects to raise student achievement by improving teachers' knowledge, understanding, and appreciation of traditional American history. Grant awards assist local educational agencies (LEAs), in partnership with entities that have extensive content expertise, to develop, document, evaluate, and disseminate innovative, cohesive models of professional development. By helping teachers to develop a deeper understanding and appreciation of traditional American history as a separate subject matter within the core curriculum, these programs improve instruction and raise student achievement.

Note: The Secretary construes traditional American history to mean the following: Traditional American history teaches the significant issues, episodes, and turning points in the history of the United States, and how the words and deeds of individual Americans have determined the course of our Nation. This history teaches how the principles of freedom and democracy, articulated in our founding documents, have shaped—and continue to shape—America's struggles and achievement, as well as its social, political, and legal institutions and relations. Traditional history puts its highest priority on making sure students have an understanding of these principles and of the historical events and people that best illustrate them.

Eligible Applicants: Local educational agencies (LEAs)—including charter schools that are considered LEAs under State law and regulations—working in partnership with one or more of the following entities:

- Institutions of higher education (IHEs);
- Non-profit history of humanities organizations; and
- Libraries and museums.

Note: Groups of LEAs interested in submitting a single application must follow the procedures for group applications in 34 CFR 75.127-75.129 of the Education Department General Administrative Regulations (EDGAR).

Notification of Intent To Apply for Funding: The Department will be able to develop a more efficient process for reviewing grant applications if it has a better understanding of the number of LEAs that intend to apply for funding under this competition. Therefore, the Secretary strongly encourages each potential applicant to notify the Department with a short e-mail noting the intent to submit an application for funding. The e-mail need not include information regarding the content of the proposed application, only the applicant's intent to submit it. The Secretary requests that this e-mail notification be sent no later than June 6, 2003, to Christine Miller at: *teachingamericanhistory@ed.gov.*

Applicants that fail to provide this e-mail notification may still apply for funding.

Deadline for Transmittal of Applications: July 7, 2003.

Deadline for Intergovernmental Review: September 5, 2003.

Estimated Available Funds: $99,350,000.

Estimated Range of Awards: Total funding per grant, for a three-year project period is $350,000–$1,000,000 for LEAs with enrollments of less than 300,000 students; $500,000–$2,000,0000 for LEAs with enrollments above 300,000 students.

Estimated Average Size of Awards: Total for all three years is $500,000.

Maximum Award Amount: The total amount of funding that an LEA may receive under this competition is $2,000,000.

Estimated Number of Awards: 100–125.

Note: The Department of Education is not bound by any estimates in this notice.

Project Period: Up to 36 months.

Please note that applicants for multiyear awards are required to provide detailed budget information for the total grant period requested. The Department will determine at the time of the initial award the funding levels for each year of the grant award.

Note: To provide the applicant the capacity to effectively plan for and carry out the comprehensive long-term activities involved in ongoing, intensive professional development, to establish partnerships to support this work, and to document and demonstrate the effectiveness of its program for future dissemination, the Secretary anticipates awarding the entire three-year grant amount for the project at the time of the initial award.

Page Limits: Applicants are strongly encouraged to limit the application narrative to no more than 20 single-sided, double-spaced pages printed in 12 point font or larger. If the applicant is addressing the competitive priority for evaluation, the narrative should be limited to 25 pages. The page limitation does not include the title page, Application for Federal Assistance (ED 424), one-page abstract, the budget summary form (ED 524) and the narrative budget justification, any curriculum vitae, the bibliography of literature cited, or the assurances and certifications.

The following standards are preferred: (1) A "page" is 8.5 × 11 (one side only) with one-inch margins (top, bottom, and sides). (2) Use 12-point font for all text in the application narrative.

The page limit does not apply to the cover sheet, the one-page abstract, budget section, appendices, and forms and assurances.

Applicable Regulations and Statute: (a) *Regulations.* The Education Department General Administrative Regulations (EDGAR) in 34 CFR parts 75, 77, 79, 80, 81, 82, 85, 86, 97, 98 and 99. (b) *Statute.* Part C, subpart 4, of Title II of the Elementary and Secondary Education Act as reauthorized by the No Child Left Behind Act of 2001.

Description of Program: Students who know and appreciate the great ideas, issues, and events of American history are more likely to understand and exercise their civic rights and responsibilities. Their understanding of traditional American history will be enhanced if it is taught as a separate academic subject and not as a component of social studies. Teachers must have strong content knowledge to teach students effectively about the significant issues, episodes, individuals, and turning points in the history of the United States.

The Teaching American History Grant program will support projects to raise student achievement in traditional American history by improving teachers' knowledge, understanding, and appreciation for American history through intensive, ongoing professional development. Project activities should enable teachers to develop further expertise in American history subject content, teaching strategies, and other essential elements of teaching to higher standards. Projects should be driven by a coherent, long-term plan and should be evaluated on the basis of their impact on teacher effectiveness and student learning. This assessment should guide subsequent professional development efforts.

This program will demonstrate how LEAs and institutions with expertise in traditional American history can collaborate over a three-year period to ensure that teachers develop the content knowledge and skills necessary to teach traditional American history effectively as a separate academic subject. In addition to any dissemination conducted directly by grantees, the Department intends to take the products and information resulting from this grant program and share the results with other communities.

Under this program, applicants must propose projects that—

• Develop and implement high-quality in-service or pre-service professional development that provides educators with content knowledge and related teaching skills to prepare all students to achieve to higher standards in American history; and

• Develop and implement strategies for sustained and on-going collaboration that will take place over the course of at least three years among teachers and outside experts to improve content knowledge and instruction in traditional American history.

Applicants should consider projects that include at least one or more of the following activities:

• Supporting participation of teams of teachers in summer institutes and summer immersion activities designed to improve content knowledge and instruction in traditional American history.

• Supporting school-based collaborative efforts among teachers, including programs that facilitate teacher observation and analyses of fellow history teachers' classroom practice to improve content knowledge and instruction.

• Developing programs to assist new history teachers in the classroom, such as programs that employ—

   (a) *Mentoring and coaching by trained mentor teachers over the entire grant period;*

   (b) *Team teaching with experienced history teachers; or*

   (c) *Providing release time for observation and consultation with experienced history teachers.*

• Providing collaborative professional development experiences for veteran history teachers.

• Supporting LEA collaboration with history departments at IHEs to improve content understanding and quality of instruction in the LEA.

• Developing programs to improve history knowledge and instruction, and therefore student achievement, in high poverty areas or for disadvantaged students.

• Establishing and maintaining professional networks, focused specifically on teaching traditional American history, that provide a forum for interaction among teachers and that allow for the exchange of information.

• Providing guidance to teachers on the use of technology to provide access to primary historical documents and develop effective presentations of historical content.

• Creating materials documenting the implementation and benefits of the program and products for other educators to use in the course of teaching American history as a separate subject within the core curriculum.

ANNUAL MEETING

Budgets must include funds for at least two project staff members to attend a two-day annual meeting of the Teaching American History Grant program in Washington, DC, each year of the project. Applicants must include funds to cover travel and lodging expenses for these training activities during each year of the project.

PRIORITIES

This competition focuses on three priorities that are explained in the following paragraphs. To be considered for funding, each applicant must address the absolute priority regarding Collaboration with Other Agencies. The competitive preference priority for evaluation allows an applicant to earn additional points beyond the 100 points provided under the selection criteria.

Absolute Priority: Collaboration With Other Agencies or Institutions

   (a) *Each applicant must propose to work in collaboration with one or more of the following entities:*

• Institutions of higher education

• Non-profit history or humanities organizations; or

• Libraries or museums.

   (b) *The applicant must identify the entity or entities with which it will collaborate and include in its application an assurance from appropriate officials of those entities that they will work with the applicant in implementing the proposal.*

Under 34 CFR 75.105(c)(3) we consider only applications that meet this absolute priority.

Competitive Preference Priority: Under 34 CFR 75.105(c)(2)(i), we award up to an additional 20 points to an application, depending on how well the application meets this competitive preference priority. These points are in addition to any points the application earns under the selection criteria. In reviewing applications that address this competitive preference priority, we consider awarding additional points only to those applicants with top-ranked scores on their selection criteria. We expect that up to 10 applicants will receive these additional competitive preference points.

Competitive preference points can be earned by a project designed to determine, through a rigorous evaluation, whether the implemented program produces meaningful effects on student achievement or teacher performance.

Evaluations using an experimental design are best for determining program effectiveness. Thus, the project will ideally use an experimental design under which participants—that is, students, teachers, classrooms, or schools—are randomly assigned (a) to receive the program being evaluated or (b) to be in a control group that does not receive the program. Evaluations using an experimental design will receive up to 20 points in addition to any points the application earns under the selection criteria.

If random assignment is not feasible, the project may use a quasi-experimental design with carefully matched comparison conditions. This alternative design attempts to approximate a randomly assigned control group by matching program participants—that is, students, teachers, classrooms or schools—with non-participants having similar pre-program characteristics. Evaluations of this type will receive up to 15 points in addition to any points the application earns under the selection criteria.

Proposed evaluations that use neither experimental designs with random assignment nor quasi-experimental designs using a matched comparison group will receive 0 points under this competitive preference priority.

The program evaluator should collect— before the program commences and after it ends—valid and reliable data that measure the impact of participation in the program or in the comparison group.

We determine points under this priority by the quality of the proposed evaluation. We consider the extent to which the applicant presents a feasible, credible plan that includes the following:

• The type of design to be used (that is, random assignment or matched comparison).

• Outcomes to be measured.

• A discussion of how the applicant plans to assign students, teachers, classrooms, or schools to the program or match them for comparison with other students, teachers, classrooms, or schools.

• A proposed evaluator, preferably independent, with the necessary background and technical expertise to carry out the proposed evaluation.

Invitational Priority: We are particularly interested in applications that meet the following priority:

Applications from high-poverty rural and urban LEAs for projects designed to improve traditional American history instruction in chronically low-performing schools and improve achievement of disadvantaged students.

Under 34 CFR 75.105 (c)(1), we do not give an application that meets the invitational priority a competitive or absolute preference over other applications.

Selection Criteria

The Secretary uses the following selection criteria to evaluate applications for grants under this competition. In all instances where the word "project" appears in the selection criteria, the reference to a Teaching American History program should be made. The maximum composite score for all of these criteria is 100 points. The maximum score for each criterion is indicated in parentheses. Within each criterion, unless otherwise noted, the Secretary evaluates each factor equally. We evaluate an application by determining how well the proposed project meets the following provisions. Please note that the *Notes* following each criterion are meant to serve as guidance to assist the applicant in creating a stronger application, and are not required by statute or regulation.

(a) Meeting the purpose of the statute. (Total of 70 points)

(1) *Quality of the project design.* (40 points)

The Secretary considers the quality of the project design for the proposed project by considering how well the applicant describes a plan for development, implementation, and strengthening of programs to teach traditional American history as a separate academic subject (not as a component of social studies) within elementary school and secondary school curricula, including the implementation of activities—

(i) *To* provide professional development and teacher education activities with respect to American history; and

(ii) To improve the quality of instruction, as demonstrated by the specific instructional activities teachers would implement to improve the quality of student work and knowledge of American History.

Note: The Secretary encourages the applicant to include a discussion of the specific history content to be covered by the grant; the format in which the applicant will deliver the history content; and the quality of the staff and consultants responsible for delivering these content-based professional development activities. The applicant may also, to the extent possible, attach curriculum vitae for individuals who will provide the content training to the teachers.

The applicant should also provide a description of plans to demonstrate how teachers are using the knowledge acquired from project activities to improve the quality of instruction. This description may include plans for reviewing how teachers' lesson planning and classroom teaching was affected by their participation in project activities.

(2) *Need for project.* (20 points)

The extent to which specific weaknesses in teacher knowledge of traditional American History and student performance in this subject have been identified and will be met by the project.

Note: The Secretary encourages the applicant to discuss the need for the proposed project and the significance of the project, including national significance. For example, the applicant could include information on: the extent to which teachers in the LEA are not certified in history or social studies; student achievement data in American history; and rates of student participation in courses such as Advanced Placement American history.

(3) *Partnership(s).* (10 points)

How well the applicant describes a plan that meets the statutory requirement to carry out activities under the grant in partnership with one or more of the following:

(i) An institution of higher education.

(ii) A nonprofit history or humanities organization.

(iii) A library or museum.

Note: The applicant should provide the rationale for selecting the partners and explain the specific activities that the partner(s) will contribute to the grant during each year of the project. The applicant should include a memorandum of understanding or detailed letters of commitment from the partner(s) in an appendix to the application narrative.

(b) Quality of the management plan. (10 points)

The Secretary considers the quality of the management plan for the proposed project. In determining the quality of the management plan for the proposed project, the Secretary considers the following factors:

(1) The adequacy of the management plan to achieve the objectives of the proposed project on time and within budget, including clearly defined responsibilities, timelines, and milestones for accomplishing project tasks.

(2) The extent to which the time commitments of the project director and other key project personnel are appropriate and adequate to meet the objectives of the proposed project.

(c) Quality of the project evaluation. (20 points)

The Secretary considers the quality of the evaluation to be conducted of the proposed project. In determining the quality of the valuation, the Secretary considers the extent to which the methods of evaluation include the use of objective performance measures that are clearly related to the intended outcomes of the project and will produce quantitative and qualitative data to the extent possible.

Note: The evaluation plan provided under this criterion should align with the project design explained under the Quality of project design criterion.

Reporting Requirements and Expected Outcomes

The Secretary requires successful applicants to submit annual performance reports that document the grantee's yearly progress toward meeting expected programmatic outcomes. These outcomes must be based on measurable performance objectives. The Secretary will use these reports to measure the success of the grantee's project, and the reports will contribute to a broader knowledge base about high-quality, effective professional development strategies that can improve the teaching and learning of American history nationwide.

In addition, grantees will be required to submit a final performance report, due no later than 90 days after the end of the project period.

Waiver of Proposed Rulemaking

Under the Administrative Procedure Act (5 U.S.C. 553) the Department generally offers interested parties the opportunity to comment on proposed selection criteria and other proposed program requirements. However, section 437(d)(2) of the General Education Provisions Act (GEPA) exempts from this rulemaking requirement those rules where the Secretary determines it would cause extreme hardship to the intended beneficiaries of the program. In order to make timely grant awards in FY 2003, the secretary has decided to issue these final regulations without first publishing them for public comment, in accordance with section 437(d)(2) of GEPA. These regulations will apply to the FY 2003 grant competition only.

Intergovernmental Review of Federal Programs

This program is subject to Executive Order 12372 (Intergovernmental Review of

Federal Programs) and the regulations in 34 CFR part 79.

One of the objectives of the Executive order is to foster an intergovernmental partnership and a strengthened federalism. The Executive order relies on processes developed by State and local governments for coordination and review of proposed Federal financial assistance.

If you are an applicant, you must contact the appropriate State Single Point of Contact (SPOC) to find out about, and to comply with, the State's process under Executive Order 12372. If you propose to perform activities in more than one State, you should immediately contact the SPOC for each of those States and follow the procedure established in each State under the Executive order. If you want to know the name and address of any SPOC, see the latest official SPOC list on the Web site of the Office of Management and Budget at the following address: *http://www.whitehouse.gov/omb/grants/ spoc.html.*

In States that have not established a process or chosen a program for review, State, area wide, regional, and local entities may submit comments directly to the Department.

Any State Process Recommendation and other comments submitted by a SPOC and any comments from State, area wide, regional, and local entities must be mailed or hand-delivered by the date indicated in this application notice to the following address: The Secretary, E.O. 12372-CFDA #84.215X, U.S. Department of Education, room 7E200, 400 Maryland Avenue, SW., Washington, DC 20202-0125.

We will determine proof of mailing under 34 CFR 75.102 (Deadline date for applications). Recommendations or comments may be hand-delivered until 4:30 p.m. (Washington, DC time) on the date indicated in this notice.

Please Note That Address Is Not the Same Address as the One to Which an Applicant Submits Its Completed Application. *Do Not Send Applications to the Above Address.*

Application Instructions and Forms

The Appendix to this notice contains forms and instructions, a statement regarding estimated public reporting burden, a notice to applicants regarding compliance with section 427 of the General Education Provisions Act, and various assurances and certifications and a checklist for applicants.

• Application for Federal Education Assistance (ED 424 (Exp. 11/30/2004)) and instructions and definitions.

• Budget Information—Non-Construction Programs (ED Form No. 524) and instructions.

• Application Narrative.

• Assurances—Non-Construction Programs (Standard Form 424B) (Rev. 7-97)

• Certifications regarding Lobbying; Debarment, Suspension, and Other Responsibility Matters; and Drug-Free Workplace Requirements (ED 80-0013, 12/98) and instructions.

• Certification regarding Debarment, Suspension, Ineligibility and Voluntary Exclusion: Lower Tier Covered Transactions (ED 80-0014, 9/90) and instructions. (NOTE: ED 80-0014 is intended for the use of grantees and should not be transmitted to the Department.)

• Disclosure of Lobbying Activities (Standard Form LLL (Rev. 797)) and instructions.

• Survey on Ensuring Equal Opportunity for Applicants and survey instructions.

You may submit information on a photocopy of the application and budget forms, the assurances, and the certifications. However, the application form, the assurances, and the certifications must each have an original signature. We will not award a grant unless we have received a completed application form.

Individuals with disabilities may obtain this document in an alternative format (*e.g.*, Braille, large print, audiotape, or computer diskette) on request to the program contact person listed under **FOR FURTHER INFORMATION CONTACT**. However, the Department is not able to reproduce in an alternative format the standard forms included in this application notice.

Electronic Access to This Document

You may view this document, as well as all other Department of Education documents published in the **Federal Register**, in text or Adobe Portable Document Format (PDF) on the Internet at the following site: *http://www.ed.gov/legislation/FedRegister.*

To use PDF you must have Adobe Acrobat Reader, which is available free at this site. If you have questions about using PDF, call the U.S. Government Printing Office (GPO), toll free, at 1-888-293-6498; or in the Washington, DC, area at (202) 512-1530.

Note: The official version of this document is the document published in the **Federal Register**. Free Internet access to the official edition of the **Federal Register** and the Code of Federal Regulations is available on GPO Access at: *http://www.access.gpo.gov/nara/index.html.*

FOR FURTHER INFORMATION CONTACT: Christine Miller, Alex Stein, Harry Kessler, or Claire Geddes, U.S. Department of Education, 400 Maryland Avenue, SW., room 5C126, Washington, DC 20202-6200. Telephone: (202) 260-8766 (Christine Miller); (202) 205-9085 (Alex Stein); (202) 708-9943 (Harry Kessler); or (202) 260-8757 (Claire Geddes) or via Internet: *teachingamericanhistory@ed.gov.*

If you use a telecommunications device for the deaf (TDD), you may call the Federal Information Relay Service (FIRS) at 1-800-877-8339.

Instructions for Transmitting Applications

If you want to apply for a grant and be considered for funding, you must meet the following deadline requirements:

(A) If you Send Your Application by Mail: You must mail the original and two copies of the application on or before the deadline date. One copy of the application should be unbound and suitable for photocopying. To help expedite our review of your application, we would appreciate your voluntarily including an additional 2 copies of your application. We will not penalize applicants who do not provide additional copies. Mail your application to: U.S. Department of Education, Application Control Center, Attention: (CFDA #84.215X), 7th and D Streets, SW., Room 3671, Regional Office Building 3, Washington, DC 20202-4725.

You must show one of the following as proof of mailing:

(1) A legibly dated U.S. Postal Service postmark.

(2) A legible mail receipt with the date of mailing stamped by the U.S. Postal Service.

(3) A dated shipping label, invoice, or receipt from a commercial carrier.

(4) Any other proof of mailing acceptable to the Secretary.

If you mail an application through the U.S. Postal Service, we do not accept either of the following as proof of mailing:

(1) A private metered postmark.

(2) A mail receipt that is not dated by the U.S. Postal Service.

(B) If You Deliver Your Application by Hand: You or your courier must hand deliver the original and two copies of the application by 4:30 p.m. (Washington, DC time) on or before the deadline date. One copy of the application should be unbound and suitable for photocopying. To help expedite our review of your application, we would appreciate your voluntarily including an additional 2 copies of your application. We will not penalize applicants who do not provide additional copies. Deliver your application to: U.S.

Department of Education, Application Control Center, Attention: (CFDA #84.215X), 7th and D Streets, SW., Room 3671, Regional Office Building 3, Washington, DC 20202-4725.

The Application Control Center accepts application deliveries daily between 8 a.m. and 4:30 p.m. (Washington, DC time), except Saturdays, Sundays, and Federal holidays. The Center accepts application deliveries through the D Street entrance only. A person delivering an application must show identification to enter the building.

(1) The U.S. Postal Service does not uniformly provide a dated postmark. Before relying on this method, you should check with your local post office.

(2) If you send your application by mail or if you or your courier deliver it by hand, the Application Control Center will mail a Grant Application Receipt Acknowledgment to you. If you do not receive the notification of application receipt within 15 days from the date of mailing the application, you should call the U.S. Department of Education Application Control Center at (202) 708-9493.

(3) If your application is late, we will notify you that we will not consider the application.

(4) You must indicate on the envelope and—if not provided by the Department—in Item 4 of the Application for Federal Education Assistance (ED 424 (exp. 11/30/2004)) the CFDA number—and suffix letter, if any—of the competition under which you are submitting your application.

Program Authority: 20 U.S.C. 2351 *et seq.*

Dated: April 30, 2003.

Michael J. Petrilli,

Associate Deputy Under Secretary for Innovation and Improvement.

Appendix

Instructions for Estimated Public Reporting Burden

According to the Paperwork Reduction Act of 1995, you are not required to respond to a collection of information unless it displays a valid OMB control number. The valid OMB control number for this collection of information is 1890-0009. Expiration date: June 30, 2005. We estimate the time required to complete this collection of information to average 65 hours per response, including the time to review instructions, search existing date sources, gather the date needed, and complete and review the collection of information. If you have any comments concerning the accuracy of the time estimate or suggestions for improving this form, please write to: U.S. Department of Education, 400 Maryland Avenue, SW., Washington, DC 20202-4651.

If you have comments or concerns regarding the status of your submission of this form, write directly to: Christine Miller, U.S. Department of Education, 400 Maryland Avenue, SW., room 5C126, Washington, DC. 20202-6200.

Instructions for Application Narrative

Applications should be concise and clearly written. Before preparing the narrative, applicants should review the closing date notice and program statue for specific guidance or requirements. Note that applications will be evaluated according to the selection criteria specified in this closing date notice.

Successful applicants will be expected to report annually on the progress of each project or study included in the grant, including a description of preliminary or key findings and an explanation of any changes in goals, objectives, methodology, or planned products or publications.

Note: The section on PAGE LIMIT elsewhere in this application notice applies to your application.

Instructions for the Abstract

For non-electronic submissions, include the name and address of your organization and the name, phone number and e-mail address of the contact person for this project.

The abstract narrative must not exceed one page and should use language that will be understood by a range of audiences. For all projects, include the project title (if applicable), goals, expected outcomes and contributions for research, policy, practice, etc. Include population to be served, as appropriate. For research applications, also include the following:

• Theoretical and conceptual background of the study (*i.e.,* prior research that this investigation builds upon and that provides a compelling rationale for this study)

• Research issues, hypotheses, and questions being addressed

• Study design including a brief description of the sample including sample size, methods, principal dependent, independent, and control variables, and the approach to data analysis.

Checklist for Applicants

Applications must include the following:
• Title Page Form—Application for Federal Education Assistance (ED 424).
• Application Abstract.
• Application Narrative.
• Curriculum Vitae (as appropriate).
• Literature Cited (as appropriate).
• Appendix (as appropriate).
• Budget Information Form (ED 524).
• General Education Provision Act (GEPA) Section 427 Statement.
• Certifications and Assurances.
• Assurances-Non-Construction Programs (Standard Form 424B).
• Certification Regarding Lobbying; Debarment, Suspension, and Other Responsibility Matters; and Drug-Free Work-Place Requirements (ED. Form 80-0013).
• Disclosure of Lobbying Activities (Standard Form LLL), if applicable.
• Certification Regarding Debarment, Suspension, Ineligibility and Voluntary Exclusion-Lower Tier Covered Transactions (ED Form 80-0014) Note: ED form GCS-0014 is intended for the use of primary participants and should not be transmitted to the Department.

BILLING CODE 4000-01-P

Federal Register / Vol. 68, No. 87 / Tuesday, May 6, 2003 / Notices   24059

Application for Federal Education Assistance (ED 424)

U.S. Department of Education
Form Approved
OMB No. 1875-0106
Exp. 11/30/2004

Applicant Information

1. Name and Address
Legal Name: GREENCASTLE-ANTRIM SCHOOL DISTRICT
Organizational Unit

Address: 500 EAST LEITERSBURG ST

GREENCASTLE
City

PA
State

FRANKLIN
County

17225 1138
ZIP Code + 4

2. Applicant's D-U-N-S Number: 3 3 9 4

3. Applicant's T-I-N: 7 7

4. Catalog of Federal Domestic Assistance #: 8 4 2 1 5 X
Title: Teaching American History Grant Program

5. Project Director: MICHAEL MEIER

Address:
CHAMBERSBURG   PA   17201
City   State   ZIP Code + 4

Tel. #:   Fax #:

E-Mail Address:

6. Novice Applicant ☐ Yes ☐ No

7. Is the applicant delinquent on any Federal debt? ☐ Yes ☒ No
(If "Yes," attach an explanation.)

8. Type of Applicant (Enter appropriate letter in the box.) **K**

A State
B Local
C Special District
D Indian Tribe
E Individual
F Independent School District

G Public College or University
H Private, Non-Profit College or University
I Non-Profit Organization
J Private, Profit-Making Organization
K Other (Specify): PUBLIC SCHOOL DISTRICT

Application Information

9. Type of Submission:

—PreApplication
☐ Construction
☐ Non-Construction

—Application
☐ Construction
☒ Non-Construction

10. Is application subject to review by Executive Order 12372 process?
☐ Yes (Date made available to the Executive Order 12372 process for review): _____
☒ No (If "No," check appropriate box below.)
☒ Program is not covered by E.O. 12372.
☐ Program has not been selected by State for review.

11. Proposed Project Dates:
Start Date: 10-1-03   End Date: 9-30-06

12. Are any research activities involving human subjects planned at any time during the proposed project period?
☐ Yes (Go to 12a.)   ☒ No (Go to item 13.)

12a. Are all the research activities proposed designated to be exempt from the regulations?
☐ Yes (Provide Exemption(s) #): _____
☐ No (Provide Assurance #): _____

13. Descriptive Title of Applicant's Project:
WHO IS THE AMERICAN; THIS NEW MAN, THIS NEW WOMAN?

Estimated Funding

14a. Federal	$	725,545 .00
b. Applicant	$	.00
c. State	$	.00
d. Local	$	.00
e. Other	$	.00
f. Program Income	$	.00
g. TOTAL	$	725,545 .00

Authorized Representative Information

15. To the best of my knowledge and belief, all data in this preapplication/application are true and correct. The document has been duly authorized by the governing body of the applicant and the applicant will comply with the attached assurances if the assistance is awarded.

a. Authorized Representative (Please type or print name clearly.)
DR. P. DUFF REARICK

b. Title
SUPERINTENDENT

c. Tel. #: 717-597-2487   Fax #:

d. E-Mail Address: rearick@greencastle.k12.pa.us

e. Signature of Authorized Representative   Date: 7-3-03

U.S. DEPARTMENT OF EDUCATION

OMB Control Number: 1890-0004

BUDGET INFORMATION

NON-CONSTRUCTION PROGRAMS

Expiration Date:

Name of Institution/Organization
Greencastle-Antrim School District

Applicants requesting funding for only one year should complete the column under "Project Year 1." Applicants requesting funding for multi-year grants should complete all applicable columns. Please read all instructions before completing form.

SECTION A - BUDGET SUMMARY
U.S. DEPARTMENT OF EDUCATION FUNDS

Budget Categories	Project Year 1 (a)	Project Year 2 (b)	Project Year 3 (c)	Project Year 4 (d)	Project Year 5 (e)	Total (f)
1. Personnel	0	0	0			0
2. Fringe Benefits	0	0	0			0
3. Travel	6,000	6,000	6,000			18,000
4. Equipment	3,000	0	0			3,000
5. Supplies	1,028	1,028	1,028			3,084
6. Contractual	185,433	185,433	185,433			556,299
7. Construction	0	0	0			0
8. Other	1,460	1,460	1,460			4,380
9. Total Direct Costs (lines 1-8)	196,921	193,921	193,921			584,763
10. Indirect Costs	4,220	4,156	4,156			12,532
11. Training Stipends	42,750	42,750	42,750			128,250
12. Total Costs (lines 9-11)	243,891	240,827	240,827			$725,545

ED Form No. 524

Abstract

Located along the Mason-Dixon Line in south-central Pennsylvania, rural Franklin County is steeped in the historic events of this nation. Franklin County is Civil War country. Because of the region's rich local history, five school districts and the state-owned Scotland School for Veterans children decided to create the Franklin County Consortium's TAH professional development project: *Who is the American: this new man, this new woman*? to explore the history of what it means to be an American. This project will assist the Consortium's 93 middle and high school history and social studies teachers in becoming scholar-teachers with a three-year, in-depth examination of how the bedrocks of American ideology were formed and translated from generation to generation from the 18th through the 20th Century. Who was the American when the nation was born; who is the American now? Through this content-rich professional development project, teachers will gain the historical knowledge and resources to reinvigorate their classroom instruction and their students' understanding of the important questions, themes and narratives of traditional American history.

In order to provide the highest quality professional development, the Consortium has formed three important partnerships with national nonprofit history organizations: National Council for History education; Facing History and Ourselves; and the Center for Learning and Media—New Media Classroom. Their commitments and program outlines are included in the Appendix.

The goal of this project is to increase teachers' content knowledge of American history to improve student instruction. Each partner has committed to providing sustained, intensive professional development to assist the Consortium in reaching its goal. Increased teacher knowledge and understanding through this professional development effort will result in students knowing and understanding the great ideas, issues and events of American history and the likelihood that they will better understand and exercise their civic rights and responsibilities.

Who is the American; this new man, this new woman?
Greencastle-Antrim School District (LEA for Franklin County Consortium)
500 Leitersburg Street, Greencastle, PA 17225
Project Director: Michael Meier
717-264-3532/mjmeier@innernet.net

Introduction

Located along the Mason-Dixon Line in south-central Pennsylvania, rural Franklin County is steeped in the historic events of this nation. Franklin County is Civil War country. It sustained more military activity during the Civil War than any comparable area in the North. Because of its strategic location in the heart of the Cumberland Valley (which stretches from Carlisle, PA to Winchester, VA), the area was the target of three major Confederate cavalry raids as well as one full-scale invasion, the Gettysburg Campaign of 1863. These events incurred severe destruction and economic hardship on the population. The final visitation by McCausland's cavalry left the county seat, Chambersburg, a smoldering ruin. At least 19 separate military engagements, most of them skirmishes, occurred in the county. This is more than any other county in the north. More than 150,000 soldiers from both sides camped at various locations in the area.

Because of the region's rich local history, five school districts and the state-owned Scotland School for Veterans children decided to create the Franklin County Consortium's TAH professional development project: *Who is the American: this new man, this new woman*? to explore the history of what it means to be an American. This project will assist the Consortium's 93 middle and high school history and social studies teachers in becoming scholar-teachers with a three-year, in-depth examination of how the bedrocks of American ideology were formed and translated from generation to generation from the 18th through the 20th Century. Who was the American when the nation was born; who is the American now? Through this content-rich professional development project, teachers will gain the historical knowledge and resources to reinvigorate their classroom instruction and their students' understanding of the important questions, themes and narratives of traditional American history.

(1) Quality of Project Design

The Franklin County Consortium has put together a comprehensive, intensive, three-pronged professional development project to take its 93 middle and high school history and social studies teachers into the content-rich environment of American history. Specifically, the Consortium has established three vital partnerships to enhance this teacher-as-scholars effort and meet the following goal and objectives.

- **GOAL: To increase teachers' content knowledge of American history to improve student instruction.**

Objective 1: *Over the three-year project, 93 educators will participate in 5-day, intensive, themed summer colloquiums and institutes provided by experts from the National Council for History Education (NCHE) and Facing History and Ourselves (FHAO).*

Activity 1.1: NCHE will conduct a 5-day History Colloquium for 36 middle and high school teachers in June of 2004. The content theme for Year 1 will be: Using the *Vital Themes of History* and *History's Habits of Mind* to examine *The 18th Century: Creating the American Nation.* Specific issues to be addressed will include: *the colonial heritage (immigration, land-owning, representative government); The American Revolution (establishing freedom); the Constitution (protecting freedom and individual rights).* Historian Dr. Kevin Brady, former director of the *Bill of Rights Institute,* learning specialist Susan Dangel from Johns Hopkins University, and master classroom teacher Bruce Lesh of Franklin HS (MD), have committed to serve on the NCHE leadership team for the 2004 Colloquium. (see Appendix)

Activity 1.2: In June 2005, NCHE will conduct a 5-day History Colloquium for 36 middle and high school teachers to examine the topic *The 19th Century American: Developing the American Nation.* Specific issues to be addressed will include: *the westward movement (securing the nation's borders, enlarging the area of democracy); immigration (the continuing discovery of America); slavery, the Civil War, and Reconstruction.*

Activity 1.3: In June of 2006, NCHE will conduct a 5-day History Colloquium for 36 middle and high school teachers to examine the topic *The 20th Century: Rediscovering the American Nation.* Specific issues to be addressed will include: *the new immigration; the changing roles of women; and the civil rights movement.*

Activity 1.4: In all three years of this project, FHAO will provide a 5-day institute for 30 teachers entitled—*Forging a Nation: Becoming American.* This institute will utilize a variety of American history materials that illustrate important decisions that citizens make about themselves and others in their community and the nation. Specific issues to be addressed include: *membership in American democracy (foundations of the Early Republic, Constitution and Bill of Rights); ideas of liberty and justice tested in 19th century America (pre-civil war society, reconstruction, immigration and the growth of American cities and industry); challenges to the ideals of American democracy (Jim Crow, social Darwinism, labor unrest); The Progressive Age: Responding to Crisis in American Democracy (the impact of scientific notions of progress on important American institutions, NAACP and the anti-lynching movement); and preserving American democratic ideals in our lifetime (the civil rights movement of the 50s and 60s, choosing to participate today).* Dr. Karen Murphy, an historian in American studies from the University of Minnesota and Mark Swaim-Fox, an FHAO staff member and former middle school history teacher will be leading this Institute.

Objective 2: *To provide professional development opportunities during the school year for 93 teachers over three years.*

Activity 2.1: Each year, Facing History and Ourselves will provide a fall one-day workshop and a spring one-day workshop for 30 teachers. Teachers will rotate through the workshop over the three-year project. Attendance at the spring workshop will be required for those who will be attending the FHAO summer institute.

- **Fall Workshop** (offered Fall 2003, 2004, 2005) *Building Community: Ordinary People in American History—Making a Difference in American Democracy: A Case Study of Ida B. Wells*

Born into slavery in Mississippi, Ida B. Wells became a school teacher, journalist, and led a national effort to stop lynching. Her campaign that inspired later civil rights efforts in the 1950's and 60's, is a real case study of how democratic advocacy, philanthropy, and journalism were used to confront violence and change laws to improve our society.

The workshop will include: the use of primary sources; strategies for locating, evaluating, and integrating historical material from the Internet in the classroom.

- **Spring Workshop** (offered Spring 2004, 2005, 2006) *Forging a Nation: Becoming American—Introduction to the "Becoming American" project*

This workshop is the prelude to the FHAO Summer Institute on *Becoming American*. It will include: an introduction to the history content (*see content listing in Activity 1.4*) and methodology to be used at the summer institute; and an introduction to the Facing History and Ourselves online campus as a tool for institute pre-work.

Activity 2.2: Four Saturday book discussion groups will take place each year (two in the fall and two in the spring) with 10 teachers participating in each Saturday session. Dr. Sarah Bair, a PhD. in American History and Chair of Wilson College's Education Department and a former history teacher in one of the Franklin County Consortium school districts will facilitate the book discussions. Dr. Bair will create a list and teachers will be surveyed at the beginning of each project year to determine which books they will read and discuss. The fall 2004 selections are *Narrative of the Life of Fredrick Douglass* by Frederick Douglass and *To Kill a Mockingbird* by Harper Lee.

Objective 3: *To increase teacher proficiency in integrating technology into the teaching of American History.*

In an effort to provide the broadest professional development experience possible, the Franklin County Consortium has also forged a partnership with The Center for Media and Learning and their project New Media Classroom, a history and humanities teaching with technology program for secondary school teachers. Through its New Media Classroom (NMC), the Center for Media and Learning will train five teams of teachers each year to become leaders of educational technology integration in their schools through a yearlong mentoring process. This training includes a summer institute, online and telephone consultations, school visits and workshops. The NMC program's role in the professional development project **Who is the American: this new man, this new woman**? is to revitalize the teaching of American History by developing strategies for using new technological tools in the classroom and advancing active learning in students.

Activity 3.1: To create five teams of two teachers per year (15 teams of two teachers over project) to participate in an intensive, sustained teaching with technology professional development program in the application of new media resources in classroom practice.

Activity 3.2: To provide a 4-day intensive summer institute in July of each year. The institute will feature presentations by history, humanities and education scholars along with new media project developers. Workshops will address themes such as the Great Migration, the Civil War, immigration, freedom and early America. Each session will involve: hands-on application, where teachers learn to employ new media effectively and comprehensively; finding and evaluating resources on the Web and CD-ROMs; creating new curriculum; and incorporating classroom management, Web design, presentation, and online writing software into instruction. These activities are also designed to foster reflective classroom practice within group, individual and team assignments.

Activity 3.3:   The New Media Classroom will provide a school year program that includes three to four classroom visits per year consisting of peer consultation on such issues as curriculum planning, identification of resources, and discussion of new scholarship. (NMC staff will issue a report of each visit with recommendations for all teacher teams and administrators.) NMC will schedule workshops for in-service days or Saturdays on topics like *Inquiry and Archive: Using Online Primary Source Collections to Teach the US History Survey; New Technology and US History Standards; and Student Multimedia History Projects.* NMC will also offer online and telephone consultations for ongoing mentoring. Resources NMC will provide include a two volume CD-ROM, *Who Built America?* (maps, graphs, film, photographs, text documents and audio from 1876 to 1946; *History Matters: Teaching the US History Survey on the Web; The Lost Museum: Exploring Antebellum American Life and Culture;* and the 10-part *Who Built America?*

The following Center for Media and Learning staff and teacher-consultants will work with the Franklin Country Consortium: Donna Thompson Ray—Director of the New Media Classroom; Dr. Ellen Noonan—Ph.D. American history (NYU); and Angela Darrenkamp—middle school teacher of social studies, Phoenixville School District (PA);

Objective 4:   *To increase Consortium teachers' professional networks focused on teaching traditional American history that provide a forum for interaction among teachers and allows for the exchange of information.*

Activity 4.1:   Eight teachers per year will attend the 5-day summer NCHE National History Academy, weeklong content-rich professional development program at Colonial Williamsburg for teachers of the high school level American History Survey Course. Participation in the Academy will provide Consortium teachers access to NCHE's national network of historians, history educators and secondary school teachers from across the country.

Activity 4.2:   Facing History and Ourselves will provide participating teachers with access to the facing History Online campus to engage with their peers and Facing History staff in a series of collaborations focused on the content and methodology of community building in American history.

Participating teachers in ***Who is the American: this new man, this new woman?*** will learn to use primary sources and other materials to help their students explore times in American history that both tested, and demonstrated, the nation's commitment to liberty and individual rights. Teachers will learn a variety of questions, activities, and classroom strategies that encourage students to think historically—that is, to place themselves and their families within the nation's master narrative.

By providing a menu of professional development opportunities from nationally recognized organizations such as the National Council for History Education, facing History and Ourselves, and The New Media Classroom, Franklin County Consortium's teachers will be able to strengthen their content knowledge of American history, improve the quality of their instruction, and link American history to the lives of their students, resulting in increased student knowledge and understanding of what it means to be an American.

(2) Need for Project

The five school districts in Franklin County (Chambersburg Area, Fannett-Metal, Greencastle-Antrim, Tuscarora and Waynesboro Area) and the state-owned Scotland School for Veterans' Children (SSVC) have combined efforts to form a professional development consortium. The schools did this because, for the most part, they are small, poor and rural districts that have discovered that working together makes better use of resources and provides meaningful interaction among staff that often feel isolated within their districts.

Because of their poverty, the schools in Franklin County have been able to access a number of state funded grants for professional development programs focused on mathematics, the sciences and educational technology. Unfortunately, because of local funding constraints, the schools have not had the means to provide parallel professional development opportunities to teachers of American history.

This is particularly unfortunate for this Consortium's teachers as Franklin County is nestled among some of the richest places in American history (Gettysburg, Antietam, the Underground Railroad), birthplace to one of this country's presidents (James Buchanan), and centrally located within a state known for its American history landmarks, historical individuals, and museum collections. Pennsylvania has been the setting for major events and the accomplishments of nationally significant figures for over three centuries.

Another development of particular interest in defining the need for this professional development project: *Who is the American; this new man, this new woman*? is the fact that Franklin County is undergoing a cultural change. Since its inception, Franklin County has been and remained rural; very Appalachian in its culture and values and its economy based on agriculture. But life in Franklin County is changing . . . and changing drastically.

Because of its proximity to the Washington DC/Baltimore corridor and the interstate highways now running through Franklin County, access to the urban economy has become easier than ever. Washington DC and Baltimore are but a 90 minute commute. Property costs are substantially lower in Franklin County, making housing more affordable and more attractive to professionals looking for a "good place to raise kids" while allowing them to maintain their career path.

Diversity has come to Franklin County; both in the variety of professionals that are moving into the southern part of the county as well as a burgeoning Hispanic population that has moved into the central part of the county to fill migrant laborer and low wage labor jobs. This influx of diversity into the Appalachian culture has caused racial tension to increase in the schools.

Teachers need ways to build common connections among all students; this can be accomplished through the teaching of the story of America; but teachers need to better understand America's history themselves before interacting with and enriching their students.

- *Need—Lack of access to public historians for content enrichment*

Franklin County is a mostly rural community. While its southernmost border lies just 90 miles from Washington DC or Baltimore, the culture of this county remains rural—which translates into isolationist and independent. There are two historical societies within the country that have small, locally focused museums but do not employ professionally trained historians. Consortium teachers do not have access to high-quality historians within this area to provide content rich professional development.

- *Need—Lack of American history as a separate matter within the core curriculum*

Among the Consortium schools, there are 93 middle and high school teachers of American history/social studies employed. Yet, in only one of the districts is there an AP course offered to students in American History. This AP offering reaches just 32 students. Most schools offer courses in pieces of American history at the high school level. Both middle and high school curriculum is timeline/factually-oriented, teaching from one particular date in American history to another; each grade level assigned a particular time period to adhere to.

According to Consortium administrators, there does not currently exist an inquiry-based, content-rich focus on the teaching of American history; but there is a definite interest among both administrators and faculty to strengthen this part of their core curriculum and make it a separate subject matter. Several districts want to add an American history AP course as an outcome of this project; a big step for small, poor districts. Professional development and a mentoring process will be the key in its successful implementation.

- *Need—Lack of student understanding of American history*

A focus group comprised of a sampling of middle and high school American history/social studies teachers revealed that students do not grasp their connection to the story of this country. Current instructional strategies that emphasize "timeline-oriented" teaching are not engaging students. While some schools are using some project-related, themed units as a part of their overall course, many teachers said that their curriculum content needs to be enriched and tied back to each student's view of their place within the community and this country. Teachers stated that they lack opportunities to grow as teacher-scholars in their field.

Currently, Pennsylvania does not include History in its state assessment,. so districts have to rely upon local assessment for student achievement in American history. A way to measure student achievement using the newly passed PA History Standards will be an outcome of this project.

- *Need—Lack of access to on-going collaboration among teachers of American history*

During the focus group, teachers also noted that they often work in isolation—even within their own district. Many noted that the current trend of focusing intensive professional development efforts on math, science and reading leaves them without access to opportunities for professional growth within their own field. By building a consortium for this project, teachers will develop a local and regional network PLUS gain access to a national network through the established partnerships.

• *Need—Lack of guidance on the use of technology and media specific to the American history classroom*

Teachers also expressed a need to better understand how to incorporate technology into their classrooms to strengthen instruction and provide access to historical documents and develop effective presentations of historical content. Many have received generalized in-service on technology provided over the past several years by the schools; but locating appropriate sites and Web-based information and using more comprehensive technology/media skills in the context of American history classroom instruction needs to be developed and supported. Teams will be developed in each school to learn these skills and mentor others.

Certification Issues

Currently, it is not necessary to study history in order to be certified as a social studies teacher in Pennsylvania. Consequently, many of the pool of 93 teachers that are the focus of this professional development project have admitted little background in American history. Most have developed their curriculum from textbooks.

Teachers of history/social studies, in fact most teachers in rural schools, tend to stay in one place for their entire career. As a result, the pool of teachers for this project has considerable longevity—many with 20 + years. This longevity is positive and negative for the schools; positive in providing staff stability, but negative in terms of stagnation of professional growth (especially in traditional American history) or in the understanding/use of technology in American history instruction. The teachers themselves have expressed a desire to learn more so they can become reinvigorated.

(3) Partnerships

In creating this professional development project—*Who is the American; this new man, this new woman?*, a focus groups of middle and high school teachers of history/social studies was convened and met several times to identify needs and brainstorm potential partners that could meet their identified needs. Because the teachers work in rural schools, often isolated from one another as well as from their peers in neighboring districts, they agreed that a consortium approach would provide a spectrum of opportunities locally that could be strengthened by engaging national partners that could provide them with far-reaching access not only to historians but to a national network of their peers.

For this project—***Who is the American; this new man, this new woman?***, three partnerships with national nonprofit history/humanities organizations have been created to meet the needs identified by the teachers and the district administrators: the National Council for History Education, Facing History and Ourselves, and The New Media Classroom of CUNY's Center for Media and Learning's American Social History Project. All three organizations worked with the Franklin County Consortium to design this project. Their detailed Memorandums of Understanding are included in the Appendix.

Partner Contributions

- **National Council for History Education:** Over the course of the project, NCHE will provide three intensive, 5-day summer colloquiums in Franklin County for 36 teachers each year. NCHE will provide the services of a leadership team to include an historian, a learning specialist, and a master teacher who will present the colloquiums as identified in the project goal and objectives section and provide follow-up activities. Materials and handouts will be provided. Participants will also be provided with NCHE memberships, increasing their collegial networking opportunities.

- **Facing History and Ourselves:** Over the course of this project, FHAO will provide three intensive, 5-day summer institutes in Franklin County, for 30 teachers each year, that include as presenters an historian and master teacher specializing in the content areas outlined in the goal/objectives section of this proposal. In addition, FHAO will provide two days of on-site workshops, one in the fall and one in the spring, as outlined in the project design. All participating teachers will be provided access to the FHAO Online Campus for networking and content/teaching strategy discussion opportunities.

- **The New Media Classroom:** This prong of the professional development project will build teams of teachers who will become proficient in utilizing the latest history and humanities scholarship to improve student performance. NMC will provide a 4-day summer institute focused on incorporating technology and media resources into the teaching of American history. In addition, NMC will provide follow-up classroom visits, online and phone consultation and three additional on-site workshops per year. All specifics are outlined in the project design portion of this proposal.

(b) Quality of the Management Plan

To implement ***Who is the American; this new man, this new woman?***, the following plan to achieve the proposed objectives through defined responsibilities, a timeline and proposed milestones has been included.

Quality of Project Personnel

Project Director: The Franklin County Consortium will contract with retired Franklin County school administrator and consultant Michael Meier for project coordination and direction. Mr. Meier, a former secondary humanities/history teacher, has a broad range of experience in coordinating grant-funded projects. A retired secondary principal, Mr. Meier has more than 30 years of experience in coordinating professional development efforts for teachers. He knows all the building administrators in Franklin County resulting in a smoother coordination effort in reaching their teachers. Since his retirement, Mr. Meier has coordinated countywide projects such as Communities That Care, coordinated a comprehensive education department review of Wilson College by the PA Department of Education, and directed a multi-district after-school project. The Project Director will provide 7 days per month to the coordination of this project. His resume is included in the Appendix.

Data Entry Clerk: The Franklin County Consortium will contract with an individual (to be determined) who will be responsible for all data entry into the project database. This person will report to the Project Director and work with the evaluator to provide data reports upon request. It is anticipated that this contracted service will be for 2 days per month for the project period.

Consultants (*see Partnership Agreements in Appendix for more details*)
NCHE: Historian Dr. Kevin Brady, former director of the *Bill of Rights Institute*, **Johns Hopkins University learning specialist Susan Dangel**, and **master classroom teacher Bruce Lesh** of Franklin HS (MD), have committed to serve on the NCHE leadership team.

FHAO: **Dr. Karen Murphy, an historian in American studies** from the University of Minnesota and **Mark Swaim-Fox**, an FHAO staff member and former middle school history teacher will be leading the Institute and workshops.

NMC: **Donna Thompson Ray**—Director of the New Media Classroom, professional developer and humanities program designer; adjunct faculty for City College of New York—Center for Worker Education; M.A. in Art History and Museum Studies. **Dr. Ellen Noonan**—Ph.D. American history (NYU); coordinator of *History Matters: Teaching the US History Survey on the Web and The Lost Museum: Exploring Antebellum American Life and Culture web sites;* curriculum developer; published writer. **Angela Darrenkamp**—middle school teacher of social studies, Phoenixville School District (PA); national faculty, NMC faculty development program—Millersville University (PA); staff developer; adjunct faculty Millersville University School of Education; M.A.

Book Discussions: **Dr. Sarah Bair**, Education Department Chair at Wilson College and PhD in American history.

Selection of Teachers for Participation

- *Summer Colloquiums/Institutes:* Beginning in the fall of 2003, the Project Director will work with each school's administrator to identify all 93 middle and high school history/social studies teachers in the consortium. A database will be created with contact information (including email) that will be used to market each professional development opportunity. Slots for each program will be created based on each school's number of eligible teachers. Schools will have the opportunity to fill their appointed slots until the final registration date after which slots will be opened to overflow requests from other schools.

- **Technology in American History Teams:** For the New Media Classroom prong, teams of two teachers each must be created at the local level. Only five teams will be participating in this prong each year. Each district will have one slot (or team) per year. Each team must be willing to conduct mentoring sessions with colleagues within their school in an effort to share their training.

- **Book Discussion Groups:** In the fall of 2003, the book selections will be advertised to all eligible teachers and registration for participation will be on a first-come, first-served basis. Also in the fall, a survey will be conducted among all project teachers to determine what books will be selected for the spring discussion groups.

Participating teachers will receive stipends for professional development activities occurring outside the regular school day as well as Act 48 professional development credits, assigned according to the number of hours of participation for each activity.

Project Timeline

Dates	Milestone
Fall 2003	Project Director contracted; database of all eligible teachers developed; Project Director and evaluator meet to discuss evaluation process; first FHAO workshop scheduled, advertised, filled and conducted. NMC teams are selected for initial training. Two book discussion sessions are held on Saturdays. Teachers surveyed to determine spring readings.
Winter 2003–04	NCHE Summer Colloquium, FHAO Summer Institute planned by team of teachers, NCHE/FHAO consultants and Project Director; recruitment begins. Slots to American History Academy offered and filled; Spring FHAO workshop scheduled, advertised and filled. NMC team training continues. Spring book discussion groups are formed, materials distributed.
Spring 2004	Spring FHAO workshop (prelude to summer institute) conducted. Final slots for each summer institute/colloquium filled before the end of school. New NMC teams are solicited for next school year; spring book discussion sessions are conducted. Survey conducted to determine fall readings.
Summer 2004	NCHE Summer Colloquium, FHAO Summer Institute take place. Teams participate in NMC Summer Institute. American History Academy participants attend national training. Evaluator and project Director meet to discuss progress and remediate processes. Fall FHAO workshop is scheduled.

Fall 2004	Fall FHAO workshop is advertised and filled by end of September. New NMC teams begin training. New book discussion groups are formed and discussions held in late fall. Survey conducted to determine spring readings.
Winter 2004–05	NCHE Summer Colloquium, FHAO Summer Institute planned by team of teachers, NCHE/FHAO consultants and Project Director; recruitment begins. Slots to American History Academy offered and filled; Spring FHAO workshop scheduled, advertised and filled. NMC team training continues. Spring book discussion groups are formed, materials distributed.
Spring 2005	Spring FHAO workshop (prelude to summer institute) conducted. Final slots for each summer institute/colloquium filled before the end of school. New NMC teams are solicited for next school year; spring book discussion sessions are conducted. Survey conducted to determine fall readings.
Summer 2005	NCHE Summer Colloquium, FHAO Summer Institute take place. Teams participate in NMC Summer Institute. American History Academy participants attend national training. Evaluator and project Director meet to discuss progress and remediate processes. Fall FHAO workshop is scheduled.
Fall 2005	Fall FHAO workshop is advertised and filled by end of September. New NMC teams begin training; New book discussion groups are formed and discussions held in late fall. Survey completed to determine spring readings.
Winter 2005–06	NCHE Summer Colloquium, FHAO Summer Institute planned by team of teachers, NCHE/FHAO consultants and Project Director; recruitment begins. Slots to American History Academy offered and filled; Spring FHAO workshop scheduled, advertised and filled. NMC team training continues. Spring book discussion groups are formed, materials distributed.
Spring 2006	Spring FHAO workshop (prelude to summer institute) conducted. Final slots for each summer institute/colloquium filled before the end of school. New NMC teams are solicited for next school year; spring book discussion sessions are conducted.
Summer 2006	NCHE Summer Colloquium, FHAO Summer Institute take place. Teams participate in NMC Summer Institute. American History Academy participants attend national training.
Fall 2006	Evaluator issues report to Consortium administrators and the USDOE.

(c) Quality of the project evaluation

This section includes the evaluation plan and discusses how the evaluation methods are appropriate for this professional development project, are objective, and provide quantifiable and qualitative data.

Who is the American; this new man, this new woman? Will be evaluated by an outside consultant with federal and state grant program evaluation experience. Dr. Kenneth Byers, a retired education administrator, will bring his background as a former assistant superintendent in charge of professional development combined with his experience as a program evaluator, to conduct a comprehensive evaluation of this project as outlined below. The evaluation will include data collection and analysis, observation of programs and classrooms, and interviews of participants. His resume is included in the Appendix.

The evaluation plan uses both quantitative (number of staff served) and qualitative (satisfaction and impact) methods to evaluate project objectives in four areas:

(1) Project Management- Evaluation of the attainment of project objectives
(2) Documentation- 　　　Specific data on the number of staff who received training
(3) Satisfaction- 　　　　Evaluation of teacher attitudes re: the quality of training received
(4) Impact- 　　　　　　Evaluation of the benefits that occurred

(1) **Project Management** issues will be addressed through the comparison of the listed activities in the proposal with the record of activities conducted over the three-year project period. The project Director will be responsible to maintain documentation for activities conducted as part of the **Who is the American?** project. This documentation will be provided to the outside evaluator and will aid him in determining whether the Franklin County Consortium and its partners have undertaken the activities and generated the deliverables as outlined in the proposal. Project Management will be evaluated on an on-going basis through communication between the Project Director and evaluator.

(2) **Documentation** will be maintained through a computerized database that will track participation in each professional development activity, contacts made between the Project Director and the teachers, contacts between teachers and history professionals, and records of materials provided to the target audience. Forms will the developed by the Project Director that will include attendance sheets, written evaluation forms, contact forms, and a materials received form that will track and document participation (who and how many) in each facet of this project.

(3) **Satisfaction** with the professional development opportunities provided through this project will be measured through written evaluations of each program. Did the participating teachers find the training well designed and useful? These written evaluations will provide the Project Director and the consortium's partners with feedback documenting the utility and other important features of each program. Adjustments can then be made to assure programs are meeting the needs of the teachers.

(4) Measuring the **impact of *Who is the American?*** project will occur in two ways: student outcome data and the Concerns-Based Adoption Model (CBAM). First, student achievement will be measured in relation to the American history area. Although Pennsylvania does not have a statewide test for American history at this time, this project is interested in measuring the impact of professional development of teachers on student achievement. Were students' levels of content knowledge in American history increased? Data to measure student impact will be gathered through the administration

of pre- and post-tests specific to American history content knowledge. Designed by the evaluator, a pre/post test for middle school students and one for high school students will be developed. One teacher per grade level per school (6 per school, grades 6–12) will take part in the pre/post testing of students. Participating teachers in this evaluation activity will agree to participate in a minimum of one intensive summer colloquium/institute each year of the project. The evaluator will collect and analyze pre/post test data and issue an annual report to the Consortium's Project Director and superintendents.

The second part of measuring the **impact** of this project is measuring the change in teachers as a result of the professional development. To do this, the evaluator will use the Concerns-Based Adoption Model (CBAM) created by Shirley M. Hord et al at the Center for R & D in Teaching at the University of Texas in Austin. The model was created to explain the lack of teacher buy-in and to propose ways of using this model to monitor and increase implementation of educational innovations. The CBAM identifies and provides ways to assess seven stages of concern regarding change. These stages have major implications for professional development. The evaluator will use the model to monitor teacher expressions of concern and levels of use of the American history content enrichment and instructional strategies learned through this project as outlined in the project objectives. The evaluator will collect this data, monitor progress and issue an annual report.

Conclusion

Franklin County Consortium's *Who is the American; this new man, this new woman?* professional development project will help to increase student achievement by improving the knowledge, understanding and appreciation for traditional American history of 93 middle and high school teachers. The critical partnerships with national American history and humanities organizations will assist teachers in learning about the significant issues, episodes and turning points in the history of the United States and how the words and deeds of individual Americans have steered the course of the nation. Increased teacher knowledge and understanding through this professional development effort will result in students knowing and understanding the great ideas, issues and events of American history and the likelihood that they will better understand and exercise their civic rights and responsibilities.

Curriculum Vitae
Partnership Agreements

- National Council for History Education
- Facing History and Ourselves
- Center for Learning and Media: New Media Classroom

NATIONAL COUNCIL FOR HISTORY EDUCATION, INC.

PROMOTING THE IMPORTANCE OF HISTORY IN SCHOOL AND SOCIETY

MEMORANDUM OF UNDERSTANDING

25 June 2003

Dr. P. Duff Rearick
Superintendent
Greencastle-Antrim School District
500 East Leitersburg Street
Greencastle, PA 17225

Dear Dr. Rearick,

Based on our understanding of your proposal to the U.S. Department of Education for a Teaching American History Grant, the National Council for History Education, Inc. (NCHE) would be pleased to partner with the Greencastle-Antrim School District (for the Franklin County Consortium) in planning for and providing professional development programs in the *Who Is the American: this new man, this new woman?*, **Professional Development Program**. This agreement will cover NCHE participation from October, 2003, to October, 2006, and will take effect only if, and when, the Greencastle-Antrim School District is awarded a grant from the U.S. Dept. of Education to fund the project.

Specifically, NCHE will conduct three, 5-day History Colloquium programs for up to 36 middle and high school teachers from the Franklin County Consortium. The Colloquia will be held during June of 2004, 2005, and 2006.

- Content theme for the June 2004 colloquium will be: Using the *Vital Themes of History* and *History's Habits of Mind* to examine the **The 18th Century: Creating the American Nation**. Specific issues to be addressed will include: *the colonial heritage (immigration, land-owning, representative government); the American Revolution (establishing freedom); the Constitution (protecting freedom and individual rights).* Historian **Kevin Brady**, recently of *The Bill of Rights Institute*, Johns Hopkins University learning specialist **Susan**

Dangel, and master classroom teacher **Bruce Lesh** of Franklin H.S. (MD), have committed to serve on the leadership team for the 2004 Colloquium.

- Content theme for the June 2005 colloquium will be: Using the *Vital Themes of History* and *History's Habits of Mind* to examine the topic **The 19th Century American: Developing the American Nation.** Specific issues to be addressed will include: *the westward movement (securing the nation's borders, enlarging the area of democracy); immigration (the continuing discovery of America); slavery, the Civil War, and Reconstruction.*

- Content theme for the June 2006 colloquium will be: Using the *Vital Themes of History* and *History's Habits of Mind* to examine the topic **The 20th Century: Rediscovering the American Nation.** Specific issues to be addressed will include: *the new immigration; the changing roles of women; and the civil rights movement.*

For each Colloquium, it is our understanding that the Greencastle-Antrim School District will provide the following:

- a Coordinator from your district to facilitate local arrangements,
- stipend or released time for the participating teachers for all days of the colloquium,
- space for the meetings (including breakout space),
- A-V equipment,
- a list of the names and home addresses of the participants, so that we may contact them with a backgrounder mailing, and
- a $41,070 fee for each colloquium ($41,070 for up to 36 participants + $1,050 each for any additional participants) to NCHE for leading each program.

Based on those assumptions, for each colloquium NCHE will do the following:

- assemble and pay a 3-member leadership team (historian, master classroom teacher, learning specialist) chosen to address your content.
- appoint and pay an NCHE Colloquium Coordinator who will work with your coordinator.
- develop and mail a pre-colloquium mailing to the participants introducing the concept of the program, the team of leaders, and inviting them to contribute to the planning of the program.
- pay for time and travel of the leadership team, and arrange and pay for meeting facilities for a planning meeting for the colloquium. Your coordinator is invited and encouraged to attend, observe, and offer suggestions to the NCHE team, but that person's time and travel will be your responsibility.
- develop presentations within the 5-day meeting agenda specifically crafted to address your topics. We will try to meet as many of the needs and desires of your district and participants as possible, but NCHE will be solely responsible for the philosophy and content (as expressed in the booklet **Building a United States History Curriculum**) of the colloquium.
- prepare materials and handouts for the program and provide participants with a packet that they can take home and use.

- hold conference calls for agenda fine-tuning, produce handouts/materials, and purchase publications for participants; pay to ship all materials to the colloquium site.
- lead participants through the planned agenda.
- arrange and pay for refreshments and lunches for all participants for the colloquium days.
- pay time and travel expenses for the leadership team to/during/from the colloquium.
- provide phone/FAX/email/postage for planning and follow-up activities.
- give NCHE memberships (or extensions for those who may already be members) to all participants, and hold a door prize giveaway for participants at the end of the colloquium.
- develop a follow-up mechanism to help carry the program beyond the end of the colloquium.

If you concur with this statement of our respective responsibilities, this letter will serve as our agreement. NCHE will conduct the three Colloquium programs, as stated above. The Greencastle-Antrim School District shall provide support as indicated above (participants, space, A-V equipment, etc.) and shall pay NCHE a total fee of $123,210 in 3 installments upon receipt of an NCHE Invoice per the following schedule: $41,070 on January 2, 2004; $41,070 on January 2, 2005; and $41,070 on January 2, 2006.

It is a pleasure to be working with the Greencastle-Antrim School District and we are looking forward to a great *Who Is the American: this new man, this new woman?*, **Professional Development Program.**

I agree to the above terms and conditions,

Elaine Wrisley Reed   25 June 2003
Elaine Wrisley Reed   Date
Executive Director
National Council for History Education, Inc.

Dr. P. Duff Rearick   July 1, 03
Dr. P. Duff Rearick   Date
Superintendent
Greencastle-Antrim School District

This agreement on the part of NCHE is void and NCHE will have no responsibility to fulfill: if the above person is not properly authorized to sign for Greencastle-Antrim School District; or if, after receiving a *TAH Grant* using this NCHE *Memorandum of Understanding* in its proposal, Greencastle-Antrim School District imposes additional contracts, reports, personnel specifications, payment schedules, or procedures not specified in this agreement. If this agreement becomes void, all terms, conditions, personnel, and payments must be renegotiated and a new *Memorandum of Understanding* must be signed before NCHE can work on this project.

FACING HISTORY AND OURSELVES

Letter of Intent to Provide Services

Dr. P. Duff Rearick, Superintendent
Greencastle-Antrim School District
500 East Leitersburg Street
Greencastle, PA 17225

Dear Dr. Rearick,

Facing History and Ourselves National Foundation, Inc. agrees to enter into partnership with the Franklin County Consortium (Greencastle-Antrim School District, fiscal agent) to provide the services described in Attachment A and as outlined in the application for the Teaching American History Grant Program entitled "Who is the American: this new man, this new woman?" These services as a partner will be provided between October 1, 2003 and September 30, 2006, at the cost outlined in Attachment B, subject to any approved re-budgeting procedures under the program regulations.

Sincerely,

Margot Stem Strom
Executive Director

June 27, 2003

Attachment A: Description of Services Provided by: Facing History and Ourselves

***Who Is the American? This New Man, This New Woman: A Professional Development Project
for Elementary and Secondary American History and Social Studies Teachers***

Fall Workshop #1 (Offered Fall 2003, 2004, 2005)

Building Community: Ordinary People in American History (1 day workshop for 30 teachers)
Making a Difference in American Democracy: A Case Study of Ida B. Wells

> Born into slavery in Mississippi, Ida B. Wells became a school teacher, journalist, and led a
> national effort to stop lynching. Her campaign inspired later civil rights efforts in the 1950's
> and 60's. Teachers may use the case study of Ida B. Wells to show that making a difference
> is not simple—it may often take many years and involve many people who are willing to
> help. It is a real case study of how democratic advocacy, philanthropy, and journalism were
> used to confront violence and change laws to improve our society.
>
>> Examination of primary resource documents
>> Use of primary American history documents in the classroom
>> Strategies for locating, evaluating, and integrating historical material using the Internet
>> Use of the Anti-lynching exhibit on the web in the classroom

Spring Workshop #2 (Offered Spring 2004, 2005, 2006)

Forging a Nation: Becoming American (1 day workshop for 30 teachers)
Introduction to the "Becoming American" project

> History is not inevitable. Individuals can make a difference. Democracy is a work in
> progress—a work that is shaped by the choices that ordinary people make day in and day
> out. Although those decisions may not seem important at the time, little by little, they
> define an individual, create a community, and ultimately forge a nation. Those choices
> build on the efforts of earlier generations and leave a legacy for those to come.
>
>> Introduction to content and methodology to be used at the summer institute
>> Introduction to the Facing History and Ourselves online campus as a tool for institute
>> pre-work

5 day Summer Institute (Offered Summer 2004, 2005, 2006)

Forging a Nation: Becoming American (5day institute for 30 teachers)

This institute will utilize a variety of American history materials that illustrate important deci-
sions that citizens make about themselves and others in their community and the nation.
Participating teachers will learn to use these materials to help their students explore times in
American history that both tested, and demonstrated, the nation's commitment to democracy.
Teachers will learn to utilize a variety of questions and activities that link American history to the

lives and experiences of their students. They will learn a methodology that encourages students to think historically—that is, to place themselves and their families within the nation's master narrative and assume the responsibility to keep that story alive for future generations.

Day One: Membership in American Democracy
Foundations of the Early Republic
Constitution and Bill of Rights: Ideas & Practice
Enlightenment notions of political freedom, individual rights and membership

Day Two: Ideas of Liberty and Justice tested in 19th century America
Pre civil war society
Reconstruction
The Immigration Experience and the growth of American cities and industry

Day Three: Challenges to the Ideals of American Democracy
Jim Crow
Social Darwinism
Labor unrest

Day Four: The Progressive Age: Responding to Crisis in American Democracy
The impact of scientific notions of progress on important American institutions
NAACP and the anti-lynching movement
Settlement house movement

Day Five: Legacies: Preserving American Democratic Ideals in our Lifetime
The civil rights movement of the 1950's and 1960's
Choosing to participate today

On- Going Teacher Follow Up Support and Technical Assistance

Individual phone consultation re curricular design and content implementation, personal web account with tech support, access to lending library, access to speakers, and other Facing History and Ourselves resources

Additional Requirements—to be provided by the lead LEA

- Workshop and Institute space
- Web connection in main presentation room with LCD projector
- Web-enabled Computer lab with at least one computer for each 2 participants
- Arranging for coffee, snacks in morning and lunches for participants and facilitators at 6 workshops and 3 (5-day) institutes

The New Media Classroom – Franklin County Consortium

Program Description

NMC will train history and humanities secondary school educators to become leaders of educational technology integration through a year-long mentoring process. This training includes a summer institute, online and telephone consultations, school visits, and workshops. The program will begin in July and end in April. Our goal is to help teachers:

- **revitalize** teaching of American history;
- rethink their **classroom practice**;
- sharpen **technology skills**;
- **develop strategies** for using new technological tools in the classroom; and
- advance **active learning** in students.

Summer Institute

A 4-day intensive summer institute is held in July. The institute features presentations by history, humanities, and education scholars along with new media project developers. Workshops will address such historical periods or themes as the Great Migration, the Civil War, immigration, freedom, and early America. Each session involves hands-on application, where teachers learn to employ new media effectively and comprehensively: to find and evaluate resources on the Web and CD-ROMs; to create new curriculum; and to incorporate classroom management, Web design, presentation, and online writing software into instruction. These activities are also designed to foster reflective classroom practice within group, individual, and team assignments.

School Year Program

To deepen the impact of the work produced during the summer institute, Franklin County Consortium-NMC teachers participate in school year activities.

>School Visits

NMC will conduct three to four classroom visits for Franklin County Consortium schools during the school year. The visits may consist of a peer consultation covering such issues as curriculum planning, identification of resources, and discussion of new scholarship. NMC staff produce a report of the visit with recommendations to the participating teacher(s) and school administrators.

>Workshops

NMC provides follow-up workshops for participating teachers. School administrators are also welcome to attend. The workshops are full or half-day in length and can be scheduled during district-wide professional development days or Saturdays.

NMC will adopt the workshop design according to the technology capabilities of the school. NMC will also consider the capability teachers have for off-site access to new media technologies when selecting resources and designing activities for classroom use. Those resources and activities address one computer classrooms, computer lab access, and distribution of primary resources found on online archives.

The thematic focus of the workshops may include such topics as: *Inquiry and Archive: Using Online Primary Source Collections to Teach the U.S. History Survey; New Technology and U.S. History Standards; Student Multimedia Projects;* and *Literacy Building & the World Wide Web.*

>Online and Telephone Consultation

Personal and group consultations inform the year-long mentoring process. The consultations will take place through email and telephone conversation.

Curriculum Resources

NMC has identified and uses a range of new digital resources—from online archives to interactive Web conferencing tools—that offer exciting opportunities to enhance content learning and develop basic literacy skills to improve student performance and motivation.

Those resources include but are not limited to ASHP/Center for Media and Learning's:

- Two volume CD-ROM, *Who Built America?*, a vast collection of primary sources including maps, graphs, film, photographs, text documents and audio chronicling the Centennial Celebration of 1876 to the Great War of 1914 (Vol. 1) and from the Great War to the Atomic Age of 1946 (Vol. II). http://www.ashp.cuny.edu/WBAcd-roms.html

- *History Matters: Teaching the U.S. History Survey on the Web. History Matters* features an annotated directory of Web sites for the history and humanities classroom, classroom-tested lessons, and a collection of primary documents in text, image, and audio dating from early civilization to colonization and settlement through to contemporary America. http://historymatters.gmu.edu

- *The Lost Museum: Exploring Antebellum American Life and Culture*, a web-based, interactive re-creation of P.T. Barnum's American Museum that examines the social, cultural, and political history of antebellum and Civil War America. http://www.lostmuseum.cuny.edu

- 10-part *Who Built America?* Web documentaries http://www.ashp.cuny.edu/video.html

- *New Media Classroom Handbook*, featuring classroom activities that use new media resources. http://www.ashp.cuny.edu/lesson.html

Participants

Classroom teachers of US history at the secondary level (middle and high school). New teachers are welcome.

Standards, Documentation, and Dissemination

The New Media Classroom

A history and humanities teaching with technology program for secondary school teachers

About The New Media Classroom

The New Media Classroom is a teaching with technology professional development program for secondary school teachers of history and the humanities. The program builds on the ASHP/Center for Media and Learning's national teaching with technology program, *The New Media Classroom-Expanding Horizons*, a six-year collaborative research project for high school and college/university faculty, funded by the National Endowment for the Humanities. To-date, the New Media Classroom has reached over 12,500 students.

The New Media Classroom program (NMC) is predicated on the belief that to train history and humanities teachers in the use of new media resources, professional development programs must deploy technology in the service of high-quality content and student-centered instruction. NMC offers sustained and ongoing teacher support with an emphasis on classroom implementation. Through a year-long program that includes an intensive summer institute and follow-up activities both, face-to-face and online, NMC helps teachers overcome the often daunting initial obstacles, both technical and pedagogical, to incorporating new media into their classroom practice. Program work and learning objectives focus on history and humanities content, student learning, technology skills, content and performance standards, and curriculum development. NMC's curriculum and professional development approach is comparable to the teaching practices and content standards administered by The Association of Supervision and Curriculum Development (ASCD), the National Council of Teachers of English (NCTE), and the National Educational Technology Standards (NETS-ISTE). In 1999 NMC was endorsed by the National Council for the Social Studies (NCSS). NMC has published and widely distributed *The New Media Classroom Teacher's Handbook,* a collection of new media-enriched resources and classroom lessons, and *Intentional Media: the Crossroads Conversations on Learning and Technology in the American Culture and History Classroom,* a collection of essays produced by NMC staff and teachers in the biannual journal, *Works & Days* (Indiana University of Pennsylvania), 1998. NMC has been documented in such publications as the OAH's *Journal of American History,* AHA's *Perspectives,* Jaime Mackenzie's *From Now On,* and Scholastic magazines.

> *[I learned] how to develop more sophisticated approaches to pedagogy using multimedia. It raised important questions and helped me focus on goals...I found the presentations that were "look what works for me"- based to be the most valuable. Thank you for always returning to the teaching element.*
>
> *High School Teacher*

NMC links multimedia curriculum to national standards in social studies/history, English/Language Arts, and technology. In an effort to document improved student learning, NMC measures teacher change by comparing curriculum units and lessons before and after training; working with teachers to create electronic portfolios of their curriculum writing and reflective work; and encouraging peer review of teacher work mounted on the NMC program Web site. NMC disseminates classroom findings at national and local education conferences and symposia.

Personnel

The following Center for Media and Learning staff and teacher-consultants will work with NMC- Franklin County Consortium Schools:

Donna Thompson Ray – director of the New Media Classroom (CML); professional developer and humanities program designer; adjunct faculty City College of New York-Center for Worker Education; M.A. in Art History and Museum Studies.

Ellen Noonan – Ph.D. American history (NYU); CML media producer; coordinator of *History Matters: Teaching the U.S. History Survey on the Web* and *The Lost Museum: Exploring Antebellum American Life and Culture* web sites. Curriculum developer. Published writer.

Angela Darrenkamp – middle school teacher of Social Studies, Phoenixville School District (PA); national faculty, New Media Classroom faculty development program-Millersville University; staff developer; adjunct faculty Millersville University School of Education; M.A.

For further information contact:
Donna Thompson Ray, Co-Director of Education/Director of New Media Education
ASHP/CML Tele: 212-966-4248 x219 email: Dthompson@gc.cuny.edu Fax: 212-966-4589

GEPA, Section 427 Statement

GEPA Section 427

Since the primary focus of this proposal is professional development for teachers, the main barrier under GEPA that could impede access or participation is disability. The Franklin County Consortium will provide for equitable access to all training opportunities offered by holding trainings in handicap accessible buildings so as not to prevent access to or participation in by any teacher. Franklin County, a mostly rural county, has a minority population under 2%; consequently other potential barriers as outlined in GEPA will not apply to this project.

OMB Approval No. 0348-0040

ASSURANCES - NON-CONSTRUCTION PROGRAMS

Public reporting burden for this collection of information is estimated to average 15 minutes per response, including time for reviewing instructions, searching existing data sources, gathering and maintaining the data needed, and completing and reviewing the collection of information. Send comments regarding the burden estimate or any other aspect of this collection of information, including suggestions for reducing this burden, to the Office of Management and Budget, Paperwork Reduction Project (0348-0040), Washington, DC 20503.

PLEASE DO NOT RETURN YOUR COMPLETED FORM TO THE OFFICE OF MANAGEMENT AND BUDGET. SEND IT TO THE ADDRESS PROVIDED BY THE SPONSORING AGENCY.

NOTE: Certain of these assurances may not be applicable to your project or program. If you have questions, please contact the awarding agency. Further, certain Federal awarding agencies may require applicants to certify to additional assurances. If such is the case, you will be notified.

As the duly authorized representative of the applicant, I certify that the applicant:

1. Has the legal authority to apply for Federal assistance and the institutional, managerial and financial capability (including funds sufficient to pay the non-Federal share of project cost) to ensure proper planning, management and completion of the project described in this application.

2. Will give the awarding agency, the Comptroller General of the United States and, if appropriate, the State, through any authorized representative, access to and the right to examine all records, books, papers, or documents related to the award; and will establish a proper accounting system in accordance with generally accepted accounting standards or agency directives.

3. Will establish safeguards to prohibit employees from using their positions for a purpose that constitutes or presents the appearance of personal or organizational conflict of interest, or personal gain.

4. Will initiate and complete the work within the applicable time frame after receipt of approval of the awarding agency.

5. Will comply with the Intergovernmental Personnel Act of 1970 (42 U.S.C. §§4728-4763) relating to prescribed standards for merit systems for programs funded under one of the 19 statutes or regulations specified in Appendix A of OPM's Standards for a Merit System of Personnel Administration (5 C.F.R. 900, Subpart F).

6. Will comply with all Federal statutes relating to nondiscrimination. These include but are not limited to: (a) Title VI of the Civil Rights Act of 1964 (P.L. 88-352) which prohibits discrimination on the basis of race, color or national origin; (b) Title IX of the Education Amendments of 1972, as amended (20 U.S.C. §§1681-1683, and 1685-1686), which prohibits discrimination on the basis of sex; (c) Section 504 of the Rehabilitation

Act of 1973, as amended (29 U.S.C. §794), which prohibits discrimination on the basis of handicaps; (d) the Age Discrimination Act of 1975, as amended (42 U.S.C. §§6101-6107), which prohibits discrimination on the basis of age; (e) the Drug Abuse Office and Treatment Act of 1972 (P.L. 92-255), as amended, relating to nondiscrimination on the basis of drug abuse; (f) the Comprehensive Alcohol Abuse and Alcoholism Prevention, Treatment and Rehabilitation Act of 1970 (P.L. 91-616), as amended, relating to nondiscrimination on the basis of alcohol abuse or alcoholism; (g) §§523 and 527 of the Public Health Service Act of 1912 (42 U.S.C. §§290 dd-3 and 290 ee 3), as amended, relating to confidentiality of alcohol and drug abuse patient records; (h) Title VIII of the Civil Rights Act of 1968 (42 U.S.C. §§3601 et seq.), as amended, relating to nondiscrimination in the sale, rental or financing of housing; (i) any other nondiscrimination provisions in the specific statute(s) under which application for Federal assistance is being made; and, (j) the requirements of any other nondiscrimination statute(s) which may apply to the application.

7. Will comply, or has already complied, with the requirements of Titles II and III of the Uniform Relocation Assistance and Real Property Acquisition Policies Act of 1970 (P.L. 91-646) which provide for fair and equitable treatment of persons displaced or whose property is acquired as a result of Federal or federally-assisted programs. These requirements apply to all interests in real property acquired for project purposes regardless of Federal participation in purchases.

8. Will comply, as applicable, with provisions of the Hatch Act (5 U.S.C. §§1501-1508 and 7324-7328) which limit the political activities of employees whose principal employment activities are funded in whole or in part with Federal funds.

9. Will comply, as applicable, with the provisions of the Davis-Bacon Act (40 U.S.C. §§276a to 276a-7), the Copeland Act (40 U.S.C. §276c and 18 U.S.C. §874), and the Contract Work Hours and Safety Standards Act (40 U.S.C. §§327-333), regarding labor standards for federally-assisted construction subagreements.

10. Will comply, if applicable, with flood insurance purchase requirements of Section 102(a) of the Flood Disaster Protection Act of 1973 (P.L. 93-234) which requires recipients in a special flood hazard area to participate in the program and to purchase flood insurance if the total cost of insurable construction and acquisition is $10,000 or more.

11. Will comply with environmental standards which may be prescribed pursuant to the following: (a) institution of environmental quality control measures under the National Environmental Policy Act of 1969 (P.L. 91-190) and Executive Order (EO) 11514; (b) notification of violating facilities pursuant to EO 11738; (c) protection of wetlands pursuant to EO 11990; (d) evaluation of flood hazards in floodplains in accordance with EO 11988; (e) assurance of project consistency with the approved State management program developed under the Coastal Zone Management Act of 1972 (16 U.S.C. §§1451 et seq.); (f) conformity of Federal actions to State (Clean Air) Implementation Plans under Section 176(c) of the Clean Air Act of 1955, as amended (42 U.S.C. §§7401 et seq.); (g) protection of underground sources of drinking water under the Safe Drinking Water Act of 1974, as amended (P.L. 93-523); and, (h) protection of endangered species under the Endangered Species Act of 1973, as amended (P.L. 93-205).

12. Will comply with the Wild and Scenic Rivers Act of 1968 (16 U.S.C. §§1271 et seq.) related to protecting components or potential components of the national wild and scenic rivers system.

13. Will assist the awarding agency in assuring compliance with Section 106 of the National Historic Preservation Act of 1966, as amended (16 U.S.C. §470), EO 11593 (identification and protection of historic properties), and the Archaeological and Historic Preservation Act of 1974 (16 U.S.C. §§469a-1 et seq.).

14. Will comply with P.L. 93-348 regarding the protection of human subjects involved in research, development, and related activities supported by this award of assistance.

15. Will comply with the Laboratory Animal Welfare Act of 1966 (P.L. 89-544, as amended, 7 U.S.C. §§2131 et seq.) pertaining to the care, handling, and treatment of warm blooded animals held for research, teaching, or other activities supported by this award of assistance.

16. Will comply with the Lead-Based Paint Poisoning Prevention Act (42 U.S.C. §§4801 et seq.) which prohibits the use of lead-based paint in construction or rehabilitation of residence structures.

17. Will cause to be performed the required financial and compliance audits in accordance with the Single Audit Act Amendments of 1996 and OMB Circular No. A-133, "Audits of States, Local Governments, and Non-Profit Organizations."

18. Will comply with all applicable requirements of all other Federal laws, executive orders, regulations, and policies governing this program.

SIGNATURE OF AUTHORIZED CERTIFYING OFFICIAL	TITLE SUPERINTENDENT
APPLICANT ORGANIZATION GREENCASTLE-ANTRIM SD.	DATE SUBMITTED 7-3-03

Standard Form 424B (Rev. 7-97) Back

CERTIFICATIONS REGARDING LOBBYING; DEBARMENT, SUSPENSION AND OTHER RESPONSIBILITY MATTERS; AND DRUG-FREE WORKPLACE REQUIRMENTS

Applicants should refer to the regulations cited below to determine the certification to which they are required to attest. Applicants should also review the instructions for certification included in the regulations before completing this form. Signature of this form provides for compliance with certification requirements under 34 CFR Part 82, "New Restrictions on Lobbying," and 34 CFR Part 85, "Government-wide Debarment and Suspension (Nonprocurement) and Government-wide Requirements for Drug-Free Workplace (Grants)." The certifications shall be treated as a material representation of fact upon which reliance will be placed when the Department of Education determines to award the covered transaction, grant, or cooperative agreement.

1. LOBBYING

As required by Section 1352, Title 31 of the U.S. Code, and implemented at 34 CFR Part 82, for persons entering into a grant or cooperative agreement over $100,000, as defined at 34 CFR Part 82, Sections 82.105 and 82.110, the applicant certifies that:

(a) No Federal appropriated funds have been paid or will be paid, by or on behalf of the undersigned, to any person for influencing or attempting to influence an officer or employee of any agency, a Member of Congress, an officer or employee of Congress, or an employee of a Member of Congress in connection with the making of any Federal grant, the entering into of any cooperative agreement, and the extension, continuation, renewal, amendment, or modification of any Federal grant or cooperative agreement;

(b) If any funds other than Federal appropriated funds have been paid or will be paid to any person for influencing or attempting to influence an officer or employee of any agency, a Member of Congress, an officer or employee of Congress, or an employee of a Member of Congress in connection with this Federal grant or cooperative agreement, the undersigned shall complete and submit Standard Form-LLL, "Disclosure Form to Report Lobbying," in accordance with its instructions;

(c) The undersigned shall require that the language of this certification be included in the award documents for all subawards at all tiers (including subgrants, contracts under grants and cooperative agreements, and subcontracts) and that all subrecipients shall certify and disclose accordingly.

2. DEBARMENT, SUSPENSION, AND OTHER RESPONSIBILITY MATTERS

As required by Executive Order 12549, Debarment and Suspension, and implemented at 34 CFR Part 85, for prospective participants in primary covered transactions, as defined at 34 CFR Part 85, Sections 85.105 and 85.110—

A. The applicant certifies that it and its principals:

(a) Are not presently debarred, suspended, proposed for debarment, declared ineligible, or voluntarily excluded from covered transactions by any Federal department or agency;

(b) Have not within a three-year period preceding this application been convicted of or had a civil judgement rendered against them for commission of fraud or a criminal offense in connection with obtaining, attempting to obtain, or performing a public (Federal, State, or local) transaction or contract under a public transaction; violation of Federal or State antitrust statutes or commission of embezzlement, theft, forgery, bribery, falsification or destruction of records, making false statements, or receiving stolen property;

(c) Are not presently indicted for or otherwise criminally or civilly charged by a governmental entity (Federal, State, or local) with commission of any of the offenses enumerated in paragraph (2)(b) of this certification; and

(d) Have not within a three-year period preceding this application had one or more public transaction (Federal, State, or local) terminated for cause or default; and

B. Where the applicant is unable to certify to any of the statements in this certification, he or she shall attach an explanation to this application.

3. DRUG-FREE WORKPLACE (GRANTEES OTHER THAN INDIVIDUALS)

As required by the Drug-Free Workplace Act of 1988, and implemented at 34 CFR Part 85, Subpart F, the grantees, as defined at 34 CFR Part 85, Sections 85.605 and 85.610.

A. The applicant certifies that it will or will continue to provide a drug-free workplace by:

(a) Publishing a statement notifying employees that the unlawful manufacture, distribution, dispensing, possession, or use of a controlled substance is prohibited in the grantee's workplace and specifying the actions that will be taken against employees for violation of such prohibition;

(b) Establishing an on-going drug-free awareness program to inform employees about:

(1) The dangers of drug abuse in the workplace;

(2) The grantee's policy of maintaining a drug-free workplace;

(3) Any available drug counseling, rehabilitation, and employee assistance programs; and

(4) The penalties that may be imposed upon employees for drug abuse violations occurring in the workplace;

(c) Making it a requirement that each employee to be engaged in the performance of the grant be given a copy of the statement required by paragraph (a);

(d) Notifying the employee in the statement required by paragraph (a) that, as a condition of employment under the grant, the employee will:

(1) Abide by the terms of the statement; and

(2) Notify the employer in writing of his or her conviction for a violation of a criminal drug statute occurring in the workplace no later than five calendar days after such conviction;

(e) Notifying the agency, in writing, within 10 calendar days after receiving notice under subparagraph (d)(2) from an employee or otherwise receiving actual notice of such conviction. Employers of convicted employees must provide notice, including position title, to: Director, Grants Policy and Oversight Staff, U.S. Department of Education, 400 Maryland Avenue, S.W. (Room 3652, GSA Regional Office Building No. 3), Washington, DC 20202-4248. Notice shall include the identification number(s) of each affected grant;

(f)   Taking one of the following actions, within 30 calendar days of receiving notice under subparagraph (d)(2), with respect to any employee who is so convicted:

(1) Taking appropriate personnel action against such an employee, up to and including termination, consistent with the requirements of the Rehabilitation Act of 1973, as amended; or

(2) Requiring such employee to participate satisfactorily in a drug abuse assistance or rehabilitation program approved for such purposes by a Federal, State, or local health, law enforcement, or other appropriate agency;

(g) Making a good faith effort to continue to maintain a drug-free workplace through implementation of paragraphs (a), (b), (c), (d), (e), and (f).

B. The grantee may insert in the space provided below the site(s) for the performance of work done in connection with the specific grant:

Place of Performance (Street address, city, county, state, zip code)

Check ☐ if there are workplaces on file that are not identified here.

**DRUG-FREE WORKPLACE
(GRANTEES WHO ARE INDIVIDUAL)**

As required by the Drug-Free Workplace Act of 1988, and implemented at 34 CFR Part 85, Subpart F, for grantees as defined at 34 CFR Part 85, Section, 85.605 and 85.610-

A. As a condition of the grant, I certify that I will not engage in the unlawful manufacture, distribution, dispensing, possession, or use of a controlled substance in conducting any activity with the grant; and

B. If convicted of a criminal drug offense resulting from a violation occurring during the conduct of any grant activity, I will report the conviction, in writing, within 10 calendar days of the conviction, to: Director, Grants Policy and Oversight Staff, Department of Education, 400 Maryland Avenue, S.W. (Room 3652, GSA Regional Office Building No.3), Washington, DC 20202-4248. Notice shall include the identification number(s) of each affected grant.

As the duly authorized representative of the applicant, I hereby certify that the applicant will comply with the above certifications.

NAME OF APPLICANT	PR/AWARD NUMBER AND/OR PROJECT NAME
GREENCASTLE-ANTRIM SD	

PRINTED NAME AND TITLE OF AUTHORIZED REPRESENTATIVE	
DR. P. DUFF REARICK, SUPERINTENDENT	

SIGNATURE	DATE
	7-3-03

ED 80-0013

Certification Regarding Debarment, Suspension, Ineligibility and Voluntary Exclusion — Lower Tier Covered Transactions

This certification is required by the Department of Education regulations implementing Executive Order 12549. Debarment and Suspension, 34 CFR Part 85, for all lower tier transactions meeting the threshold and tier requirements stated at Section 85.110.

Instructions for Certification

1. By signing and submitting this proposal, the prospective lower tier participant is providing the certification set out below.

2. The certification in this clause is a material representation of fact upon which reliance was placed when this transaction was entered into. If it is later determined that the prospective lower tier participant knowingly rendered an erroneous certification, in addition to other remedies available to the Federal Government, the department or agency with which this transaction originated may pursue available remedies, including suspension and/or debarment.

3. The prospective lower tier participant shall provide immediate written notice to the person to which this proposal is submitted if at any time the prospective lower tier participant learns that its certification was erroneous when submitted or has become erroneous by reason of changed circumstances.

4. The terms "covered transaction," "debarred," "suspended," "ineligible," "lower tier covered transaction," "participant," "person," "primary covered transaction," "principal," "proposal," and "voluntarily excluded," as used in this clause, have the meanings set out in the Definitions and Coverage sections of rules implementing Executive Order 12549. You may contact the person to which this proposal is submitted for assistance in obtaining a copy of those regulations.

5. The prospective lower tier participant agrees by submitting this proposal that, should the proposed covered transaction be entered into, it shall not knowingly enter into any lower tier covered transaction with a person who is debarred, suspended, declared ineligible, or voluntarily excluded from participation in this covered transaction, unless authorized by the department or agency with which this transaction originated.

6. The prospective lower tier participant further agrees by submitting this proposal that it will include the clause titled "Certification Regarding Debarment, Suspension, Ineligibility, and Voluntary Exclusion-Lower Tier Covered Transactions," without modification, in all lower tier covered transactions and in all solicitations for lower tier covered transactions.

7. A participant in a covered transaction may rely upon a certification of a prospective participant in a lower tier covered transaction that it is not debarred, suspended, ineligible, or voluntarily excluded from the covered transaction, unless it knows that the certification is erroneous. A participant may decide the method and frequency by which it determines the eligibility of its principals. Each participant may but is not required to, check the Nonprocurement List.

8. Nothing contained in the foregoing shall be construed to require establishment of a system of records in order to render in good faith the certification required by this clause. The knowledge and information of a participant is not required to exceed that which is normally possessed by a prudent person in the ordinary course of business dealings.

9. Except for transactions authorized under paragraph 5 of these instructions, if a participant in a covered transaction knowingly enters into a lower tier covered transaction with a person who is suspended, debarred, ineligible, or voluntarily excluded from participation in this transaction, in addition to other remedies available to the Federal Government, the department or agency with which this transaction originated may pursue available remedies, including suspension and/or debarment.

Certification

(1) The prospective lower tier participant certifies, by submission of this proposal, that neither it nor its principals are presently debarred, suspended, proposed for debarment, declared ineligible, or voluntarily excluded from participation in this transaction by any Federal department or agency.

(2) Where the prospective lower tier participant is unable to certify to any of the statements in this certification, such prospective participant shall attach an explanation to this proposal.

NAME OF APPLICANT	PR/AWARD NUMBER AND/OR PROJECT NAME
GREENCASTLE-ANTRIM SD	
PRINTED NAME AND TITLE OF AUTHORIZED REPRESENTATIVE	
DR. P. DUFF REARICK, SUPERINTENDENT	
SIGNATURE	**DATE**
	7-3-03

ED 80-0013

24072 Federal Register/Vol. 68, No. 87/Tuesday, May 6, 2003/Notices

DISCLOSURE OF LOBBYING ACTIVITIES

Complete this form to disclose lobbying activities pursuant to 31 U.S.C. 1352

(See reverse for public burden disclosure.)

Approved by OMB
0348-0046

1. Type of Federal Action:	2. Status of Federal Action:	3. Report Type:
b a. contract b. grant c. cooperative agreement d. loan e. loan guarantee f. loan insurance	**a** a. bid/offer/application b. initial award c. post-award	**a** a. initial filing b. material change **For Material Change Only:** year _____ quarter _____ date of last report _____

4. Name and Address of Reporting Entity:

☐ Prime   ☐ Subawardee

Tier _____, *if known* :

GREENCASTLE-ANTRIM SD
500 LEITERSBURG ST
GREENCASTLE PA 17225

Congressional District, *if known* :

5. If Reporting Entity in No. 4 is a Subawardee, Enter Name and Address of Prime:

N/A

Congressional District, *if known* :

6. Federal Department/Agency:

US DEPT OF ED.

7. Federal Program Name/Description:

CFDA Number, *if applicable* : __84.215 X__

8. Federal Action Number, *if known* :

9. Award Amount, *if known* :

$

10. a. Name and Address of Lobbying Registrant
(if individual, last name, first name, MI):

N/A

b. Individuals Performing Services *(including address if different from No. 10a)*
(last name, first name, MI):

N/A

11. Information requested through this form is authorized by title 31 U.S.C. section 1352. This disclosure of lobbying activities is a material representation of fact upon which reliance was placed by the tier above when this transaction was made or entered into. This disclosure is required pursuant to 31 U.S.C. 1352. This information will be reported to the Congress semi-annually and will be available for public inspection. Any person who fails to file the required disclosure shall be subject to a civil penalty of not less that $10,000 and not more than $100,000 for each such failure.

Signature: _____

Print Name: DR. P. DUFF REARICK

Title: SUPERINTENDENT

Telephone No.: 717-597-2187   Date: 7-3-03

Federal Use Only

Authorized for Local Reproduction
Standard Form LLL (Rev. 7-97)

PROPOSAL #3

FEDERAL EMERGENCY MANAGEMENT AGENCY

Grants for State and Local Homeland Security Activities

AGENCY: Office of National Preparedness (ONP), Federal Emergency Management Agency (FEMA)

ACTION: Notice of availability of fiscal years 2002 supplemental funds for State and local all-hazards emergency operational planning, Citizen Corps activities, and development or improvement of Emergency Operations Centers.

SUMMARY: FEMA gives notice of the availability of funds for fiscal year (FY) 2002 for State and local all-hazards emergency operations planning; for the development or improvement of State and local Emergency Operations Centers (EOCs); and for further development of Citizen Corps, including funds for Citizen Corps Councils and for Community Emergency Response Team (CERT) training. Funding of $100 million is available for planning, $56 million for EOCs, and $25 million for Citizen Corps.

FOR FURTHER INFORMATION CONTACT:

Gil Jamieson, Federal Emergency Management Agency, Office of National Preparedness, 500 C Street, SW., Washington, DC 20472, (202) 646-4090 or e-mail: *gil.jamieson@fema.gov.*

SUPPLEMENTARY INFORMATION:

Authority and Appropriation

The legislative authority for the program activities described in this notice are the Robert T. Stafford Disaster Relief and Emergency Assistance Act (Stafford Act), 42 U.S.C. 5121-5206;. The 2002 Supplemental Appropriations Act For Further Recovery From and Response To Terrorist Attacks on the United States, P.L. 107-206.

Applicant Eligibility

States are eligible to apply for the assistance described in this notice. The term "State" as used in this notice and consistent with the Stafford Act, 42 U.S.C. 5122(4), means any State of the United States, the District of Columbia, Puerto Rico, the Virgin Islands, Guam, American Samoa, and the Commonwealth of the Northern Mariana Islands.

Local governments may receive assistance as subgrantees of the States in which they are located. The term "Local government" as used in this notice shall have the meaning set forth in the Stafford Act, 42 U.S.C. 5122(6).

Activities To Be Funded

State and Local All Hazards Emergency Operational Planning

The FY 2002 supplemental funding will provide comprehensive planning assistance to State and local governments to conduct Emergency Operations Plan (EOP) updating for all hazards with special emphasis on incidents of terrorism including use of weapons of mass destruction (WMD).

The funds for planning grants will be allocated among the States on the basis of population and will require no cost share. Each State grantee of these planning funds will be required to pass through at least 75 percent of the amount received to local governments.

Coordinated planning at the State and local levels is essential to meet urgent needs for improving the planning initiatives of State and local emergency management and first responder organizations to effectively request and use future resources and thereby build and enhance our Nation's capability to respond to and recover from the imminent threat or actual occurrence of a terrorist attack including use of WMD.

States will receive supplemental 2002 funding to modify and enhance their EOPs, as needed, so that they address all hazards, to include terrorism using WMD or conventional means. Funds should also be used for

the following emergency planning objectives:

- Incorporate interstate and intrastate mutual aid agreements,
- Facilitate communication and interoperability protocols,
- Establish a common incident command system, * Address critical infrastructure protection,
- Conduct State and local assessments to determine emergency management planning priorities,
- Address State and local continuity of operations and continuity of government, and
- Provide for coordination and effective use of volunteers in response and preparedness activities.

Citizen Corps

Grants under the Citizen Corps initiative will be available to establish Citizen Corps Councils, to support the oversight and outreach responsibilities of the councils, and to expand CERT training. Of the $25 million appropriated for Citizen Corps, $4 million will be used for grants related to Citizen Corps Councils, $17 million will be used for grants related to CERT training, and $4 million will be used by FEMA for activities essential for developing the Citizen Corps initiative.

Citizen Corps funds will be allocated to States using the percentages prescribed in Section 1014 of the USA Patriot Act, Pub. L. 107-56. Each State will be allocated a base amount of not less than 0.75 percent of the total amount available except that the Virgin Islands, Guam, American Samoa, and the Commonwealth of the Northern Mariana Islands each will be allocated a base amount of 0.25 percent. The remaining Citizen Corps grant funds will be allocated on the basis of population and added to the base amounts. Citizen Corps grants and subgrants described in this notice will carry no cost-share requirement.

Grantees will be expected to develop and implement a jurisdiction-wide strategic plan for Citizen Corps, including forming local Citizen Corps Councils, CERT training, public education and outreach, and volunteer opportunities that promote community and family safety. Local governments receiving grants may use the funding for Citizen Corps Council organizing activities; for outreach and public education campaigns to promote Citizen Corps and community and family safety measures, to include printing, marketing, advertising, and special events; for organizing, training, equipping, and maintaining CERTs; and for defraying the added expense of liability coverage for CERT participants.

Each grantee of Citizen Corps funds will be required to subgrant at least 75 percent of those funds to local governments with no cost share. Grantees are expected to give priority to local governments that have demonstrated a commitment to community and family safety or to local governments that have a high-risk profile based on crime, disaster vulnerabilities, and public health issues. A commitment to community and family safety is shown by such activities as having established or planned a Citizen Corps Council, having programs to promote community and family safety, having conducted community-based events that promote safety, having established mutual aid agreements with other jurisdictions, and having demonstrated a commitment to citizen participation in crime prevention and disaster mitigation, preparedness, response, and recovery.

Emergency Operations Centers (EOCs)

The funding for EOCs will be awarded in two phases. Each State will be allocated a $50,000 Phase 1 grant, which is targeted for an initial assessment of the hazards, vulnerabilities, and resultant risk to the existing EOC. If a State has already completed a vulnerability assessment of its existing State EOC, it may apply to use the funds to conduct initial assessments of local EOCs. Phase 1 EOC activity will be 100 percent federally funded, *i.e.*, will require no cost share.

Phase 2 EOC grants will use the remaining funds to address the most immediate EOC deficiencies nationwide. The Phase 2 EOC grants will require a 50–percent non-Federal cost share.

During Phase 2, we invite the States to submit grant applications that reflect deficiencies documented in a completed self-assessment that reflects statewide needs, is consistent with national priorities, and considers characteristics associated with a fully functioning EOC. EOC self-assessment criteria will be provided in the grant guidance package.

Project applications will be evaluated and selections made for funding on the basis of the following order of national priorities:

- Physical modifications to the EOC to support secure communications equipment;
- New EOC construction where the most cost effective action is new construction (Cost-benefit ratio should be greater than 1);
- Corrective construction to address deficiencies determined by the Risk Assessment;
- Architectural and Engineering services for EOC projects in FY 2003 and out years;
- Creation of State Alternate EOC at an existing building for Continuity of Operations;
- Physical modifications to enhance security, but not the hiring of guards;
- Retrofits of existing EOCs with collective protection systems for Chemical, Biological, Radiological, or Nuclear (CBRN) agents;
- Redundant communications; and
- Others projects to increase the survivability of existing State or local EOCs.

FEMA will conduct the final environmental review and approval for all activities in accordance with Title 44, Code of Federal Regulations, Part 10 (44 CFR part 10) prior to awarding any grants. The approval for some activities, including the risk/vulnerability assessments of EOCs, is automatic through the categorical exclusion under the National Environmental Policy Act, per 44 CFR 10.8. However, some EOC projects, including physical modifications to EOCs for secure communications equipment, may require a more extensive environmental review, sometimes resulting in an environmental assessment. To expedite the approval process, States should consult with the FEMA Regional office as they develop their environmental documentation. Until FEMA has completed its environmental review, States may not initiate work on these projects.

EOC construction projects supported by these grants are subject to the provisions of the Davis-Bacon Act. All laborers and mechanics employed by contractors or subcontractors in performance of construction work assisted by these EOC grants must be paid wages at rates not less than those prevailing on similar construction in the locality as determined by the Secretary of Labor in accordance with Davis-Bacon and related Acts.

Grant Application Process

The chief elected official of each eligible jurisdiction will receive a letter from FEMA describing the grant activity and requesting that a point of contact (POC) and alternate be appointed. Guidance and grant application packages will be provided to the POCs.

A single grant application may be used to apply for the planning, Citizen Corps and Phase 1 EOC program elements. A separate application should be prepared for the Phase 2 EOC program element. The grant application for the planning, Citizen Corps, and Phase 1 EOC program elements should include:

- Application for Federal Assistance, Standard Form 424;
- Budget Information "Non-Construction Program, FEMA Form 20-20;
- Budget Narrative;
- Summary Sheet for Assurances and Certification, FEMA Form 20-16;
- Assurances "Non-Construction Program, FEMA Form 20-16A;
- Certification Regarding Lobbying; Debarment, Suspension and Other Responsibility Matters; and Drug-Free Workplace Requirements, FEMA Form 20-16C;
- Disclosure of Lobbying Activities, Standard Form LLL; and,
- Program Narrative identifying the activities for which funding is requested.

The Program Narrative should include the following:

• Description of how States will work with local governments including Tribal governments and communities and the process that the State will use to solicit, prioritize, and select subgrants;

• Activity title and number;

• Individual activity costs, including Federal and nonfederal shares;

• Activity-specific scopes of work, including a list of properties, if applicable;

• Recommendations and documentation regarding the environmental review required by 44 CFR 10, Environmental Considerations, and other applicable laws and executive orders; and

• Certification that the State has evaluated the included projects and that they will be implemented in accordance with 44 CFR part 13, Uniform Administrative Requirements for Grants and Cooperative Agreements to State and Local Governments.

The Phase 2 EOC grant application should include all of the above with the following construction program forms substituted for the non-construction versions:

• Budget Information, Construction Programs, FEMA Form 20-15;

• Assurances, Construction Programs, FEMA Form 20-16B;

FEMA regional personnel will work directly with the States providing technical assistance, as required, as state and local governments carry out work under the grants.

Administrative Costs

Costs to administer each of the programs will be limited to 5 percent of the grant award. The amount that grantees and subgrantees choose to apply toward administrative costs will not be in addition to the grant and subgrant amounts. For grants with the 75-percent pass-through requirement, administrative costs for the grantees will be based on the portion of the grant that the State retains (i.e., States may use no more than 5 percent of the 25 percent of the total grant award

they retain for administrative costs). Administrative costs for each subgrantee will be limited to 5 percent of their subgrant award. Administrative costs may be used to support grants management activities such as the review and award of subgrant applications, the preparation of quarterly reports, and monitoring subgrants. Costs related to staffing to implement program activities are eligible costs under each of the grants and do not need to be charged to the administrative costs. For example, hiring a staff person to update the State's Emergency Operations Plan is an eligible activity under the Planning grant. Indirect costs should also be included in administrative costs and must be supported with a current Indirect Cost Rate approved by a Federal Cognizant Agency. In compliance with 44 CFR 13.20, all administrative costs must be supported by source documentation. If the Indirect Cost Rate exceeds the 5-percent administrative costs allowance after all other eligible administrative costs have been identified and budgeted, the grantee must submit a request for a waiver with justification to validate the need for additional administrative costs.

Sensitive Information

FEMA will make every effort as permitted by law to protect sensitive or confidential information submitted in the grant process. If FEMA receives a third-party request for an applicant's information, both the Freedom of Information Act and FEMA's regulations contain provisions that may protect sensitive or confidential information that is determined by FEMA to be exempt from disclosure. These determinations are made on a case-by-case basis. Applicants should advise FEMA of the sensitive or confidential nature of information at the time such information is submitted. To ensure proper handling in the mail distribution process, the sensitive or confidential information should be placed in an envelope plainly marked to indicate the nature of its contents. This envelope should be placed in a second envelope marked "To be opened by

addressee only" and mailed "Certified Receipt Requested."

Reporting Requirements

The States are required to submit quarterly financial and performance reports 30 days after the end of each quarter, per 44 CFR 13.40 and 41. Reporting dates are: January 30, April 30, July 30, and October 30. The performance reports will provide a comparison of actual accomplishments to the objectives approved for the period. Where the output of the project can be quantified, that information shall be provided. The States must also report the progress of each subgrantee award in their quarterly reports. When the Department of Health and Human Services (HHS) Payment Management System (SMARTLINK) is used for advanced or reimbursement payments, the grantee is required to submit a copy of Federal Cash Transaction Report (HHS/PMS 272) to FEMA when it is submitted to HHS. In addition, final financial and performance reports are required 90 days after the close of the grant, per 44 CFR 13.50.

ADDRESSES: FEMA Regional Offices:

FEMA Region I — *Serving the States of Maine, New Hampshire, Vermont, Rhode Island, Connecticut, and Massachusetts:* 442 J.W. McCormack POCH, Boston, MA 02109-4595.

FEMA Region II — *Serving the States of New York and New Jersey, the Commonwealth of Puerto Rico and the Territory of the U.S. Virgin Islands:* 26 Federal Plaza, Rm. 1337, New York, NY 10278-0002.

FEMA Region, III — *Serving the District of Columbia and the States of Delaware, Maryland, Pennsylvania, Virginia, and West Virginia:* 1 Independence Mall, 6th Floor, 615 Chestnut Street, Philadelphia, PA 19106-4404.

FEMA Region IV — *Serving the States of Alabama, Florida, Georgia, Kentucky, Mississippi, North Carolina, South Carolina and Tennessee:* 3003 Chamblee Tucker Road, Atlanta, GA 30341.

PHASE 2
EMERGENCY OPERATIONS CENTER UPGRADE

VOLUME I
COMPETITIVE GRANT PROPOSAL

Prepared for:

FEMA REGION IX
Federal Emergency Management Agency
U.S. Department of Homeland Security

Prepared by:

DEPARTMENT OF MILITARY AFFAIRS
OFFICE OF CIVIL DEFENSE
GOVERNMENT OF GUAM
P.O. BOX 2877, HAGATÑA, GUAM 96932

May 2003

Table of Contents

PROGRAM NARRATIVE

I. OBJECTIVE

The objective of Guam's Comprehensive EOC Upgrade Grant Proposal is to assure that Guam, through the Office of Homeland Security/Office of Civil Defense, will have the opportunity to assure the continuity of government by maintaining command and control through a comprehensive emergency management and response capability that can only be realized via an Emergency Operations Center (EOC) that is in line with FEMA's objective of building a nationwide network of fully functioning EOCs. The ultimate goal of this grant proposal is to improve Guam's emergency preparedness and management by ensuring that its EOC has the facility, decision support, and telecommunications capabilities that will provide flexibility, sustainability, security, survivability, and interoperability. Furthermore, it is Guam's conviction that the approval of this grant will provide emergency managers the capability to effectively and efficiently manage and respond to the vast range of natural and manmade hazards and threats in order to minimize the loss of life, injuries, damage to property, and insure the continuance of essential government functions without interruption.

II. JUSTIFICATION

A. Guam's Strategic Importance

Guam is located southeast of Japan and east of the Philippine Islands, about 3 hours flying time from both Tokyo and Manila, and less than 5 hours flying time from nearly every nation in Asia as well as Australia. Because of our proximity to Asia and the fact that we are a U.S. flagged territory, Guam is widely known in the region as "America in Asia."

Over the last decade Guam has enjoyed a steady population growth. The 1990 census reports a population of 133,152, a 20.4 percent increase since 1980. Population estimates for 1997 indicated Guam had grown to 153,000 people. The 2000 census data for Guam is currently unavailable but preliminary findings suggest a continued increase in population growth with an estimated totality in excess of 160,000.

Throughout the 20th Century, Guam has had significant strategic value as a crossroads of the western Pacific and Asia for the United States' military and commercial interests. **The island's critical infrastructure including power, water, port, airport, and communications are considered vital assets. Today, at the beginning of the 21st Century, and in the wake of the war the nation is conducting against global terrorism, Guam's strategic value is greater than ever.**

Guam is home to forward deployed Air Force and Navy detachments that have within their mission responsibility millions of square miles of air and sea space. Since the start of the war on terrorism and the war with Iraq, both have played a strategic role in the movement and positioning of weapons, supplies, troops, and humanitarian aid to points west of here. In addition, Guam houses a number of facilities that support and serve both the commercial and military interests of the United States. These facilities include Andersen Air Force Base, US Coast Guard Pacific Command, US Army Reserve, National Guard, three major marine cable installations, Apra Harbor, Guam Naval Station, and Naval Magazine.

Aside from these military components, Guam is home to many federal installations maintained by the State Department, the National Weather Service, U.S. Geological Survey, and the Federal Emergency Management Agency (FEMA). In addition, the island is home to a U.S. District Court building, FBI Field Office, U.S. Attorney's Office, ATF Field Office and several other federal agencies.

B. Guam's Vulnerability To Terrorism

As the closest US territory to Asia and an international tourist destination, Guam could easily become the stepping stone for terrorist activities aimed toward the United States. The threat of terrorist activities entering through the port and occurring on Guam and/or its neighboring islands is likely to transpire and the threat should not be underestimated. Guam is particularly vulnerable to illegal activity given its strategic geographical location and proximity to numerous countries like the Philippines, North Korea, China and Indonesia, which have unstable governments that promote anti-American politics. Due to Guam's geographic location, the island presents itself as an ideal entry port for terrorists from the Philippines, Malaysia and Indonesia. Each of these countries has a past and present affiliation with Osama Bin Laden and his terrorist organization. **It is a vital priority that the emergency management and response deficiencies of Guam be addressed and new measures are employed immediately.**

The presence of the Air Force and Navy detachments and federal agencies give us increased visibility as a target for those who would want to harm U.S. interests in this part of the world or send a message to the United States that it is not welcome in this part of the world.

The war against terrorism requires that the island rely on its own civil resources to develop the capability to manage and respond to man-made threats and on the potential use of weapons of mass destruction against its residents.

This vulnerability further identified and hampered our ability to address the security issues arising out of the 9/11 tragedies that later resulted in the war on terrorism, a war in which Guam is the geographically closest United States location to the threat of identified terrorist organizations that have made their presence known through several terrorist related bombings in the Philippines, Indonesia and the Asian continent.

C. Guam's Vulnerability To Natural Disasters

The island has a rich history with natural disasters that include typhoons, earthquakes, landslides, flooding, etc. Guam sits in Typhoon Ally and is situated along the Ring of Fire making the island highly vulnerable to the frequent occurrence of natural disasters.

The most recent events, Typhoons Chata'an and Pongsona, occurred in the same year and within a few months of each other and reached super typhoon strengths that caused extensive damage throughout the island with millions of federal and local dollars required for repair and restoration.

In addition to typhoons, Guam also recently experienced earthquakes of Richter magnitudes 7.0 and 7.1 in October of 2001 and April of 2002. The Great Earthquake that occurred on August 8, 1993 with Richter Magnitude 8.0 was one of the most damaging earthquakes in Guam's history.

D. Financial Shortfalls/Needs

Aside from natural disasters, the war against terrorism, border security, and other man-made threats require that the island rely on its own civil resources to develop the capability to manage and respond to potential threats of terrorism and weapons of mass destruction. **Unfortunately, this requires an economic and financial capability that our island does not possess on its own in building a fully functional EOC to provide effective emergency management and response.** We humbly recommend that FEMA make significant investments to protect Guam's residents, its delicate infrastructure, and its strategically vital military and federal installations not only from natural disasters but also from acts of terrorism, espionage, and criminal activity.

By all accounts, Guam's proposal should be a high priority because of the critical national assets that are housed on island and its importance in serving as a critical link to America's defense posture. Guam is vital to trade, national security, and serves as the catalyst for America's domestic and international trade. Guam and its diverse commercial and military shipping operations offer easily accessible ports of entry to terrorism and illegal activity.

To further exacerbate the current situation, Guam's economy is struggling from the impact of an unprecedented combination of natural disasters and complex economic forces over which Guam has little or no direct control, and is straining the limited resources of both public and private sector organizations. If Guam continues to be affected by the Asian economic crisis for an extended period, progress that is needed to reduce the General Fund deficit will be halted, bond ratings will be affected, infrastructure projects critical to the implementation of Guam's overall economic development may be subject to capital rationing, and key programs in the areas of aviation and maritime security, public safety, health, education, and solid waste management may be severely compromised. Over the last 8 years, as the Asian economic crisis continues to deepen, government revenues have decreased by more than 50%. This constitutes a reduction from the 1995 annual budget of $660 million to the current annual budget of less than $350 million.

III. PHASE 1 EOC ASSESSMENT

A. General

The EOC is in desperate need of upgrade and renovation. Guam's EOC, in particular, is an extremely active emergency operations center that constantly deals with disaster and emergency responses. With the recent threat of terrorism, the activity in North Korea, the outbreak of SARS in Hong Kong and neighboring countries, the consistent typhoon occurrences, and the potential of major earthquakes, the EOC is an essential element of day-to-day operations on Guam.

The Emergency Operations Center (EOC) Upgrade Competitive Grant Proposal will provide an opportunity to secure unlimited but warranted funding for the much needed upgrade and renovation of the EOC. The first phase of Guam's grant application process through the completion of the comprehensive assessment of the existing facility has identified shortfalls and needs requiring modifications that are necessary in building a fully functioning EOC and thus improving emergency preparedness and management. As per FEMA guidelines, the comprehensive assessment provides the technical data for Guam to have the facility, decision support, and telecommunications capabilities that will provide flexibility, sustainability, security, survivability, and interoperability in its emergency management and response functions.

B. Comprehensive Assessment Report

The EOC Comprehensive Assessment Report prepared under the Phase 1 EOC Assessment Grant identified over 100 deficiencies. The report provides a detailed description of the current EOC condition, a general discussion of the EOC deficiencies' operational impacts and their proposed solutions and a completed EOC Assessment Checklist. Three detailed listings of identified deficiency descriptions, proposed solutions and estimated corrective construction costs are provided in table format sorted by technical discipline, by operational impact and by site location. Detail sheets (field inspection report forms) with some photos and proposed solution sketches complete the report package. The assessment report is included as Volume II of the Grant Application Package for your reference.

The operational impact of each deficiency listed in the assessment report was categorized using the evaluation factors presented in the March 26, 2003 Grant Guidance entitled "Evaluation and Process Overview and Factors for the Review of Phase 2 Emergency Operations Center Competitive Grant Proposals". The evaluation factors are P- Permanent Disruption, M – Moderate Disruption, T – Temporary Disruption, L - Limited Disruption and I – Inconvenience Disruption.

IV. PROPOSED GRANT ACTIVITIES

A. General

The EOC Assessment Report categorized the deficiencies into two groups based on geographical location. After extensive evaluation of the assessment report the deficiencies and proposed solutions were further divided into functional groups (to identify proposed grant activities) based on operational impact subcategories and proposed scopes of work.

B. Individual Activity Locations

Two individual activity locations identified and described in the EOC assessment report are:
- the existing EOC Facility in Agana Heights and
- the proposed alternate EOC Facility at the Department of Public Works Complex Traffic Management Center building in Tamuning.

In addition, based on proposed grant activities, the existing EOC Facility location can further be divided into three activity locations: the existing EOC facility, the proposed EOC facility expansion and the proposed emergency access road upgrade. Since the proposed EOC facility expansion and the proposed emergency access road upgrade are stand alone line items we felt two individual activity locations were sufficient. See Figure 1 on the next page for the existing EOC site plan and the proposed EOC facility expansion plan.

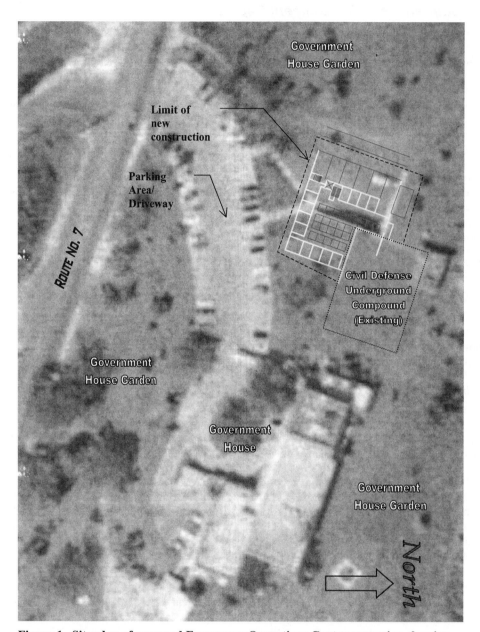

Figure 1. Site plan of proposed Emergency Operations Center expansion showing limits of construction.

C. Functional Group Descriptions

1. ALTERNATE EOC GROUP 1 - ESTABLISH ALTERNATE EOC MISSION CRITICAL OPERATING CAPABILITIES (P3)

This group builds upon a basic premise of facility planning: preparedness for and maintenance of emergency response and recovery operations requires redundancy in critical capabilities. The proposed solutions to identified deficiencies in this functional group specifically address achieving redundancy in Guam's OCD mission critical capabilities of 1) emergency communications; 2) coordination and management of emergency response; and 3) maintenance of a Joint Information Center. The completion of this group results in the fitting out of a modern building shell as a fully functional, secure and capable center for emergency operations. This includes electrical power, lighting, data/communications, PA systems, and air-conditioning systems, as well as fixed furniture and equipment. Given the frequency of disasters on Guam, and the age of the existing EOC, the alternate EOC capability also provides the opportunity to complete long needed work on the main EOC.

2. ALTERNATE EOC GROUP 2 - PROVIDE ALTERNATE EOC PHYSICAL SECURITY MEASURES (M2)

The establishment of an alternate EOC will require its reasonable protection, which becomes more important under conditions of increased threat. Realizing this importance, and the potential for disruption of operations from various sources, physical security protection measures then become increasingly important aspects of normal EOC operation. The completion of this group will result in the installation of security component systems such as access control, video surveillance, monitoring and physical barriers.

3. EOC GROUP 1 - MITIGATE EFFECTS OF RELEVANT RISKS (P2)

The current condition of the EOC leaves the facility open to certain risks. The lack of fire protection equipment creates a very real hazard, considering the bunker-type construction, limited means of access from all parts of the building and occasional use of the facility for storage and distribution of materials/supplies. The underground construction combined with the heavy rainfall encountered in this part of the world mean an increased hazard of flooding. The completion of this group of tasks will provide for increased fire protection through the installation of an automatic sprinkler system, as well as alleviate drainage and flooding problems experienced during heavy rain storms.

4. EOC GROUP 2 - PROVIDE PROTECTION AGAINST INDIRECT EFFECTS OF WMD (M1)

Guam's EOC is vulnerable to attacks or threats to indirect airborne contaminants and/or Weapons of Mass Description. Building mechanical systems controlling the indoor environment were designed over 20 years ago during a much different time and with little thought given to the current threats. The completion of this group will allow for the upgrade of air conditioning equipment both within the building and externally, providing continuity of operations and added protection against chemical, biological and radiological threats. This will be accomplished through the improvement of air intake, filtration and distribution capabilities, as well as through the installation of shielding to protect the EOC against electromagnetic radiation.

5.   EOC GROUP 3 - PROVIDE PHYSICAL SECURITY MEASURES (M2)

The EOC is currently operating without the benefit of functional security measures.   This is especially critical since the site on which the EOC is located in not controlled, and is accessible from all directions.   The completion of this group will provide the necessary security upgrades to deter threatening activity, provide early warning of potential threats and protect building systems and occupants against identified risks and threats.   This will be accomplished through a combination of measures, including a fully automated Access Control System to include Biometrics integration, an ID Badging System and interface with CCTV system. Improvements to the building such as hardening and securing access to utility systems will also provide added protection.   It is further recommended that a second line of defense against unauthorized access be implemented in the form of "Man Trap" security measures at each of the existing entry points to the EOC facility.   The use of Digital Video Recording and CCTV system with remote capabilities via a secured line is also recommended.   To augment these surveillance measures described above, we recommend locking access points to several key facilities such as the water storage tank access, fuel system tank access, and mechanical/electrical equipment enclosure access.

6.   EOC GROUP 4 - UPGRADE POWER GENERATOR SYSTEM (M3)

As with any facility on Guam, protection of power systems can be problematic.   Reliable and trouble-free generation capacity is crucial to maintaining critical operations especially during and immediately after major storm events, when response and recovery operations are at their busiest. The EOCs power supply is susceptible to damage from heavy winds, as well as damage from unauthorized personnel through open primary handholes. This group of solutions proposes to resolve these issues through the construction of hardened and secure utility infrastructure, as well as the installation of voltage suppression and uninterrupted power supply capabilities.   New generation equipment will be installed in a new location outside the EOC to alleviate operation and maintenance burdens associated with the current underground installation.

7.   EOC GROUP 5 - UPGRADE EMERGENCY COMMUNICATIONS (M5)

The EOCs emergency communications capabilities are currently limited.   In order to upgrade the relevant systems, physical improvements to existing spaces must be made to harden telecommunication service access points and areas surrounding the secure communications area. These improvements should be coordinated with the implementation of security measures to insure necessary space requirements are met.

8.   EOC GROUP 6 - UPGRADE EMERGENCY COMMUNICATION ACCESS ROUTE (M5)

Redundancy and multiple points of entry are critical features of a well planned facility which must remain operational.   Telecommunications at the EOC have a single entry point, making the primary service vulnerable to attack.   Further, access to and from the EOC under all conditions may not be possible with a single route for ingress/egress.   The item in Group 6 allows for the enhancement of both access and communications, by providing an enhanced vehicular access complete with curbs and guide rails, which can also be used for an alternate routing for primary service or fiber optic communications.

9. EOC GROUP 7 - UPGRADE/REPAIR BUILDING SYSTEMS FOR CODE COMPLIANCE (T1)

As can be expected from a 20+ year old facility, building systems are not at optimum operating capability. The EOC requires several fixes which relate to its ability to provide basic service to occupants. This group includes repairs to existing building systems, such as structural crack repairs, architectural renovations to meet code requirements, and upgrades to exhaust and drainage systems .Work on the building air conditioning system is also required to restore design cooling rates.

10. EOC GROUP 8 - PROVIDE SUFFICIENT TELECOMMUNICATIONS RESOURCES, PERIPHERALS AND ROUTES (T2&3)

In order to alleviate the vulnerability of the EOC's single communications trunk line, this group of proposed solutions provides an alternate primary service through the installation of a separate drop. It also provides for the expansion of inadequate communications and data-transmission facilities by upgrading the existing peer-to-peer network capability with a new client-server system. The increased speed of communications will be accompanied by increased capacity for access by federal staff to augment local personnel during response efforts.

11. EOC GROUP 9 - MODIFY EOC TO ALLOW HI-TECH EMERGENCY MONITORING & COMMAND AREAS (T5)

The EOC is currently set up for large emergency management and response efforts in a centralistic, paper based fashion. Modern response and management operations utilize a smaller group for monitoring and planning with computer based information systems for instant access and response. This group proposes to upgrade Guam's ageing EOC setup to be current with other EOCs regionally and nationally by dividing the existing EOC into two spaces; one for emergency monitoring functions and one space for emergency management and conference functions (see sketch below).

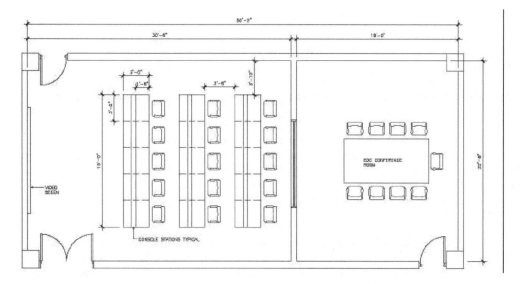

12. EOC GROUP 10 - EXPAND EOC FACILITY TO PROVIDE FUNCTIONAL ANNEX MULTI-FUNCTION SPACE (T5)

The Guam EOC, as configured, is inadequate for the scope and magnitude of response, recovery and mitigation efforts encountered during the course of its emergency response operations. Several key functions (media briefing, conference, etc.) are not provided for within the existing EOC layout. Further, operational flexibility is lacking due to the constraints of the space and layout. For example,

- ❏ The existing EOC houses a minimum of 86 people and can reach over 150 people in an approximately 1300 SF space;
- ❏ Response Activity Coordinators (RACs) from different GovGuam, military, federal, non-profit, and private sector entities responsible for implementing the GERP's Functional Annexes all operate within this space, creating a crowded and excessively noisy environment;
- ❏ Due to the layout of the site in relation to existing parking, EOC staff and RACs are unprotected from the weather and other hazards when attempting to access emergency operations vehicles;
- ❏ The location of the existing unprotected entry to the EOC allows for frequent flooding of the facility due to wind driven rain and storm water during the frequent typhoons and tropical storms.

Although originally submitted as an expansion to incorporate multi-functional space for functional annexes during emergency responses and additional space for mitigation and recovery staff during day-to-day operations, EOC Group 10 has been revised to include only the space necessary for efficient EOC operations and correction of the issues identified above.

Based on past activations and lessons learned, there was a need to address the shortfalls of the EOC and the Office of Civil Defense (OCD) logistical support functions before, during, and immediately after a major disaster. Dating back to Super typhoon Paka in 1997 and subsequent presidential declared disasters thereafter, the same setbacks were always present.

The Guam Emergency Response Plan (GERP) is patterned after the Federal Response Plan (FRP). Operating under the ICS system, the GERP utilizes all Government of Guam assets and resources in response to any emergency. In the case of a major event and implementing a Unified Command type of management, it provides guidance, process, and structure for the coordinated, systematic, and efficient delivery of assistance and response in addressing any and all disaster related activities.

As experienced in the past, the EOC, as the nerve center of GovGuam's response and recovery effort, has had to deal with challenges that are always a part of any activation. During a major disaster event, over 100 personnel (local, federal, military, non-profit organizations, and private sector) report to the EOC. Because of its current size, this has been a logistical and operational nightmare. It is a challenge that many Federal officials, most especially FEMA, is aware of and has experienced first hand.

Because the intent of the GERP is to mirror the objectives and functions of the FRP, it is critical that all aspects of the recovery effort be addressed. Aside from its RACs (response activity coordinators) that represent all primary and support response agencies, there are additional federal personnel that are immediately activated that need to be co-located with local emergency managers. An example of this co-location is the integration of the FRP's 12 ESFs to the GERP's primary and support agencies to address all relevant Functional Annexes.

In the past FEMA has had to spend additional monies to establish a DFO to house these functions aside from its contingent of recovery personnel. Though it is inevitable that FEMA will establish a DFO, the size and subsequent cost can be reduced by having a permanent and fully functioning EOC to support its ESFs.

For Guam to follow FEMA's objective of developing fully functional EOCs as a national standard, all four emergency management functions (preparation, response, mitigation, and recovery) must be addressed in the EOC upgrade.

Group 10 provides for the alleviation of these issues through the expansion of the OCD site to include a new 4300 sq.ft. extension and a 2475 sq.ft. garage at the front of the existing space.

The existing EOC is comprised of approximately 1300 sq.ft. of space for emergency response personnel. The following table indicates the various agencies tasked to respond during an event, as outlined in the Guam Emergency Response Plan.

Guam Emergency Operations Center - Emergency Response Plan Personnel

	Primary Agency	Functional Annexes	No. of Annexes	Minimum Personnel Assigned
1	Office of the Governor	C,D,J	3	4
2	Dept of Administration	J,M	2	2
3	Dept of Education	A,G,K	3	2
4	Dept of Public Health and Social Services Guam Memorial Hospital Authority	A,B,K	3	2
5	Dept of Public Works	A,B,K	3	4
6	Guam EPA	A,B	2	2
7	Guam Police Department	A,K,L	3	2
8	Guam Fire Department	A,K,L	3	2
9	Guam Office of Civil Defense	A,C,D,E,F,G,H,I,J,K,L,M,O	13	20

Support Agency

1	Bureau of Budget & Management Research	J	1	2
2	Bureau of Planning	A	1	2
3	Dept of Agriculture	A	1	2
4	Dept of Commerce / GEDCA	A	1	2
5	Dept of Labor	A	1	2
6	GHURA	A,K	2	2
7	GIAA	A	1	2
8	Guam Legislature	J	1	2
9	Guam National Guard	K,L	2	2
10	GPA	A	1	2
11	GTA	A	1	2
12	Guam Visitors Bureau	A,D,	2	2
13	GWA	A	1	2
14	Mayors Council of Guam	A,B,D,G,K	5	4
15	Port Authority of Guam	A	1	2
16	American Red Cross	A,K,O	3	2
17	Guam Hotel and Restaurant Association	D,G	2	2
18	Salvation Army	K,O	2	2
19	VOAD	K	1	2
20	US Air Force	D,L,H	2	2
21	US Coast Guard	D,L,H	2	2
22	US Navy	D,L,H	2	2

	Estimated Minimum Personnel	*86*

Based on the number of responding agencies and the functional annexes required to respond to disasters, the space requirements exceed the existing size of the EOC. The following table provides some detail of the space required and the allotments in the revised proposed expansion.

Guam Emergency Operations Center Space Requirements

Space Desciption	Location	EOC Agency Served	Minimum Personnel	Area
1 Command / Response Room	Existing EOC Room	Primary RACs / OCD	15	800 SF
2 Executive Conference Room	Existing EOC Room	Governor / RACs	10	500 SF
3 Media Room	Proposed Expansion	Press / Media / Public	2	200 SF
4 Conference/Breakout Rooms	Proposed Expansion	RACs (Primary, Support)	59	2100 SF
5 Secure Entry Lobby / Elevator	Proposed Expansion	All	n/a	450 SF
6 Emergency exits, corridors	Proposed Expansion	All	n/a	1550 SF
7 Secure / Weatherproof Garage	Proposed Expansion	OCD / RACs (Primary, Support)	n/a	2475 SF

See proposed Group 10 EOC facility expansion below.

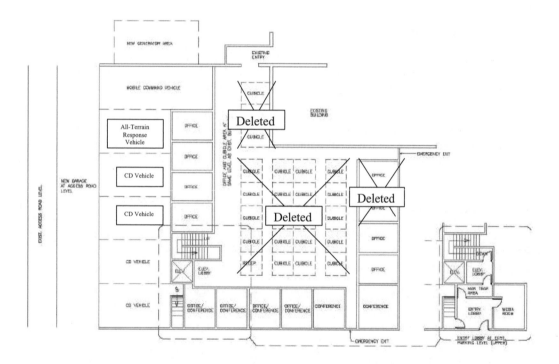

13. EOC GROUP 11 - PROVIDE/REPAIR EXTERIOR LIGHTING SYSTEM (I1)

The EOC is located on an unsecured site, in close proximity to several public areas and thoroughfares. The documented lack of security provisions coupled with the vulnerability of key site utility structures and personnel access points should dictate a cautious approach to facility surveillance. Group 11 proposes to address some deficiencies so as to allow for increased lighting around the site to deter any activity, which may compromise the EOC or its utility infrastructure. Provisions for typhoon rated light posts for exterior area lighting will be installed under this group.

14. EOC GROUP 12 - MINOR REPAIR/MAINTENANCE ITEMS (I3)

The EOC has suffered from regular wear and tear over the last 20+ years and has managed to remain in fairly good shape. Although not critical in nature, there are a few minor repairs which require some attention to enhance EOC operations (PA and Communications) and prevent further deterioration to the structure (spalling, cracks, etc.). This group proposes to address these minor repairs at one time.

D. Detailed Functional Group Scopes of Work

Detailed discrepancy descriptions and proposed solution scopes of work are listed in Table 2. The technical discipline that identified each discrepancy and the corresponding field inspection report forms are indicated on Table 2 by the Detail Sheet No. The field inspection report forms are filed by their Detail Sheet No. in Appendix E of the EOC assessment report and can, therefore, be reviewed as required.

V. COST SUMMARY

Summarized total budgetary costs and both total Federal and total non-Federal shares, are listed by activity location and by functional group in Table 1 (below). Individual activity budgetary costs and both Federal and non-Federal shares, are listed in Table 2 at the end of the Program Narrative.

The total budgetary costs are based on the construction and equipment cost amounts from the assessment report plus 6% of construction costs for architectural-engineering design, 0.5% of construction costs for other architectural-engineering costs, 9.5% of construction costs for contract administration and construction management costs and 0.13% for miscellaneous items such as reproduction costs.

TABLE 1

PHASE 2 EOC UPGRADE GRANT PROPOSAL - SUMMARY COST BREAKDOWN BY ACTIVITY LOCATION AND FUNCTIONAL GROUP

FUNCTIONAL GROUP NAME	Budgetary Total Costs	Budgetary Federal Share Costs	Budgetary Matching Share Costs
ALTERNATE EOC GROUP 1 - ESTABLISH ALTERNATE EOC MISSION CRITICAL OPERATING CAPABILITIES **(P3)**	$ 427,940.39	$ 320,955.29	$ 106,985.10
ALTERNATE EOC GROUP 2 - PROVIDE ALTERNATE EOC PHYSICAL SECURITY MEASURES **(M2)**	$ 68,517.84	$ 51,388.38	$ 17,129.46
GROUP SUBTOTAL - ALTERNATE EOC ACTIVITY LOCATION	$ 496,458.23	$ 372,343.67	$ 124,114.56
EOC GROUP 1 - MITIGATE EFFECTS OF RELEVANT RISKS **(P2)**	$ 61,004.10	$ 45,753.08	$ 15,251.03
EOC GROUP 2 - PROVIDE PROTECTION AGAINST INDIRECT EFFECTS OF WMD **(M1)**	$ 145,352.47	$ 109,014.35	$ 36,338.12
EOC GROUP 3 - PROVIDE PHYSICAL SECURITY MEASURES **(M2)**	$ 257,817.07	$ 193,362.80	$ 64,454.27
EOC GROUP 4 - UPGRADE POWER GENERATOR SYSTEM **(M3)**	$ 211,023.02	$ 158,267.27	$ 52,755.76
EOC GROUP 5 - UPGRADE EMERGENCY COMMUNICATIONS **(M5)**	$ 60,716.19	$ 45,537.14	$ 15,179.05
EOC GROUP 6 - UPGRADE EMERGENCY COMMUNICATION ACCESS ROUTE **(M5)**	$ 377,022.31	$ 282,766.74	$ 94,255.58
EOC GROUP 7 - UPGRADE/REPAIR BUILDING SYSTEMS FOR CODE COMPLIANCE **(T1)**	$ 228,530.68	$ 171,398.01	$ 57,132.67
EOC GROUP 8 - PROVIDE SUFFICIENT TELECOMMUNICATIONS RESOURCES, PERIPHERALS AND ROUTES **(T2&3)**	$ 53,403.30	$ 40,052.47	$ 13,350.82
EOC GROUP 9 - MODIFY EOC TO ALLOW HI-TECH EMERGENCY MONITORING & COMMAND AREAS **(T5)**	$ 114,526.13	$ 85,894.60	$ 28,631.53
EOC GROUP 10 - EXPAND EOC FACILITY TO PROVIDE FUNCTIONAL ANNEX MULTI-FUNCTION SPACE **(T5)**	$ 1,160,477.08	$ 870,357.81	$ 290,119.27
EOC GROUP 11 - PROVIDE/REPAIR EXTERIOR LIGHTING SYSTEM **(I1)**	$ 41,807.50	$ 31,355.62	$ 10,451.87
EOC GROUP 12 - MINOR REPAIR/MAINTENANCE ITEMS **(I3)**	$ 13,570.02	$ 10,177.51	$ 3,392.50
GROUP SUBTOTAL - EOC UPGRADE ACTIVITY LOCATION	$ 2,725,249.87	$ 2,043,937.40	$ 681,312.47
GRAND TOTAL ALL FUNCTIONAL GROUPS	$ 3,221,708.09	$ 2,416,281.07	$ 805,427.02

VI. 44 CFR PART 10 ENVIRONMENTAL REVIEW

A. Proposed Action

The proposed action is to expand the existing Civil Defense Building an additional 6775 square feet to address deficiencies relative to the Emergency Operations Center. Civil Defense is housed in an underground bunker compound located west of Government House in Agana Heights, Guam. Government House, also known as the Governor's Mansion, serves as the formal residence of the Governor of Guam and his family. An asphalt- paved parking area and driveway serves patrons and employees of Civil Defense and Government House. Brick-paved walkways and gardens also occupy the Government House grounds.

The footprint for the additional Civil Defense Building area will be located on previously disturbed Government of Guam property (Figure 1). Earthmoving activities during the construction of the underground bunker compound have disrupted the surrounding soils. The proposed expansion may involve removal of existing structures and pavement to accommodate the new facilities, and the lawn area will be excavated to achieve the necessary grade. Heavy equipment will be staged in the existing parking area/driveway fronting the Civil Defense Building.

B. Impacts To Historic And Archaeological Properties

The existing Civil Defense Building was designed in 1977 and constructed in 1980. The 23-year old facility is not an historic structure. Clearance from the State Historic Preservation Officer, however, will be needed prior to construction.

The Adjacent Government House was constructed in 1952. Portions of the House were reconstructed in 1977 following the aftermath of Typhoon Pamela in May 1976. The Historic Resources Division of the Guam Department of Parks and Recreation is currently researching the historic significance of Government House. The House and its grounds may be evaluated for nomination to the Guam and National Registers of Historic Places.

C. Impacts To The Natural Environment

The natural environment encompassed by the project area is comprised of a maintained lawn landscaped with ornamental tree species (see Figures 3 and 4 on following page). No sensitive species or threatened and endangered species occur within the proposed project site, nor does the site serve as a critical habitat for any of these species.

Figure 2
View facing south of existing open lawn adjacent and west of the Civil Defense/EOC Building.
The proposed EOC facility expansion will occupy this lawn area, and may displace a few
landscaped trees and existing utilities.

Figure 3
View of front of Civil Defense/EOC Building facing northeast. The lawn area in the foreground
and ramp in the left of the photo will be disturbed by new construction for the building expansion.

VII. ASSURANCE OF 44 CFR PART 13 COMPLIANCE

Guam Civil Defense certifies that the proposed projects have been evaluated and that the projects will be implemented in accordance with 44 CFR Part 13, Uniform Administration Requirements for Grants and Cooperative Agreements to State and Local Governments.

VIII. CONCLUSION

As the methodology of Homeland and Maritime Security becomes infused into national defense policies, Guam, a strategic asset of the United States, would greatly benefit from the archetype that this competitive grant proposal presents. Adopting and funding this proposal will provide Guam with the essential vehicle (EOC), knowledge, expertise, and assets to maintain an effective and efficient emergency management and response capability as well as to provide a proactive defense posture. It will enhance the ability, effectiveness, efficiency and capability of long and short-term initiatives of the various organizations involved in the Unified Command Structure. Although Guam has at its disposal Department of Defense components and several federal agencies, these organizations are not mandated to provide neither the capability nor the assets required to provide the island with adequate civil command and control.

As never before, and in the aftermath of the tragic events of September 11, 2001, it has become evident that in emergency situations, Guam is dependent upon rapid access to and the application of numerous types of modern technology and accurate intelligence information that enable proactive management and responses. Protecting Guam and its valuable assets are critical to the United States, its international interests, and economic growth.

Given the urgency and scale of what is now confronting Guam and the United States as it constantly faces natural disasters and participates in the global campaign against terrorism, illegal alien migration, and contraband seizure, we anticipate the continued demands upon Guam by the Federal Government to increase. Because Guam plays a valuable role in the US international defense posture, where efficient mitigation programs, effective and timely preparation and response, and immediate recovery efforts are critical issues, it is advantageous that Guam receives the necessary funding required to upgrade its Emergency Operations Center and overall facility.

TABLE 2
PHASE 2 EOC UPGRADE GRANT PROPOSAL - DETAILED DEFICIENCY LISTING AND COST BREAKDOWN BY FUNCTIONAL GROUP

Site P= Primary A = Alternate	Detail Sheet No.	Location/System***	Deficiency Description, Dimensions, Pre-Existing Conditions, Etc.	Impact Type* (P,M,T,L or I)	Sub-Type	Relevant Char.** (Sur, Sus, Sec, Int, or Flx)	Qty/Area	Units	Recommended Solution/Fix	Budgetary Total Costs	Budgetary Federal Share Costs	Budgetary Matching Share Costs
A	ARCH11	ALTERNATE EOC	NON-EXISTING. TO BE ESTABLISHED	P	3	SUR			LOCATION AND CENTER IS BEING PLANNED ACCORDING TO MEET LOCAL AND FEDERAL EOC REQUIREMENTS.ARCHITECTURAL ITEMS	$ 164,566.31	$ 123,424.74	$ 41,141.58
A	ELEC15	Power	There is no existing panelboard and electrical distribution system at the area. Existing Distribution Panel of the Main Building is supported by a back-up generator.	P	3	Sur	1		Provide new panelboard and electrical distribution system at the area. New feeder and panelboard shall be connected to existing 208Y/120V, 3 phase Distribution Panel of the Main Building. UPS power supply system shall be provided for critical equipment.	$ 21,298.60	$ 15,973.95	$ 5,324.65
A	ELEC16	Lighting	No existing lighting at area.	P	3	Sur	1		Provide new energy efficient fluorescent lighting.	$ 18,128.19	$ 13,596.15	$ 4,532.05
A	ELEC17	Telephone	No existing telephone system at area. Main building contains a telephone service cabinet.	P	3	Sur	1		Provide new telephone service by connecting to existing telephone service cabinet of Main Building.	$ 9,854.95	$ 7,391.21	$ 2,463.74
A	ELEC18	Networking	No existing networking system at area.	P	3	Sur	1		Provide new Data Networking system.	$ 34,354.95	$ 25,766.21	$ 8,588.74
A	ELEC19	CATV	No existing Cable TV system at area. Main building contains a TV service cabinet.	P	3	Sur	1		Provide new CableTV service by connecting to existing TV service cabinet of Main Building.	$ 934.86	$ 701.15	$ 233.72
A	ELEC20	Fire Alarm	No existing Fire Alarm system at area. Main building contains a FA system.	P	3	Sur	1		Provide new FA system by connecting to existing FA system of Main Building.	$ 1,747.79	$ 1,310.84	$ 436.95
A	ELEC21	PA/ Intercom	No existing PA/Intercom system at area.	P	3	Sur	1		Provide new PA/Intercom system.	$ 4,267.85	$ 3,200.89	$ 1,066.96
A	MECH15	Air Conditioning System	No A/C system currently installed; new system needed with protection against CBR threats	P	3	Sus, Sec	2300		Provide new redundant 10ton chilled water system with 2-ea 5-ton fan coil units; ducting and terminal devices.	$ 87,749.29	$ 65,811.97	$ 21,937.32
A	MECH16	Plumbing System	Stub-outs for water/sewer provided, but no fixtures or finished spaces; plumbing fit-out required	P	3	Sus, Flx	2		Provide new ADA compliant restroom and showers; kitchen	$ 20,323.09	$ 15,242.32	$ 5,080.77
A	MECH17	Water Storage System	Alternate EOC has insufficient storage capacity	P	3	Sus, Flx	1		Provide new aboveground tank and pump system dedicated to EOC operations. Provide security cameras for protection against vandalism.	$ 60,969.26	$ 45,726.95	$ 15,242.32
A	STRU14	Perimeter Walls	Vulnerability with Existing Window Openings	P	3	Sec	36	SF	Seal w/ Reinforced Concrete	$ 522.59	$ 391.95	$ 130.65
A	STRU15	Perimeter Walls	Vulnerability with Existing Wall Openings	P	3	Sec	18	SF	Seal w/ Reinforced Concrete	$ 261.30	$ 195.97	$ 65.32
A	STRU16	Interior Walls	Vulnerability w/ Existing Wall Openings at Ceiling	P	3	Sec	60	SF	Seal w/ CMU & Reinforced Concrete	$ 870.99	$ 653.24	$ 217.75
A	STRU17	Perimeter Walls	Vulnerability with Entry Door Security	P	3	Sec	48	SF	Seal w/ Reinforced Concrete	$ 696.79	$ 522.59	$ 174.20
A	STRU18	Perimeter Walls	Vulnerability with Entry Door Security	P	3	Sec	48	SF	Open New Main Entry Doors	$ 1,393.58	$ 1,045.19	$ 348.40
ALTERNATE EOC GROUP 1 - ESTABLISH ALTERNATE EOC MISSION CRITICAL OPERATING CAPABILITIES **(P3)**									SUBTOTAL	$ 427,940.39	$ 320,955.29	$ 106,985.10

1 of 6

TABLE 2
PHASE 2 EOC UPGRADE GRANT PROPOSAL - DETAILED DEFICIENCY LISTING AND COST BREAKDOWN BY FUNCTIONAL GROUP

Site P= Primary A = Alternate	Detail Sheet No.	Location/System***	Deficiency Description, Dimensions, Pre-Existing Conditions, Etc.	Impact Type* (P,M,T,L or I)	Sub-Type	Relevant Char.** (Sur, Sus, Sec, Int, or Fix)	Qty/Area	Units	Recommended Solution/Fix	Budgetary Total Costs	Budgetary Federal Share Costs	Budgetary Matching Share Costs
A	CIV07	Sewer manhole	Existing manhole cover is not secured.	M	2	Sec	1		Replace existing cover with lockable lid and cover.	$ 929.06	$ 696.79	$ 232.26
A	SEC28	Main Entry / ACS	(1) No Existing Access Control System; (2) Foyer does not allow for "Mantrap" Requirements	M	2	Sec	2		(1) Provide Fully Functional Access Control System devices with Biometric System Interface; (2) Provide New Entry to meet "Mantrap" Requirements	$ 10,451.87	$ 7,838.91	$ 2,612.97
A	SEC29	Traffic Management Center Exterior Hallway / Physical Security	Possible Access Entry (Fan Exhaust) Point not Secured	M	2	Sec			Close off Fan Exhaust; Covered by Architechtural Assesment	$ -	$ -	$ -
A	SEC30	Main Entry / CCTV	No Existing Video Surveillance	M	2	Sec	1		Install Fixed Camera to include vandal proof and weather proof housing for main entry	$ 2,090.37	$ 1,567.78	$ 522.59
A	SEC31	Building Entry / CCTV	No Existing Video Surveillance for Entry Hallway / Front Hallway	M	2	Sec	1		Install Fixed Camera to include vandal proof and weather proof housing	$ 2,090.37	$ 1,567.78	$ 522.59
A	SEC32	West Side of Traffic Management Building / CCTV	No Existing Video Surveillance	M	2	Sec	1		Install Fixed Camera to include vandal proof and weather proof housing	$ 2,090.37	$ 1,567.78	$ 522.59
A	SEC33	Traffic Management Building 1st Floor Stairwell / CCTV	No Existing Video Surveillance	M	2	Sec	1		Install Fixed Camera to include vandal proof and weather proof housing	$ 2,090.37	$ 1,567.78	$ 522.59
A	SEC34	Rear of Traffic Management Building (Covered Parking) / CCTV	No Existing Video Surveillance	M	2	Sec	1		Install Fixed Camera to include vandal proof and weather proof housing	$ 2,090.37	$ 1,567.78	$ 522.59
A	SEC35	Rooftop / CCTV	No Existing Video Surveillance	M	2	Sec	2		(1) Install fixed Camera to include vandal proof and weather proof housing; (2) Provide typhoon proof enclosure for camera housing; (3) Provide Digital Video Recording with motion tracking alert capabilities	$ 4,180.75	$ 3,135.56	$ 1,045.19
A	SEC36	2nd Floor HVAC / CCTV	No Existing Video Surveillance	M	2	Sec	1		(1) Install fixed Camera to include vandal proof and weather proof housing; (2) Provide typhoon proof enclosure for camera housing; (3) Provide Digital Video Recording with motion tracking alert capabilities	$ 2,090.37	$ 1,567.78	$ 522.59
A	SEC37	Utility Room Doors / ACS	No Existing Access Control System	M	2	Sec	2		Install Access Control System Devices	$ 3,483.96	$ 2,612.97	$ 870.99
A	SEC38	Proposed Water Tank / CCTV	No Existing Video Surveillance	M	2	Sec	1		(1) Install fixed Camera to include vandal proof and weather proof housing; (2) Provide typhoon proof enclosure for camera housing; (3) Provide Digital Video Recording with motion tracking alert capabilities	$ 2,090.37	$ 1,567.78	$ 522.59
A	SEC39	ACS	No Existing Access Control System	M	2	Sec	1		Access Control System Equipment	$ 4,645.28	$ 3,483.96	$ 1,161.32
A	SEC40	Digital Video Recorder	No Existing Digital Video Recorder	M	2	Sec	1		Closed Circuit Television Equipment	$ 30,194.30	$ 22,645.73	$ 7,548.58
ALTERNATE EOC GROUP 2 - PROVIDE ALTERNATE EOC PHYSICAL SECURITY MEASURES (M2)									SUBTOTAL	$ 68,517.84	$ 51,388.38	$ 17,129.46
P	CIV05	Catch basin / drain pipe.	Existing 8" diameter 170 feet in length of drain pipe is clogged up from the catch basin to the end pipe which is daylighted to the west side of the property	P	2	Sus	170		Expansion of EOC will alleviate this problem, however, interim pressure jetting of 8" drain pipe is required to clear debris and restore performance.	$ 2,369.09	$ 1,776.82	$ 592.27
P	MECH12	Fire Protection System	No automatic fire protection system in place	P	2	Sur, Sus	8400		Provide fire protection system within all areas of the EOC	$ 58,635.01	$ 43,976.26	$ 14,658.75
EOC GROUP 1 - MITIGATE EFFECTS OF RELEVANT RISKS (P2)									SUBTOTAL	$ 61,004.10	$ 45,753.08	$ 15,251.03
P	ELEC11	Interior/Network System	Main Hub for the entire network system is located at the Communication Officer Room. CAT5 cabling are exposed.	M	1	Fix	1		Install cables is conduit and surface mounted raceway for protection against physical damage. Provide EM shielding in EOC.	$ 31,355.62	$ 23,516.72	$ 7,838.91
P	MECH01	Outside Air Intake	OA intake structure does not provide adequate CBR threat protection	M	1	Sur, Sec	1		Provide angled screens; install security cameras	$ 17,419.79	$ 13,064.84	$ 4,354.95
P	MECH02	Outside Air Intake	Unfiltered outside air into building provides exposure pathway; system provides inadequate protection against CBR; excessive OA requirements due to generator	M	1	Sur, Sec	1		Reduce volume of OA by relocating radiator or generator; provide filtration system to protect against CBR	$ 79,157.27	$ 59,367.95	$ 19,789.32
P	MECH03	Air Conditioning System	Control system for A/C system not functional, do not provide adequate modulation of OA or protection in the event of attack	M	1	Sur, Sec	1		Provide new digital control system integrated with security to allow for immediate shutdown in the event of CBR attack.	$ 17,419.79	$ 13,064.84	$ 4,354.95
EOC GROUP 2 - PROVIDE PROTECTION AGAINST INDIRECT EFFECTS OF WMD (M1)									SUBTOTAL	$ 145,352.47	$ 109,014.35	$ 36,338.12

TABLE 2
PHASE 2 EOC UPGRADE GRANT PROPOSAL - DETAILED DEFICIENCY LISTING AND COST BREAKDOWN BY FUNCTIONAL GROUP

Site P= Primary A = Alternate	Detail Sheet No.	Location/System***	Deficiency Description, Dimensions, Pre-Existing Conditions, Etc.	Impact Type* (P,M,T,L or I)	Sub-Type	Relevant Char.** (Sur, Sus, Sec, Int, or Fix)	Qty/Area	Units	Recommended Solution/Fix	Budgetary Total Costs	Budgetary Federal Share Costs	Budgetary Matching Share Costs
P	ARCH03	STAIRCASE TO THE GOVERNORS HOUSE	OPEN NON SECURED TO GOVERNORS HOUSE STAIRCASE IS NON-A.D.A. COMPLIANT	M	2	SEC			EXTEND WALL AND PLANTER BOX AT THE TOP OF THE STAIRCASE TO CLOSE OPENING AND PROVIDE SECURE EXIT ONLY DOORS BY PLANTERS AREA AND SECURITY DOORS TO GOVERNORS HOUSE. PROVIDE WHEEL CHAIR LIFT FOR A.D.A.	$ 6,421.63	$ 4,816.22	$ 1,605.41
P	ARCH04	REAR ENTRY AT THE BOTTOM OF STAIRS	NON OPERABLE DOORS, NON-SECURED	M	2	SEC			THE 2 DOUBLE EXISTING REAR ENTRY/FOYER AREA IS TO BE CONVERTED TO A MAN TRAP AREA WITH EXTRA SECURITY MEASURES	$ 4,180.75	$ 3,135.56	$ 1,045.19
P	ARCH07	TEL. EQUIP. ROOM	2 OF THE 4 WALLS ARE GYP. BD. WALLS, NON-SECURED ROOM WHICH WILL ALLOW EASE OF TAMPERING.	M	2	SUS	99	SF	ALL GYP. BD. WALLS TO BE HARDENED WITH A HIGH	$ 6,953.98	$ 5,215.49	$ 1,738.50
P	CIV01	Underground water storage	Existing manhole cover is not secured.	M	2	Sec	1		Replace existing cover with lockable lid and cover.	$ 929.06	$ 696.79	$ 232.26
P	CIV04	Chain barrier.	Chain is being used as barrier in the entrance and exit of the emergency access road.	M	2	Sec	2		Remove existing chain and install double swing gates	$ 9,290.55	$ 6,967.92	$ 2,322.64
P	MECH08	Fuel System / UST	Access manhole not secure; no detection/security provisions; vent pipe only 4-ft from ground	M	2	Sur, Sus, Sec	1		Provide lockable cover, security cameras; extend vent	$ 7,251.28	$ 5,438.46	$ 1,812.82
P	MECH09	Water Storage System	Access manhole not secure; no detection/security provisions; vent pipe only 4-ft from ground	M	2	Sur, Sus, Sec	1		Provide lockable cover, security cameras; extend vent (see Civil for locking manhole cost)	$ 4,229.52	$ 3,172.14	$ 1,057.38
P	MECH14	Chilled Water System / Exterior Equipment Enclosure	Access to equipment plant not secure;	M	2	Sur, Sus, Sec	1		Provide lockable barriers across grating; provide surveillance cameras	$ 3,483.96	$ 2,612.97	$ 870.99
P	SEC01	Foyer 103 / ACS	Exisitng Access Control System non-functional and insufficient for security requirements	M	2	Sec	2		(1) Provide Access Control System devices to include Biometric System Interface; (2) Add "Mantrap" security setup with interior double door	$ 10,451.87	$ 7,838.91	$ 2,612.97
P	SEC02	Rm 102 Lobby / CCTV	Video Surveillance is non-functional; Conduit needs to be changed out due to security reasons	M	2	Sec	1		Replace camera with new and provide vandal and weather proof housing	$ 929.06	$ 696.79	$ 232.26
P	SEC03	Corridor 117 / CCTV	No Video monitoring on adjacent hallway surrounding EOC	M	2	Sec	8		Install Cameras to monitor all movement in hallways leading to EOC	$ 4,064.62	$ 3,048.46	$ 1,016.15
P	SEC04	Telecommunications Rooms 120 / ACS	(1) No Access Control to main telecommunications room; (2) Walls insufficient for security requirements	M	2	Sec	1		(1) Provide Access Control Equipment; (2) Change Existing wall to solid concrete	$ 1,741.98	$ 1,306.48	$ 435.49
P	SEC05	EOC Doors / Access Control System	No Access Control to EOC	M	2	Sec	1		Install Access Control Equipment to all three entry doors	$ 5,225.94	$ 3,919.45	$ 1,306.48
P	SEC06	RM 113, 114, & 115 / ACS	(1) No Access Control to Homeland Security Room; (2) Walls insufficient for security requirements	M	2	Sec	2		(1) Provide Access Control Equipment; (2) Add "Mantrap" Security Setup to enter double door; (3) Change Existing wall to solid concrete	$ 10,451.87	$ 7,838.91	$ 2,612.97
P	SEC07	Alternate 911 Dispatch Room / ACS	No Access Control to Alternate 911 Dispatch room	M	2	Sec	1		Install Access Control System Device	$ 1,741.98	$ 1,306.48	$ 435.49
P	SEC08	Main Entry / Metal / Bomb Detectors	No Metal or Bomb Detectors in Place	M	2	Sec			Install Metal/Bomb Detectors at Main Entry Location	$ -	$ -	$ -
P	SEC09	Room 103 Main Entrance / Fire Alarm System	Non-Compliant Fire Alarm System / Non Compliant with 2003 NFPA Codes; Not ADA Compliant	M	2	Sec			Provide fully functional Fire Alarm System interfaced with Security Access Control System for Emergency Egress	$ -	$ -	$ -
P	SEC10	Egress Releases all ACS	Fire Alarm System Interfaced with ACS non-existing	M	2	Sec			Provide fully functional Fire Alarm System interfaced with Security Access Control System for Emergency Egress	$ -	$ -	$ -
P	SEC11	Room 121 (Gen Rm.) / ACS	No Access Control for Generator Room	M	2	Sec	1		Install Access Control Equipment	$ 1,741.98	$ 1,306.48	$ 435.49
P	SEC12	Room 104 / ACS	Exisitng Access Control System non-functional and insufficient for security requirements	M	2	Sec	2		(1) Provide working Access Control System devices to include Biometric System Interface; (2) Add "Mantrap" security setup with interior double door	$ 10,451.87	$ 7,838.91	$ 2,612.97
P	SEC13	All Administrative Doors / ACS	No Existing Access Control System	M	2	Sec	12		Install Access Control Equipment	$ 20,903.75	$ 15,677.81	$ 5,225.94
P	SEC14	ACS	Access Control System Equipment (No detail sheet)	M	2	Sec	1		Access Control System Equipment	$ 60,388.60	$ 45,291.45	$ 15,097.15
P	SEC15	Badging System	Badging System (no detail sheet)	M	2	Sec	1		Badging System	$ 17,419.79	$ 13,064.84	$ 4,354.95
P	SEC16	Digital Video Recorder	Digital Recorder Equipment (No detail sheet)	M	2	Sec	1		Digital Recorder Equipment & Software; 2 ea. 16 camera inputs	$ 37,162.22	$ 27,871.66	$ 9,290.55
P	SEC17	All Vehicle Entrances; CCTV	No video monitoring	M	2	Sec	1		Install Fixed Camera to include vandal proof housing to monitor all entries and exits to facility parking lot	$ 2,090.37	$ 1,567.78	$ 522.59
P	SEC18	Generator Fuel Tanks / CCTV	(1) Fuel Tank Covers are not secure; (2) No existing video surveillance	M	2	Sec	1		(1) Install fixed Camera to include vandal proof and weather proof enclosure for camera housing; (2) Provide typhoon proof enclosure for camera housing; (3) Provide security measures to enable locking of manhole covers; (4) Provide Digital Video Recording with motion tracking alert capabilities	$ 2,671.03	$ 2,003.28	$ 667.76

TABLE 2

PHASE 2 EOC UPGRADE GRANT PROPOSAL - DETAILED DEFICIENCY LISTING AND COST BREAKDOWN BY FUNCTIONAL GROUP

Site P= Primary A = Alternate	Detail Sheet No.	Location/System***	Deficiency Description, Dimensions, Pre-Existing Conditions, Etc.	Impact Type* (P,M,T,L or I)	Sub-Type	Relevant Char.** (Sur, Sus, Sec, Int, or Flx)	Qty/Area	Units	Recommended Solution/Fix	Budgetary Total Costs	Budgetary Federal Share Costs	Budgetary Matching Share Costs
P	SEC19	HVAC / CCTV	No existing Video surveillance for exterior access to AHU and chillers	M	2	Sec	1		(1) Install fixed Camera to include vandal proof and weather proof housing; (2) Provide typhoon proof enclosure for camera housing; (3) Provide Digital Video Recording with motion tracking alert capabilities	$ 2,090.37	$ 1,567.78	$ 522.59
P	SEC20	Radio Antennas / CCTV	No existing Video Surveillance on antennas	M	2	Sec	1		(1) Install fixed Camera to include vandal proof and weather proof housing; (2) Provide typhoon proof enclosure for camera housing; (3) Provide Digital Video Recording with motion tracking alert capabilities	$ 2,090.37	$ 1,567.78	$ 522.59
P	SEC21	GH Generator / CCTV	No existing Video Surveillance	M	2	Sec	2		(1) Install fixed Camera to include vandal proof and weather proof housing; (2) Provide typhoon proof enclosure for camera housing; (3) Provide Digital Video Recording with motion tracking alert capabilities	$ 4,180.75	$ 3,135.56	$ 1,045.19
P	SEC22	Facility Perimeter / Physical Security	No Security barriers to restrict vehicles from driving straight to building above or to the side	M	2	Sec	25	EA	Install bollards around perimeter of the EOC to restrict vehicles approaching EOC	$ 8,709.89	$ 6,532.42	$ 2,177.47
P	SEC23	Generator Room Shaft and antenna location / Physical Security	Existing generator radiator exhaust is not protected from entry, vandalism or possible bomb threat	M	2	Sec			(1) Install metal grids inside ducting to prevent objects from being thrown inside;	$ 1,161.32	$ 870.99	$ 290.33
P	SEC24	Ramp to Main Entry / CCTV	Insufficient Security Measures for bomb threats	M	2	Sec	1		(1) Build up concrete enclosure and relocate main entry at least 50 feet from current location; (2) Provide fixed camera with Vandal & Weather Proof Housings	$ 2,090.37	$ 1,567.78	$ 522.59
P	SEC25	Stairway to Room 101 / ACS	Insufficient for Security Requirements	M	2	Sec	2		(1) Enclose Stairwell leading to EOC; (2) Add new security door with Access Control equipment to newly enclosed stairwell	$ 4,645.28	$ 3,483.96	$ 1,161.32
P	SEC26	Stairway to Room 101 / CCTV	No Video Surveillance	M	2	Sec	1		Install Camera to include vandal & weather proof housing	$ 2,090.37	$ 1,567.78	$ 522.59
P	SEC27	Water Tank / CCTV & ACS	(1) Tank Covers are not secure; (2) No existing video surveillance	M	2	Sec	1		(1) Install fixed Camera to include vandal proof and weather proof housing; (2) Provide typhoon proof enclosure for camera housing; (3) Provide security measures to enable locking of manhole covers; (4) Provide Digital Video Recording with motion tracking alert capabilities	$ 580.66	$ 435.49	$ 145.16
EOC GROUP 3 - PROVIDE PHYSICAL SECURITY MEASURES (M2)									**SUBTOTAL**	$ 257,817.07	$ 193,362.80	$ 64,454.27
P	ARCH10	NEW GENERATOR RM.	NEW ROOM NON-EXISTING. OLD ROOM SUSEPTABLE TO MECHANICAL, GAS HAZARDS AND MAINTENANCE. OLD GENERATOR IS INSUFFICIENT TO PROVIDE POWER TO NEW NEEDED OFFICE LAYOUT.	M	3	SEC	450	SF	PROVIDE NEW GENERATOR ROOM IN SECURED GARAGE. THIS WILL ALLOW FOR BETTER MAINTENANCE ACCESSIBILITY REDUCE HAZARDS WITHIN THE BUILDING.	$ 42,504.29	$ 31,878.22	$ 10,626.07
P	ELEC01	Exterior/Primary / Power Connection	Existing riser pole is wood.	M	3	Sur	1		Harden pole	$ 6,967.92	$ 5,225.94	$ 1,741.98
P	ELEC02	Exterior/Primary / Power Connection	Primary handhole is damaged	M	3	Sur	1		Replace handhole with manhole	$ 4,645.28	$ 3,483.96	$ 1,161.32
P	ELEC04	Electrical Room/ Electrical Service Equipment	Presently there is no protection from transient voltage.	M	3	Sur	1		Provide new Transient Voltage Surge Suppressor.	$ 12,000.00	$ 9,000.00	$ 3,000.00
P	ELEC05	Electrical Room/ups	Critical equipment are presently supported by stand-alone UPS systems with limited battery back-up capacity.	M	3	Sur	1		Provide larger UPS unit with sufficient capacity to support all critical equipment	$ 52,000.00	$ 39,000.00	$ 13,000.00
P	ELEC06	Electrical Room/Generator	Existing generator has exceeded its useful life and is unreliable.	M	3	Sus	1		Provide new generator of adequate capacity. Provide secondary back-up by connecting to the adjacent building's generator. Provide pre-wired connection to a portable generator.	$ 92,905.54	$ 69,679.16	$ 23,226.39
EOC GROUP 4 - UPGRADE POWER GENERATOR SYSTEM (M3)									**SUBTOTAL**	$ 211,023.02	$ 158,267.27	$ 52,755.76
P	ARCH01	VIDEO CONF. ROOM	NEW ROOM NON-EXISTING	M	5	SEC	535	SF	HIGH SECURITY ROOM WITH HARDENED WALLS AND A MAN TRAP AREA PROVIDED.	$ 55,963.51	$ 41,972.63	$ 13,990.88
P	ARCH02	RADIO EQUIP. ROOM	EXISTING ROOM WILL NEED TO HAVE NEW ACCES DEPENDING ON THE NEW VIDEO CONFERENCE ROOM.	M	5	SEC	180	SF	THE RADIO RM. & VIDEO EQUIP. RM. WILL HAVE TO BE COMBINED WITH THE RADIO RM. DOOR AS NEW ENTRY. THE WIDTH OF THE ROOMS WILL HAVE TO BE REDUCED TO ACCOMMODATE MORE SPACE FOR VIDEO CONFERENCE RM.	$ 4,752.68	$ 3,564.51	$ 1,188.17
EOC GROUP 5 - UPGRADE EMERGENCY COMMUNICATIONS (M5)									**SUBTOTAL**	$ 60,716.19	$ 45,537.14	$ 15,179.05
P	CIV03	Emergency access road	Existing emergency access road is approximately 1,510 feet long and has a width varying from 8 feet to 12 feet.	M	5	Sur	1510		Reconstruct existing access road to 24-ft wide w/ curb, gutter and guardrails to accommodate larger vehicles	$ 377,022.31	$ 282,766.74	$ 94,255.58
EOC GROUP 6 - UPGRADE EMERGENCY COMMUNICATION ACCESS ROUTE (M5)									**SUBTOTAL**	$ 377,022.31	$ 282,766.74	$ 94,255.58

TABLE 2
PHASE 2 EOC UPGRADE GRANT PROPOSAL - DETAILED DEFICIENCY LISTING AND COST BREAKDOWN BY FUNCTIONAL GROUP

Site P= Primary A = Alternate	Detail Sheet No.	Location/System***	Deficiency Description, Dimensions, Pre-Existing Conditions, Etc.	Impact Type* (P,M,T,L or I)	Sub-Type	Relevant Char.** (Sur, Sus, Sec, Int, or Flx)	Qty/Area	Units	Recommended Solution/Fix	Budgetary Total Costs	Budgetary Federal Share Costs	Budgetary Matching Share Costs
P	ARCH06	INTERIOR WALLS	HIGH PENETRATION, NON SEALED OR TAPED GYP. BD. WALLS AT JOINTS ABOVE CEILING LINE, SOME WALLS ALONG ADMIN SIDE ARE NOT FULL HEIGHT WALLS. NONE OF THE GYP. BD. WALLS ARE FIRE RATED.	T	1	SEC			ALL GYP. BD. WALLS TO BE FIRE RATED, FULL HEIGHT AND TAPED/SEALED AT ANY PENETRATION THROUGH WALL.	$ 18,774.35	$ 14,080.76	$ 4,693.59
P	ARCH09	COORIDORS	NO FIRE SPRINKLER SYS., DOORS ARE NOT FIRE RATED OUTDATED LIFE SAFETY CONDITIONS.	T	1	SUR		SF	PROVIDE SPRINKLER SYS., CHANGE OUTDATED CEILING TILES TO ACCOMMODATE SPRINKLER SYS. AND OUTDATED FALLING TILE MISHAPS. ALL DOORS TO BE FIRE RATED.	$ 92,227.33	$ 69,170.50	$ 23,056.83
P	CIV02	Water meter.	Existing water meter is above ground and connected from waterline for Gov.House	T	1	Sec	1		Replace existing meter, provide new meter and piping below ground with secure valve/meter box and locking cover.	$ 2,322.64	$ 1,741.98	$ 580.66
P	DATA01	Network Cables	Network cables and RJ45 connector box on floor subject to damage	T	1	Sur, Sus, Sec	1		Install cabling in conduit above floor and mount RJ45 box	$ 580.66	$ 435.49	$ 145.16
P	ELEC03	Transformer Well	Kilowatt hour meter is located inside Transformer Well. Meter reader needs access. Grating to secure well is always open	T	1	Sur	1		Relocate kwhr meter above Transformer Well and secure grating	$ 1,161.32	$ 870.99	$ 290.33
P	ELEC07	Interior/General Receptacle Outlets	Receptacle outlets in toilets and kitchen counter are not GFI type.	T	1	Sus	1		Provide new GFI type outlets to meet Code Requirement	$ 1,161.32	$ 870.99	$ 290.33
P	ELEC10	Interior/Telephone Distribution	Majority of telephone cables, if not all, runexposed (no conduit) inside drop ceiling and onwalls and floors. Cables at the Operations Room enter the room from a floor mounted junction box and are routed below the Conference Desk exposed.	T	1	Flx	1		Install cables inside conduits and surface mounted raceways for protection against physical damage.	$ 15,097.15	$ 11,322.86	$ 3,774.29
P	ELEC12	Interior/CATV System	Service entrance into the facility is via the ventilation louvers installed in the Generator Room. The cables then enter the adjacent Telephone Equipment Room through the ceiling. TV's are provided at the Operations Room and above the door to the Main Entrance. Cables are routed exposed in the ceiling. No outlets are provided.	T	1				Install service entrance CATV cables through a conduit from exterior to the interior of the building. Install wiring inside conduit and provide wall mounted outlet.	$ 5,225.94	$ 3,919.45	$ 1,306.48
P	ELEC13	Interior/Fire Alarm System	Fire Alarm System is sub-standard. System consists of manual pull station and bells. No visual alarm and no detection are provided as required by codes.	T	1	Flx	1		Provide new Code complying Fire Alarm System. Include direct connection to the Fire Department for transmission of alarm.	$ 9,290.55	$ 6,967.92	$ 2,322.64
P	MECH04	Exhaust System / Mechanical Room	Exhaust shaft discharge pattern and proximity to OA intakes results in recycling; poor roof drainage results in water infiltration	T	1	Sus	1		Modify discharge structure to improve performance and eliminate water infiltration. (see MECH01 for cost)	$ -	$ -	$ -
P	MECH05	Air Conditioning System / Fan Coil Units	No control of OA/Return Air modulation to maintain IAQ; return fans not functioning, resulting in poor cooling performance.	T	1	Sus	1		Upgrade fan coil units; replace non-functional dampers; replace return fans; test, adjust and balance	$ 28,603.29	$ 21,452.47	$ 7,150.82
P	MECH06	Exhaust System / Men/Women Rest Room	Fans not operational; do not provide code required ventilation rates	T	1	Sus	1		Replace exhaust fans	$ 6,152.67	$ 4,614.50	$ 1,538.17
P	MECH07	Fuel System / Mechanical Room	Vent pipe for day tank terminates inside mech room creating health and safety hazard	T	1	Sus	1		Extend day tank vent pipe through exhaust shaft to building exterior	$ 870.99	$ 653.24	$ 217.75
P	MECH10	Drainage System / Mechanical Room	Sump pump is simplex unit; no redundancy	T	1	Sur	1		Provide duplex pump system for redundancy	$ 7,850.52	$ 5,887.89	$ 1,962.63
P	MECH11	Piping System / Mechanical Room	Piping penetrations in exterior wall have lost water seal; resulting infiltration has damaged wall tiles	T	1	Sus	50		Remove tile, clean and reseal penetrations; replace tile. (see Structural for Cost)	$ -	$ -	$ -
P	MECH13	Chilled Water System / Exterior Equipment Enclosure	Secondary chiller not functional; expansion tank leaking; chilled water pump submerged due to poor drainage	T	1	Sur, Sus	1		Replace secondary chiller and pump; repair expansion tank; modify drainage system	$ 36,000.90	$ 27,000.67	$ 9,000.22
P	STRU01	Generator Rm.	Cracks in Wall with Moisture	T	1	Sus	15	LF	Repair with Epoxy Injection	$ 609.69	$ 457.27	$ 152.42
P	STRU03	Exit Stairwell	Wall Cracks and Leaks	T	1	Sus	10	LF	Repair with Epoxy Injection	$ 406.46	$ 304.85	$ 101.62
P	STRU04	Exit Stairwell	Wall Cracks and Leaks	T	1	Sus	10	LF	Repair with Epoxy Injection	$ 406.46	$ 304.85	$ 101.62
P	STRU06	Exit Stairwell	Roof Cracks and Leaks	T	1	Sus	10	LF	Repair with Epoxy Injection	$ 406.46	$ 304.85	$ 101.62
P	STRU07	Exit Stairwell	Roof Cracks and Leaks	T	1	Sus	10	LF	Repair with Epoxy Injection	$ 406.46	$ 304.85	$ 101.62
P	STRU08	Exit Stairwell	Roof Cracks and Leaks	T	1	Sus	10	LF	Repair with Epoxy Injection	$ 406.46	$ 304.85	$ 101.62
P	STRU09	Exit Stairwell	Concrete Spall at End Wall	T	1	Sus	2	SF	Repair with Modified Concrete	$ 81.29	$ 60.97	$ 20.32
P	STRU10	Exit Stairwell	Concrete Spall at End Wall	T	1	Sus	2	SF	Repair with Modified Concrete	$ 81.29	$ 60.97	$ 20.32
P	STRU11	Main Entry	Wall Cracks	T	1	Sus	10	LF	Repair with Epoxy Injection	$ 406.46	$ 304.85	$ 101.62
EOC GROUP 7 - UPGRADE/REPAIR BUILDING SYSTEMS FOR CODE COMPLIANCE (T1)									SUBTOTAL	$ 228,530.68	$ 171,398.01	$ 57,132.67

TABLE 2

PHASE 2 EOC UPGRADE GRANT PROPOSAL - DETAILED DEFICIENCY LISTING AND COST BREAKDOWN BY FUNCTIONAL GROUP

Site P= Primary A = Alternate	Detail Sheet No.	Location/System***	Deficiency Description, Dimensions, Pre-Existing Conditions, Etc.	Impact Type* (P,M,T,L or I)	Sub-Type	Relevant Char.** (Sur, Sus, Sec, Int, or Flx)	Qty/Area	Units	Recommended Solution/Fix	Budgetary Total Costs	Budgetary Federal Share Costs	Budgetary Matching Share Costs
P	DATA03	Network System / EOC	Peer-to-peer network is inadequate for enhanced EOC operations, email capability and user-level security and access control to sensitive data. Web-based notification and information access is not possible with current network equipment and configuration.	T	2	Sus, Flx	1		Provide client-server network for enhanced EOC operations. Include provisions for e-mail and web-site for enhanced communication and public notification.	$ 45,000.00	$ 33,750.00	$ 11,250.00
P	ELEC09	Telephone System Equipment	Telephone service to facility is via underground 4"conduit to the Telephone Equipment Room. Only one service with a 200 pr cable is installed.	T	3	Sus	1		Provide alternate separate service drop for redundancy. Consolidate telephone ystem by providing a Private Branch Exchange (PBX). System shall have the capability of automatic switchover between two telephone service drops.	$ 8,403.30	$ 6,302.47	$ 2,100.82
EOC GROUP 8 - PROVIDE SUFFICIENT TELECOMMUNICATIONS RESOURCES, PERIPHERALS AND ROUTES (T2&3)									SUBTOTAL	$ 53,403.30	$ 40,052.47	$ 13,350.82
P	ARCH05	EOC	OUTDATED EMERGENCY MONITORING SYSTEMS ROOM IS TOO LARGE, WASTE OF SPACE	T	5	SUS	1137	SF	UPGRADE ROOM TO ACCOMMODATE HI-TECH EMERGENCY MONITORING SYSTEMS AND PROCEDURES. DIVIDE LARGE ROOM INTO TWO SMALLER, MORE FUNCTIONAL AREAS.	$ 114,526.13	$ 85,894.60	$ 28,631.53
EOC GROUP 9 - MODIFY EOC TO ALLOW HI-TECH EMERGENCY MONITORING & COMMAND AREAS (T5)									SUBTOTAL	$ 114,526.13	$ 85,894.60	$ 28,631.53
P	ARCH08	FRONT ENTRY SECURED GARAGE	OPEN, NON-SECURED ENTRY INTO FACILITY WITH NO ACCESS CONTROL POINT, GARAGE NON-EXISTING; INADEQUATE OPERATIONAL SPACE FOR FEDERAL AND RESPONSE OPERATIONS.	T	5	SEC	8500	SF	ENTRY WILL BE COORDINATED ACCORDINGLY WITH NEW SECURED GARAGE AND HOMELAND SECURITY, RECOVERY AND MITIGATION LAYOUT PROVIDED WITH A MAN TRAP AREA	$ 1,160,477.08	$ 870,357.81	$ 290,119.27
EOC GROUP 10 - EXPAND EOC FACILITY TO PROVIDE FUNCTIONAL ANNEX MULTI-FUNCTION SPACE (T5)									SUBTOTAL	$ 1,160,477.08	$ 870,357.81	$ 290,119.27
P	ELEC08	Exterior/Area Lighting	Light poles sustained damage during the last typhoon.	I	1	Sur	12		Replace with stronger Light Pole rated to withstand 170 mph winds.	$ 41,807.50	$ 31,355.62	$ 10,451.87
EOC GROUP 11 - PROVIDE/REPAIR EXTERIOR LIGHTING SYSTEM (I1)									SUBTOTAL	$ 41,807.50	$ 31,355.62	$ 10,451.87
P	DATA02	Communications Systems	Antennas and aerials mounted on utility structure at facility are currently not in use. Most equipment is no longer functional and radio transmission facilities are underutilized.	I	3	Sur, Sus	1		Remove all unused equipment from utility structure and seal conduit penetrations for future use if required.	$ 1,161.32	$ 870.99	$ 290.33
P	ELEC14	Interior/PA System	Equipment is located in the Telecom Switchboard Room and installed on a desk. All wiring installed exposed inside the drop ceiling and on walls. There appears to be sufficient number of speakers for all the rooms.	I	3	Flx			Install equipment on a rack. Install wiring inside conduits and surface raceways for protection against physical damage.	$ 5,806.60	$ 4,354.95	$ 1,451.65
P	STRU02	Generator Rm.	Cracks in Slab on Grade	I	3	Sus	50	LF	Repair with Epoxy Injection	$ 2,032.31	$ 1,524.23	$ 508.08
P	STRU05	Exit Stairwell	Concrete Spall at Stair Riser	I	3	Sus	1	SF	Repair with Modified Concrete	$ 40.65	$ 30.48	$ 10.16
P	STRU12	Equipment Encl.	Spalled Concrete at Top of Curb	I	3	Sus	40	SF	Repair with Modified Concrete	$ 1,625.85	$ 1,219.39	$ 406.46
P	STRU13	Exterior Shelter	Cracked Floor Slab and Soil Erosion	I	3	Sus	5	CY	Repair with Concrete & Fill	$ 2,903.30	$ 2,177.47	$ 725.82
EOC GROUP 12 - MINOR REPAIR/MAINTENANCE ITEMS (I3)									SUBTOTAL	$ 13,570.02	$ 10,177.51	$ 3,392.50
									Grand Total (All Projects)	$ 3,221,708.09	$ 2,416,281.07	$ 805,427.02

PROPOSAL #4

FLORIDA DEPARTMENT OF EDUCATION

Request for Proposal
for
Competitive Grants

Bureau/Office	Office of Family and Community Outreach
Title	Florida Learn & Serve (Competitive)
Specific Funding Authority	Corporation for National and Community Service, Learn & Serve America School-Based Programs—CFDA #94.004
Funding Purpose	Engage students in service learning—school and/or community service activities that apply academic curricula and education standards—to improve student performance, provide for civic engagement and career exploration, and address real community needs. Build infrastructure at the school and district levels for sustained service-learning efforts.
Target Population	All K-12 students
Eligible Applicants	• Public school districts, on behalf of individual schools or for district-wide efforts • School district consortia (Heartland, NEFEC, PAEC)
Application Due Date	April 30, 2004. Proposals must be <u>received</u> by the close of business. The deadline refers to receipt by the DOE and is not a postmark deadline.
Delivery Address	Florida Department of Education Bureau of Grants Management, Unit C 325 West Gaines Street, Room 325 Tallahassee, FL 32399-0400 850-245-6304
Contact Person(s)	Joe Follman, Florida Learn & Serve Project Coordinator 850-488-9661, SunCom 278-9661, Fax: 850-922-2928 E-mail: jfollman@admin.fsu.edu, Website: www.fsu.edu/~flserve Marv Patterson, Florida DOE, 850-245-0821, Suncom 205-0821, Email: Marv.Patterson@fldoe.org
Total Funding Amount	$339,082

Range of Awards	1. School Projects: up to $12,000 for 1 school, up to $15,000 for 2+ schools 2. District Infrastructure Projects: up to $50,000
Budget Period	Pending receipt of federal funds, September 1, 2004 – August 1, 2005
Additional Years of Funding	• Schools projects can apply competitively for renewal awards in 2005-06, contingent upon the prior year's project performance and the future availability of federal funds. • District Infrastructure projects (1-2) can apply non-competitively for funds in 2005-06. Awards for 2005-06 are contingent upon annual project performance and the future availability of federal funds.
Funding Method	Federal Cash Advance
Local Match	Match (cash or in-kind) is required. Cash match is funds contributed or dedicated to the project. In-kind match is services, goods, or materials contributed to the project. Match must be directly applied to the project. Cash match is valued more highly than in-kind match. Requirements: • 33% for first-time or previously unsuccessful Florida Learn & Serve (FL&S) applicants (e.g., $3,000 for a $9,000 request) • 50% for proposals receiving a second year of funding • 100% for proposals receiving funding for a third year or more

General Terms, Assurances and Conditions for Participation in Federal and State Programs

The Department of Education has developed and implemented a document entitled, General Terms, Assurances and Conditions for Participation in Federal and State Programs, to comply with:

- 34 CFR Part 76.301 of the Education Department General Administration Regulations (EDGAR) which requires local educational agencies to submit a common assurance for participation in federal programs funded by the U.S. Department of Education;
- applicable regulations of other federal agencies; and
- state regulations and laws pertaining to the expenditure of state funds.

In order to receive funding, applicants must have on file with the Department of Education, Office of the Comptroller, a signed statement by the agency head certifying applicant adherence to these General Assurances for Participation in State or Federal Programs. The complete text may be found at http://www.firn.edu/doe/comptroller/gbook.htm

School Districts, Community Colleges, Universities and State Agencies

The certification of adherence filed with the Department of Education Comptroller's Office shall remain in effect indefinitely unless a change occurs in federal or state law, or there are other changes in circumstances affecting a term, assurance, or condition; and does not need to be resubmitted with this application.

Conditions for Acceptance

1. DOE 100A—Project Application Form with original signature by the agency head.
2. DOE 101—Budget Narrative Form

The original proposal and four duplexed copies must be received by the specified date above. If the signature on the DOE 100A is other than that of the agency head, a letter must be enclosed from the agency head authorizing that individual to sign. Place the DOE 100A and DOE 101 forms in the front of the proposal, followed by the Budget Justification and Match, the project narrative, and attachments.

Technical/Format Requirements

- One single-sided original and four two-sided copies
- Font size and color—12 points or larger, black
- Margins—At least 1 inch on all sides
- Budget Justification and Match—up to 2 single-spaced pages
- Proposal Narrative—Up to 6 single-spaced, numbered pages (includes required timeline)
- Attachments—Up to 6 pages (includes letters and other attachments)

Clip original. Staple duplexed copies in the upper left corner. Do not submit proposals in binders, folders, or covers. Do not use tabs or dividers. One side of a page equals one page. Only information in these sections and within allowed page limits will be reviewed. Additional pages will be removed prior to review.

Funding Priorities

Not Applicable

Program Guidance & Requirements

Florida public schools and school systems/districts are invited to apply for funds under Florida Learn & Serve (FL&S). FL&S is a federally funded initiative supporting school-based student service learning to enhance academic performance and meet real needs. Awards are also designed to improve student attendance and graduation rates, promote career exploration, increase civic participation, expand the use of adult volunteers in schools, and build infrastructure at the school and district levels for sustained service-learning efforts.

Projects funded under Florida Learn & Serve must engage K-12 students in curriculum-based service learning. In service-learning projects, students practice skills, knowledge, and behaviors they need to learn through service to others in their school or community. Projects need to address education standards and be integrated in students' course assessments. Activities can take place during or after school. Effective projects include the elements of preparation, action, demonstration, reflection, youth empowerment, collaboration, and recognition.

Before writing and submitting a proposal under this program, applicants need to understand the elements of service learning and integrate them into proposed activities. See Attachment 4 and the FL&S web site (http://www.fsu.edu/~flserve/), which provide definitions, examples, links with education standards, and many other service-learning resources.

Proposed service-learning activities must focus on one or more of the following key need areas. Sample activities are included that can be implemented at multiple grade levels, across many disciplines, and with students of all knowledge, skill, and ability levels:

- **Reading**—e.g., students serving as reading tutors for other students or for adults; creating books or other written materials for other students, the public, or web sites; reading and writing for seniors or the infirm/sick; editing brochures or other documents; teaching reading to young children; translating documents for people who do not speak English; promoting reading through advocacy campaigns, public service announcements (PSAs), book drives, or public readings; designing and constructing reading areas; and dramatic, artistic, or musical performances of texts and literature.

- **Civics/history**—e.g., conducting, compiling, recording, publishing, filming, or depicting histories of a local community, individuals in a community, or historic locations (cemeteries, buildings, natural features/sites, forts, Native American sites); advocacy campaigns on topics in the public interest; gathering and disseminating information about local services available to residents and visitors; creating murals depicting local history; teaching peers about democratic processes through events, student-made videos, performances (including puppet shows), lessons, and hands-on activities; creating children's history books; serving as museum docents; reenacting historic events; restoring or recreating historic structures; forums on topics of public interest; oral histories focusing on different eras; teaching about the importance of voting; producing tip sheets or guidebooks on how to effect positive community change.

- **Drug/violence prevention**—e.g., teaching other students or the community how to avoid/respond to conflict, drugs, STDs, teen pregnancy, alcohol, and other self-destructive choices. Strategies could include lessons, presentations, dramatic performances, videos, artistic displays, music, advocacy campaigns, PSAs, forums, coloring books, conflict mediation, serving on Teen Courts, and safety presentations for the home, car, or neighborhood.

- **Intergenerational interaction**—e.g., service projects for and with seniors to include health screenings, exercise programs, teaching use of computers, oral histories, pen pal programs, concerts and dances with (not just for) seniors, creating art or gardens at senior centers, working with seniors to put on public forums on issues of importance to both groups, and activities at nursing homes to provide patients with physical and mental stimulation (working on arts and crafts together, exercise, games, etc.). Students can also teach others about seniors through lessons, publications, presentations, performances, brochures, web sites, and advocacy campaigns.

- **Environment**—e.g., restoration of degraded areas; exotic plant removal; propagation and planting of native plants; water, flora, and fauna testing/monitoring; research on endangered species; erosion abatement efforts; management of public lands to include trail and outdoor classroom design and maintenance; raise-and-release efforts; energy audits for homes, schools, and communities; and mapping. Demonstration elements include teaching, presenting, creating brochures and web sites, giving tours and field days, making videos, composing information to place in kiosks and translating it into foreign languages, performances, advocacy campaigns, public service announcements, web sites, and fundraising to preserve natural areas.

All proposals must relate in some form to the "Just Read, Florida!" reading initiative by including some reading/writing element(s).

Strong student roles are hallmarks of effective projects, in which students
- Are involved in project design and planning, with meaningful leadership roles (including needs identification and helping to decide what service activities will be conducted). Teachers in effective projects assign students organizing and logistical duties involved in arranging, providing, measuring, evaluating, reporting, and celebrating service activities.
- Conduct a lot of service over time. Projects should be at least a semester in duration, and students need to conduct an average minimum of 20 service hours each semester. Service hours include hands-on service activities as well as demonstration, presentation, teaching, and program evaluation activities. Reflective writing and discussion, recognition, and general preparation activities such as conducting research do not count as service hours.

Proposals should detail how activities are tied to lesson plans, curricula, and education standards (Sunshine State, Goal 3, or Applied Technology). Funds can support lesson planning and curriculum development. All projects should also form a project advisory committee representing key project stakeholders including school staff, students, and community partners. This group can provide guidance and assistance with the overall proposal, share project responsibilities, and help with aspects of project implementation.

Partnerships are a key component of successful projects. Collaborations with community partners are required, and partnerships with private schools and faith-based organizations are encouraged. All proposals must identify proposed partners and describe the roles partners will play in helping meet project goals and objectives. Include a description of the contributions that partners will provide (cash, in-kind match, donations, expertise, materials, waiver of fees, sites for activities, etc.). Collaborations with other Corporation for National and Community Service programs (AmeriCorps, VISTA, RSVP) are strongly encouraged, but cannot be counted as match.

Narrative Requirements

Funds will be awarded in two categories:

1. School-Based Service-Learning Projects
2. District Infrastructure-Building Projects

1. School-Based Service-Learning Projects

Public schools, including charter and alternative schools, may apply under this category. Only one award will be issued per school, but an award may support multiple activities. Awards are for one year, with an option to reapply for future funding in 2005-06 if funds are available. Applicants may request up to $12,000 for one school, and up to $15,000 for two or more schools working together. Multiple-school awards must engage students from each school in providing service learning.

Not all applicants will be funded. Proposed activities and budgets are subject to revision. Some proposals earning a score above 70%, but in the lowest range of those to be funded, might be issued as $1,000-$2,000 planning grants.

<u>Information for All Applicants in this Category</u>

Successful applicants use service learning as a strategy to reach specific academic and affective goals for students. Such goals could include raising student academic performance, increasing FCAT scores in specific areas such as reading or math, improving attendance, reducing conflict, fostering career exploration, enhancing school/community collaboration, or as a prevention and intervention strategy for at-risk students. Service is the hands-on mechanism for students to practice academic and affective skills they need to learn; it is both a means and an application of learning. Therefore, <u>service-learning projects must be tied to one or more actual courses and the participating students' grades for the course(s)</u>.

Activities should directly address identified needs and apply needed skills and behaviors. Having 10th graders who test poorly in math tutor 6th graders in math can help students in both grades; having those 10th graders sing at a retirement center will not likely improve math performance.

Effective projects have clear objectives for both servers (the students) and the served (community members and sites, or other students). Such projects also include elements in which students demonstrate what they have learned through teaching others—peers, younger students, or the community—about their efforts. This teaching can take the form of presentations, lessons, products (brochures, videos, web sites, etc.), advocacy, or performances. Every project should include some demonstration elements.

Some specific strategies that new and renewal applicants should consider include the following:

- For school projects, no more than 50% of the total funds requested may be used to support salaries and benefits for project coordination, planning, extra duty time, evaluation, and supervision.
- Identify ways to show/tell how service learning advances the mission of the school.
- Create service-learning courses—such as a Leadership, Peer Counseling, or Community Service elective—in which the students' curriculum is to help the teacher (and other teachers) plan and implement service learning.
- Involve schools in your feeder pattern in activities to expand the scope of service learning and build partnerships with future students and their parents.
- Include fundraising (i.e., presentations, grant writing) as a project element and student assignment. Part of the students' grades would be based on their efforts.

- Put information on and definitions of service learning in school planners and calendars that are given to teachers and students.
- Have an agenda item on service learning at teacher meetings.
- Add a regular feature on service-learning activities in announcements, assemblies, recordings callers to the school hear when they are put on hold, and in-school TV; have teacher and student recognitions each year, semester, or month.
- Use funds to free a school service-learning coordinator for one period each day to plan or assist other teachers. Or, focus a portion of funds to support extra duty time of the coordinator or a service-learning team to plan and coordinate activities.
- Devote a portion of the funds for a youth service-learning council. Youth councils develop, market, disseminate, review, and select applications for service-learning mini-grants. Mini-grants would focus on one or more of the key need areas. The council should be part of a class, and must have a teacher or staff advisor.
- Cultivate relationships with key media outlets in the area that will provide ongoing publicity about service-learning efforts.
- Assign students to conduct interviews, surveys, and focus groups of partners to assess the partners' needs and levels of satisfaction with the project.
- Train teachers, students, and administrators as service-learning trainers/mentors.
- Work with the district professional development office so service-learning trainings qualify for in-service credit.
- Integrate a service-learning element—a handout, update, newsletter, presentation, training—into teacher planning days.

Information for Renewal Applicants in this Category

Renewal applicants are classified as having received a Learn & Serve award in 2003-04. Renewals must describe previous activities, the degree to which approved goals and objectives were met, and how outcomes and impacts were assessed. This information must be provided even if the 2004-05 proposal involves different activities and/or staff.

Renewal applicants need to describe how proposed 2004-05 efforts will build on, expand, improve, disseminate, and sustain prior service-learning activities. Successful renewal applicants will be committed to enriching the activities, support, policies, staffing, partnerships, and training to institutionalize their efforts. In addition, they include or examine ways to provide assistance to other schools interested in adopting, adapting, or replicating service learning.

Dissemination activities include, but are not limited to site visits; providing tours of the school's service-learning efforts and infrastructure; creating displays to show to others; producing and disseminating brochures, videos, manuals, guides, and how-to booklets; creating web sites; giving presentations and trainings at other schools by teachers and/or students; providing assistance with project design and implementation at other schools; giving conference presentations and trainings; organizing a multi-school service-learning working group; mentoring in person, on the phone, or via e-mail; designing large-scale trainings involving student and teacher trainers from the school; offering mini-grants to other schools; and assigning students in a service-learning course to provide assistance to other teachers.

2. District Infrastructure-Building Projects

Florida Learn & Serve currently supports five multi-year awards to school districts and can fund only a few more in 2004-05. This category is only for school districts that (a) can demonstrate past and present service-learning success and positive impacts on students and the communities they helped and (b) are committed to enriching the activities, support, policies, staffing, partnerships, and training over three years to institutionalize service-learning efforts at the district and school levels.

Applicants in this category will propose efforts at the district level to create or build the foundation for sustaining service learning as an ongoing and well-supported strategy for education and community building. Such districts are in the best position to make a long-term commitment to providing service-learning opportunities to the schools and students in their district as a tool to reach established goals and policies. Some suggested strategies are provided, and many others can be effective. Note: A number of the strategies previously listed in Category 1 apply in Category 2—please see the previous section, as the similar strategies are not repeated here.

- Use some, most, or (if necessary) all the funds to support the creation of a part- or full-time district service-learning coordinator to implement and oversee efforts. Part of the coordinator's responsibility would be to seek other sources of funding to support district efforts.
- Target some funds to provide service-learning training and seed grants to teachers-of-the-year and teachers who have or are seeking certification from the National Board for Professional Teaching Standards. Thousands of teachers nationally have addressed the Board's fifth core proposition, "Teachers are members of learning communities," through service learning.
- Assist teachers in designing and implementing service-learning projects by providing resources, training or access to training, and networking opportunities.
- Service-learning activities address the goals and objectives of other education programs including the federal Title programs. Districts choose how to focus Title and other funds and can include service learning as one strategy being supported by those funds.
- Form a district service-learning task force or advisory group, representing stakeholders from schools, the school district, and the community. This task force, formed with the support of the superintendent, identifies policies, goals, strategies, and activities to pursue to have service learning recognized, adopted, and supported as a strategy to meet district goals. The approved report then serves as a policy tool and instrument.
- Identify and show/tell how service learning advances the existing school district mission.
- Examine how service learning can advance other district initiatives, policies, special events, or interests of key administrators or principals.
- Focus some service-learning efforts to improve FCAT scores in key areas such as reading.
- Conduct a training and presentation on service learning for the school board.
- Focus a portion of the funds to provide stipends for the extra duty time of one or more school service-learning coordinators who plan and coordinate activities at their schools.
- Seek formal partnerships with local colleges of education to place pre-service education students with veteran service-learning teachers for their student teaching experience. Doing so can also serve to help recruit new teachers interested in using service learning as pedagogy.

- Apply to get a full-time, free VISTA from FL&S to help implement service-learning projects. Several districts have used VISTAs to coordinate service-learning efforts.
- Increase in-service and training opportunities for teachers and students with the goal that they become ongoing at the school and capacity is developed for providing assistance to other schools in the district.
- Train administrators, teachers, and students as service-learning trainers/mentors. Try to have a trainer at as many schools as possible.
- Work with the district professional development office so service-learning trainings qualify for in-service credit. Train key district professional development providers in service learning, and work to make training in service learning a regular in-service offering in the district. Ensure all new teachers receive this training before they begin teaching in the district.

Application Narrative Requirements and Scoring Criteria

Applicants should only answer the narrative questions in each section that are applicable to the particular grant category for which they are applying. As an aid and courtesy to reviewers who will score your proposal, please use the same alphanumeric outline as in the RFP.

1.   **Needs, Participants, Courses, and Standards Narrative Questions—20% of Score**
   - Describe the primary academic and/or affective needs of students to be addressed by the project. Describe the primary district or community needs to be addressed. Provide data to support claims. Do <u>not</u> list needs or issues the project will not address.
   - As applicable, project the numbers of students and adults who will participate/do service and those who will be served. List the grades levels involved as well as the course(s) into which service will be integrated, and how. Identify the primary (no more than five) Sunshine State, Goal 3, and/or Applied Technology Standards the project will address.
   - Identify the five key need area(s) that will be addressed (reading, civics/history, drug/violence prevention, intergenerational, or environment), and specify reading and writing elements that can support "Just Read, Florida!"
   - <u>Additional for renewal school applicants</u>: Describe current/past project activities and impacts on servers and served. Include current award amount(s), numbers of those serving and served, activities and products, hours of service, projected and actual impacts, and links with standards and course assessments. Describe how new efforts will build on, evolve, expand, and consolidate current or past activities. (Worth 8 of the 20 points in this section.)
   - <u>Additional for district infrastructure applicants</u>: Describe past and current levels of service-learning activity and success in the district, and how the proposal will complement, build on, sustain, and consolidate current or past activities.

   Scoring Criteria—Needs, Participants, Courses, and Standards (20 Points)
   - Applicant clearly defines the primary academic and/or affective needs of students as well as the primary district or community needs to be addressed by the project. Clear and relevant data are provided to support claims.
   - The proposal provides clear and quantifiable projections on numbers of participants who will be serving and served as well as the grade levels and course(s) involved into which

service will be integrated, and how. Applicant identifies the education standards the project will address.

- It is evident that proposed activities will address at least one of the five key need areas (reading, civics/history, drug/violence prevention, intergenerational, or environment), and the proposal specifies how reading and writing will be incorporated into the project and support "Just Read, Florida!"
- <u>Renewal school proposal</u> defines how the proposed project will build on past successes and provides detail about 2003-04 efforts including descriptions of past activities, projected and actual impacts on servers and served, products, hours of service, and links with standards and course assessments. (Worth 8 of the 20 points in this section.)
- <u>District infrastructure proposal</u> offers evidence of past and current service-learning activity and success in the district and describes how the new efforts will complement, build on, sustain, and consolidate current or past activities.

2. Activities, Elements, Scale, and Timeline Narrative Questions 30%

- Describe planned activities and how they will incorporate the elements of service learning (see Attachment 4) and be integrated with curricula, standards, and course-based assessments. Include descriptions of student roles.
- Project the scale and scope of the project—i.e., numbers of service activities, their frequency, products, and the average number of hours of service students will provide (min. 20 per semester). Include a project timeline in the narrative section.
- Describe planned strategies to disseminate and market service learning/project successes to appropriate populations through assistance, information, training, resource materials, site visits, or other activities.
- <u>Renewal school and district infrastructure applicants</u>: Describe activities to expand and improve service-learning efforts through new programs, additional financial and technical support, creating dedicated service-learning staff, and linking with school and district policies.

Activities, Elements, Scale, and Timeline Scoring Criteria—30 Points

- Proposal provides an effective and realistic service-learning plan that incorporates the elements of service learning and integrates activities with curricula, standards, and course-based assessments. Clear student roles in project design and implementation are provided.
- The scale, scope, and frequency of proposed activities are clear, and minimum student service hour requirements (20 hours per semester) are addressed. A clear and realistic timeline is provided.
- Proposal identifies and plans effective methods to disseminate and market service-learning/project successes to other interested in replicating or adapting service-learning programs.
- <u>Renewal school and district infrastructure proposals</u> include solid plans to expand and improve service-learning through new programs, additional support, creating dedicated service-learning staff, and linking with school and district policies.

3. Partnerships, Letters, Advisory Committee Narrative Questions 15%

- List key project partners, their roles in project design and implementation, and how they will contribute to project success. Include letters from primary partners that detail/confirm partner roles and contributions.

- Describe the formation, make-up and goals/roles of the school or district service-learning advisory committee. How often will it meet?
- <u>Additional for renewal school and district infrastructure applicants</u>: Describe plans to seek short- and long-term support and to strengthen or expand existing partnerships to meet project objectives.

Partnerships, Letters, Advisory Committee Scoring Criteria—15 Points

- Proposal describes substantive collaborations to help meet project goals and objectives, to include contributions by partners, and provides letters from partners that confirm and buttress statements in the narrative about partner roles and contributions.
- Applicant proposes to include a school or district service-learning advisory committee that represents key stakeholders and will contribute to project design and implementation.
- <u>Renewal school and district infrastructure applicants</u> describe clear plans to seek short- and long-term project support and to strengthen or expand existing partnerships to meet project objectives.

4. Evaluation Plan Narrative Questions 20%

Describe plans to submit final report that includes (in addition to a narrative description of project activities) the following:

- Outputs: numbers of participants (serving and served), service hours provided, and projects completed; courses involved; products or materials produced; advisory meetings held; and standards addressed. Project what these outputs will be and state how they will be measured/assessed. <u>Additional outputs for renewal school and district infrastructure applicants</u>: numbers of ongoing and new projects, funds raised, trainings provided; and site visits conducted. Project what these outputs will be and state how they will be measured/assessed.
- Service Outcome: One outcome/impact of the project (not a number) on the people, sites, needs, or organization(s) that are served by the project. Effective projects will have students conduct this evaluation through surveys, interviews, focus groups, observations, and reports. Project what this outcome will be and state how it will be measured/assessed.
- <u>Additional for school applicants</u>: Academic Outcome: One academic outcome that can be averaged/aggregated across the students serving (or of a subset of the participants if the project involves many courses and activities). Examples include improvement in grades/in the course(s) involved, GPA, FCAT reading or math scores, skill mastery, or meeting of standards (comparing the students with their previous performance or with other students who did not participate). Project what this outcome will be and state how it will be measured/ assessed.
- <u>Additional for renewal school and district infrastructure applicants</u>: Policy Outcome: One outcome of efforts to have service learning recognized, accepted, and promoted as a strategy and policy tool for meeting district education goals. Project what this outcome will be and state how it will be measured/assessed.

Evaluation Plan Scoring Criteria—20 Points

- Applicant commits to and details plans for a final report that will provide narrative and quantitative detail on project activities, challenges, and accomplishments.
- Proposal includes clear projections and plans to collect key output data on project service hours, activities; courses involved, products or materials; advisory meetings; and standards

addressed. <u>Renewal school and district infrastructure applicants</u> also project numbers of new projects, funds raised, training, and site visits to be conducted and detail how outputs will be measured.

- Proposal includes clear projections and plans to measure an impact/outcome of the service students will do, selects the appropriate assessment to measure the outcome, and involves students in assessment activities.

- <u>School applicants</u> identify and commit to measuring an academic outcome directly related to the curriculum-based need identified for student participants, selects the appropriate assessment to measure the outcome, and projects what the outcome will be.

- <u>Renewal school and district infrastructure applicants</u> identify and commit to measuring a policy outcome that demonstrates the recognition, acceptance, and promotion of service learning as a strategy and policy tool for meeting district education goals, selects the appropriate assessment to measure the outcome, and projects what the outcome will be.

5. Proposal Budget (15%)

- Budget Narrative Form (DOE 101–Attachment 2). Provide a clear breakdown and calculation by category of the resources needed to support the project.

   For school projects, no more than 50% of the total request may support salaries and benefits for project coordination, planning, extra duty time, evaluation, and supervision. Requests should be directly related to proposed service-learning activities and appropriate to meet proposed goals and objectives. Include up to $750 for expenses to attend a required sub-grantee meeting to be held in fall 2004 in Orlando.

- Budget Justification and Match (up to 2 pages, Attachment 5). Complete the Budget Justification and Match, explaining major requests and detailing required cash and/or in-kind match. Match should only include contributions that are focused on project goals and objectives and are reasonable and realistic. Most budget cuts occur because of insufficient explanation of items in the budget.

Proposal Budget Scoring Criteria—15 Points

- Cost-basis for expenditures is explained.
- Convincing justification is provided for all major budget items.
- All expenditures are necessary to achieve project objectives.
- Claimed match is realistic, will directly support project efforts, and represents a clear commitment by partners to help the project succeed.

<u>A score of 70% is the minimum standard of the Florida Department of Education to approve a project for funding. Project staff will review applications. Program and budget recommendations are subject to modification.</u>

Fiscal Requirements

Awards are designed to support service learning and build the infrastructure to initiate, improve, expand, and sustain such activities. Allowable expenditures may support activities to prepare for, design, develop lesson plans or curricula for, secure teaching or raw materials/supplies for, train for, travel to, engage in, demonstrate learning from, reflect on, evaluate, report on, coordinate, promote, teach others about, or recognize student service learning.

Substitute, trainer, and consultant costs are counted as salary. Driver salary and benefits are considered transportation expenses. School project budget requests cannot exceed 50% of the total for salary and benefits.

Restrictions on expenditures include the following:

- Travel/trips supported by grant funds can only be (1) to provide service, (2) to familiarize students with service sites or prepare them for service-learning activities, (3) to attend service-learning training or provide training or assistance to others interested in service learning, and (4) to attend the required sub-grantee meeting—include up to $750 for expenses associated with attending this meeting, to be held in fall 2004 in Orlando (per diem, hotel, tolls, mileage, substitutes, etc.).
- Award funds cannot pay for general field trips, travel to conferences not related to service learning, travel to recognition or award ceremonies, or reward trips.
- Grant funds may not be used for indirect or administrative expenses. The applicant may claim its district state-approved indirect rate as match for the project.
- Funds cannot be spent on stipends, allowances, or other financial incentives for students or service beneficiaries except to reimburse transportation, meals for out-of county travel (see next item), or other reasonable out-of-pocket expenses directly related to the project.
- Funds may not be used to pay for food or refreshments other than those associated with (1) out-of-county travel (at the state rate of $21 per day) or (2) training in remote locations that would be disrupted if participants had to travel to procure food.
- A small portion of funds may be spent on identification items (such as T-shirts that students design and wear while performing activities), recognition, and awards. Awards should be primarily symbolic in nature (certificates, ribbons, etc.).
- Funds cannot buy "off-the-shelf" gifts for service recipients (food, flowers, cards, etc.).
- Florida Learn & Serve is not designed to purchase books for school libraries or to supplant funding for regular school materials and supplies.
- Proposals for school-site plant beautification, landscaping, ornamental gardens, outdoor classrooms, nature trails, boardwalks, purchasing greenhouses, or similar projects <u>cannot be funded</u>. On-site environmental projects such as growing food for the needy, plant/feed areas for birds and butterflies being studied, energy audits, water testing (other than at manmade holding ponds), and exotic removal <u>can be funded</u>.
- Funds may support after-school programs—such as tutoring, coaching, or conflict mediation—<u>if</u> the student service learning is provided as part of or as an assignment for a credit-bearing class.

Funds do not support the purchase of equipment (cameras, TVs, VCRs, computers, printers, etc.) unless all three criteria below are met. These criteria are also applied to other permanent or large budget items, including salary, supplies, materials, transportation, and consultants:

1. The item is critical to the project; i.e., the project cannot meets objectives without it.
2. Evidence is provided that there is no other way to pay for, obtain, or use the item.
3. The dedicated and permanent use of the item will be for service learning.

Required Attachments

- Project Application Form (DOE 100A)

- Budget Narrative Form (DOE 101) This information will be considered as part of the score for the Budget section, which is worth 15% of the overall score.

- Budget Justification and Match (Attachment 5 – template) Provide an explanation and justification for all major budget requests as well as a listing and accounting of cash and in-kind contributions provided by project partners. This information will be considered as part of the score for the Budget section, which is worth 15% of the overall score.

- Letters of Commitment from Primary Partners, and other attachments up to 6 pages.

Place the DOE 100A and DOE 101 forms in the front of the proposal, followed by the Budget Justification and Match, the project narrative, and attachments.

Method of Answering Frequently Asked Questions or Providing Changes or Addenda

Frequently asked questions received by phone or at application workshops, any changes in dates, clarifications, or addenda to the RFP will be posted on the project web site (http://www.fsu.edu/~flserve/). The last date that questions will be answered is April 27, 2004. A series of free Proposal Technical Assistance Workshops will be provided statewide in March. See Attachment 3 for locations, dates, and times of these workshops.

Notice of Intent to Apply

The deadline date to notify the contact person of intent-to-apply is April 1, 2004. However, providing the intent-to-apply is not required for an application to be considered. In addition, eligible organizations that file an intent-to-apply are not required to apply.

Method of Selection

A cadre of service-learning practitioners statewide will review proposals. Reviewers will be trained and instructed to review proposals based on the evaluation criteria in this RPF. Every proposal will have at least three reviews, and proposals will be ranked based on average scores. Applicant scores will guide the program office's recommendations for funding to the Commissioner of Education. The minimum score required by the DOE to recommend a project for funding is 70.

Implementation Requirements

Requests for project amendments, extensions, early terminations, or other changes will be addressed using rules and procedures outlined in the <u>Project Application and Amendment Procedure for Federal and State Programs Administered by the Department of Education</u> (Green Book).

Reporting Outcomes

By January 31, 2005, awardees will submit a mid-year progress report giving an update on how the project is progressing toward meeting matching requirements and objectives stated in the awardees proposal. By October 20, 2005, awardees shall submit a final report addressing requirements described in the Proposal Instructions. By October 20, 2005, awardees shall submit financial reports to the Comptroller at the DOE. Awardees shall also submit (at a date to be determined) a required report summarizing project outputs/numbers to the Corporation for National and Community Service.

Attachments to the RFP

1. Project Application Form (DOE 100A)

2. Budget Narrative Form (DOE 101)

3. Proposal Technical Assistance and Workshop Schedule

4. School-Based Service Learning: Definitions, Examples, and Resources

5. Budget Justification and Match Templates

COPY

FLORIDA DEPARTMENT OF EDUCATION
PROJECT APPLICATION

TAPS Number

5C006

Please return to:	A) Program Name:	DOE USE ONLY
Florida Department of Education Bureau of Grants Management Room Turlington Building 325 West Gaines Street Tallahassee, Florida 32399-0400 Telephone: (850) Suncom:	**Florida Learn & Serve 2004-2005 School Project: Marine Studies Program** Monroe	Date Received *2004 APR 29 10: 55 BUREAU OF GRANTS MANAGEMENT RECEIVED*

B) Name and Address of Eligible Applicant:	Project Number (DOE Assigned)
Coral Shores High School 89901 Old Highway Tavernier, FL 33070	

C) Total Funds Requested:	D) Applicant Contact Information	
$ 12,000.00		
DOE USE ONLY Total Approved Project: $12,000.00	Contact Name: David Makepeace	Mailing Address: 89901 Old Highway Tavernier, FL 33070
	Telephone Number: 305- 853-3222 x327	SunCom Number:
	Fax Number: 305-853-3228	E-mail Address: makepeaced@monroe.k12.fl.us

CERTIFICATION

I, John R. Padget, do hereby certify that all facts, figures, and representations made in this application are true, correct, and consistent with the statement of general assurances and specific programmatic assurances for this project. Furthermore, all applicable statutes, regulations, and procedures; administrative and programmatic requirements; and procedures for fiscal control and maintenance of records will be implemented to ensure proper accountability for the expenditure of funds on this project. All records necessary to substantiate these requirements will be available for review by appropriate state and federal staff. I further certify that all expenditures will be obligated on or after the effective date and prior to the termination date of the project. Disbursements will be reported only as appropriate to this project, and will not be used for matching funds on this or any special project, where prohibited.

Further, I understand that it is the responsibility of the agency head to obtain from its governing body the authorization for the submission of this application.

E) _____
        Signature of Agency Head

DOE 100A
Revised 01/03

Page 1 of 2

Jim Horne, Commissioner

ATTACHMENT 2

A) <u>CORAL SHORES HIGH SCHOOL</u>
   Name of Eligible Recipient:

B) _____

Project Number: **(DOE USE ONLY)**

TAPS Number
5C006

FLORIDA DEPARTMENT OF EDUCATION
BUDGET NARRATIVE FORM

(1) OBJECT	(2) ACCOUNT TITLE AND NARRATIVE	(3) FTE POSITION	(4) AMOUNT
100	Program Manager Supplement		$ 3,000.00
200	Benefits (17%)		$ 510.00
310	Professional Services: Consultants for RECON training and Artificial Reef Monitoring project supervision		$ 1,400.00
330	Travel for presentations and grantee meeting:		$ 900.00
396	16 Seagrass restoration boat trips @ $200/ trip ($3200), 4 artificial reef monitoring trips and 1 video training trip @ $300/trip ($1500)		$ 4,700.00
510	Equipment and supplies for restoration, aquaculture and Video documentaries		$ 990.00
750	Substitute teachers: Provide coverage Marine Studies Program teacher for grantee meeting, presentations and field activities.		$ 500.00
		C) **TOTAL**	**$ 12,000.00**

Budget Justification

Object	Category	Justification/Explanation	Amount
120	Program manager	Needed for management of budget, compiling reports, maintaining web page, contacting press, supervising field activities on afternoons and weekends and attending grantee and other meetings	$3000.00
200	Benefits: Retirement/ Social Security	For program manager supplement	$510.00
310	Consultants for RECON training and Artificial Reef Monitoring project supervision	RECON and monitoring protocol requires expertise not available without consultants. The cost represents a 75 % discount.	$1400.00
330	Travel for presentations and grantee meeting:	Grantee meeting is required and presentations are part of our dissemination plan	$900.00
510	Equipment and supplies for restoration, aquaculture and Video documentaries	The equipment and supplies are necessary for the activities and there are no funds available from the school budget.	$990.00
396	16 Seagrass restoration boat trips @ $200/ trip ($3200), 4 artificial reef monitoring trips and 1 video training trip @ $300/trip ($1500)	The boat trips are necessary for completion of seagrass restoration, artificial reef monitoring and video documentation.	$4700.00
750	Substitute teachers: Provide coverage Marine Studies Program teacher for grantee meeting, presentations and field activities.	There is no funding for substitute teachers from the school District.	$500.00
	Total requested from F L & S		**$ 12000.00**

Cash and In-Kind Match Contributions

Match Source/Description	How total was Calculated	Cash Match	In-Kind Match	Total Match
Restoration training from NOAA and Florida DEP	8 sessions @ $300/ session.		$2400.00	$2400.00
Seagrass awareness and fundraising event	Proceeds from tickets and silent auction	$1500.00		$1500.00
75 % discounted consultant fee for RECON training and artificial reef monitoring supervision from Loretta Lawrence	20 students X $200 = $4000 X .75 = $3000 4 events X $400 = $1600 X .75 = $1200		$4200.00	$4200.00
2 RECON training trips with Tavernier Dive Center	$600 per trip		$1200.00	$1200.00
50 % discount on 4 artificial reef monitoring trips and 1 Underwater Video Training trip	$600 X .50 = $300/trip = $900		$1500.00	$1500.00
30 complimentary individual dive trips for RECON surveys and 20 complimentary individual dive trips for underwater video	50 trips @ $50/trip = $2500		$2500.00	$2500.00
Aquaculture training from Keys Marine Conservancy	4 sessions @ $200/session		$800.00	$800.00
Juvenile Queen Conch and Diadema specimens from Keys Marine Conservancy	600 specimens @ $2.00/ specimens		$1200.00	$1200.00
Fundraising events	Proceeds from raffle and donations	$1500.00		$1500.00
Total:		**$3000.00**	**$13800.00**	**$16800.00**

Coral Shores High School
Marine Studies Program
An Environmental Project Funding Proposal for:
Florida Learn and Serve
Project Narrative

Needs, Participants, Courses and Standards: Found in the Upper Keys, the Coral Shores High School Marine Studies Program is a project based service learning program. Students enrolled in the 2 credit program pursue a Marine Science credit and either a Research or Television Production credit. The class is offered for the entire year during the last period of Coral Shores High School's 4 X 4 block schedule. *Credit is earned through logs, reflections and web based portfolio.* The students plan their activities and are assessed in part with the assistance of a 47 item Marine Science Learner Outcome Rubric *(attachment 1.)* Enrollment for the Marine Studies Program is projected to be 25 students.

Curriculum-based needs: The student-projects to be performed in the Marine Studies Program satisfy a variety of curriculum needs but by far the most significant need satisfied is the *need for real-world applications* of the Science, Language Arts, Mathematics and Social Studies curriculum. The Marine Studies Program will also provide *day to day opportunities for **inquiry based learning***. The program also helps students **develop work place skills**. As is the nature with all service learning, the students will design and implement activities that are relevant, contextual and engaging. The primary project will be seagrass restoration. Other student-projects will include coral reef and artificial reef assessments and aquaculture. The students will also produce documentary videos and instructional Power Points. Some of these projects will require data analysis and formal reports to agencies and all will require the development of and adherence to strict scientific protocol. Additionally every project will be required to have a detailed description and documentation for the student electronic portfolio.

Sunshine State Standards in Science: In S*cience* the standards that are almost universally addressed by the Marine Studies Program projects are:

1. SC.H.1.4: *The student uses the scientific processes and habits of mind to solve problems.* This standard is addressed from project design through implementation and analysis. Most of the projects are field based and require frequent use of scientific problem solving.
2. SC.G.2.4: *The student understands the consequence of using limited natural resources.* This standard is addressed in most of the monitoring projects. It is also addressed frequently when the students take on an advocacy role related to an environmental issue.
3. SC.F.1.4: *The student describes the structure and function of living things.* This standard is addressed in the fish survey and reef assessment projects as well as the aquaculture, video and Power Point projects. There are at least 3 other science standards that are frequently addressed in the student projects.

Sunshine State Standards in Language Arts: In *Language Arts* the standards that are most frequently addressed are:

1. LA.A.1.4: *The student uses the reading process effectively.* This standard will be addressed with most of the projects during preparation and at times during analysis.
2. LA.B.2.4: *The student writes to communicate ideas and information effectively.* Along with a more general writing standard this standard will be addressed for the compilation of reports to agencies and while developing scripts for videos and Power Points. For every student project this standard will also be addressed in the production of the web based portfolios and in written reflections.

1

Sunshine State Standards in Mathematics addressed: In *Mathematics* the standard most frequently addressed is:

1. MA.B.1.4: *The student measures quantities in the real world and uses the measures to solve problems.* This standard, along with several other "real world" related mathematics standards, will be addressed in the compilation analysis and reporting of data including seagrass restoration site assessments, fish counts and artificial reef assessment data. Other mathematics standards including those related to metric measurement and use of units of measure will also be also addressed in student-projects.

Other standards addressed: Student-projects like the seagrass restoration project occasionally involve an environmental issue or issues. These issues often have a socioeconomic or governmental connection. In those cases several of the *Social Studies Standards* will be addressed. Because of the use of technology in field work, project implementation and documentation many of the *Applied Technology Standards* will also be addressed in the program.

Community Needs addressed: The Florida Keys has been designated as an **"Area of Critical Concern"** by the State of Florida because of a myriad of environmental problems. Our seagrass habitats and our coral reefs are on the brink of disaster because of boat groundings, loss of biodiversity and water quality problems. An estimated 100,000 acres of seagrass in and around the Keys have been lost in the past 20 years. One of the major causes of seagrass depletion is propeller damage or prop scarring. Restoration of prop scars will be a focal point of this proposal. The coral reefs are experiencing similar problems. Corals are dieing off at a rate so rapid that two species, elk horn and stag horn, are being considered for endangered species status. Assessment of corals reefs and artificial reefs, which may be needed to replace lost habitat, will also be part of this project. The populations of two important reef inhabitants, Diadema sea urchins and queen conch, are less than 5% of their pre-1975 levels. The aquaculture portion of this project will address this problem.

Seagrass Restoration: For this project we plan to restore and monitor at least 100 square meters of prop-damaged seagrass in the nearshore waters of the Upper Keys. Research has shown that without this intervention the prop scars would not heal in less than 7-15 years. We will also host a seagrass awareness event to help reduce future damage. This is a **new project** for this proposal.

Reef Assessment: Using an Ocean Conservancy protocol called RECON or REef CONdition our students will assess the health and biodiversity of our coral reefs. The Florida Keys National Marine Sanctuary covers more than 3000 square miles. Because of staff limitations and the remoteness of some reefs the resource managers can't assess <u>all</u> the reef areas so the data we will provide will help them identify where potential problems may be occurring.

Artificial Reef Habitat Monitoring: From 1999-2001 we produced and deployed concrete modules called "Reef Balls" at 2 sites off the Upper Keys. We plan to conduct semiannual monitoring visits to the 2 sites to provide data for the FKNMS on the efficacy of this method of habitat enhancement. The Florida Keys National Marine Sanctuary (FKNMS) gets several applications for artificial reefs every year. Our data will help FKNMS to develop permit criteria.

Depleted Species Aquaculture: For this project we plan to maintain queen conch and Diadema sea urchin grow-out tanks on our aquaculture "patio" adjacent to our Marine Science room. We will care for the conch and urchins until they are large enough to be released. Both Queen Conch and Diadema produce planktonic larva. Our goal is to create breeding colonies for each species so that they can send their larva all over the reef tract to increase the populations in other areas.

Video Documentaries: For this project, in collaboration with our TV Production program, we plan to use our underwater digital video systems and editing computer to produce video programs for our local cable network, school and presentations. The videos will document the activities of the Marine Studies Program or focus on our local habitat. The videos will increase the awareness of our program, promote service learning and increase awareness of our fragile marine environment.

2

Numbers of students and adults: The enrollment for next years Marine Studies Program is projected to be 25 students. They should be evenly distributed between the 11th and 12th grade. The service activities will be fully integrated into Marine Science, Research and TV Production classes. We estimate that 7 adults from the community will work with Marine Studies students with some participating infrequently while others will interact with the students on almost a daily basis.

Just Read, Florida! Integration: Though the Marine Studies Program is a field based project class there will be a considerable amount of reading done by the students to prepare, implement, analyze and report the activities. The reading done by the Marine Studies students is usually essential to the success of their projects so they actually want to read. Because of the need to read for comprehension and their level of engagement their reading skills are likely to improve dramatically. Also the type of reading they do is often technical in nature. Outside of Vocational classes this type of reading is inconsistently required and needs to be practiced more often. Here is an example of reading integration: A group of students wants to produce a video documentary on the Mangrove Community. Prior to developing a plan for their production they will need to read extensively about the Mangrove Community.

Current/past project activities: This 2004-5 proposal is a continuation of our 2003-4 project with the addition of seagrass restoration as a new and major component. Here is a progress report for the 6 sub-projects of our 2003-4 Florida Learn and Serve project:

Water Quality Sampling for the Village of Islamorada: We proposed to conduct 8 sampling events involving 8 students for each event. We far exceeded or projected student participation with 22 students participating in 4 events in November and 19 students scheduled to participate in April. The project will **continue with Village funding** but is not part of our 2004-5 FL L & S project.

Reef Assessment Training: We proposed to have 6 students become certified as RECON Instructors and then provide training for their classmates. Four students achieved RECON instructor status and helped train all 19 of their classmates. Three of those RECON instructors will be in the program next year and are scheduled to assist in RECON training for their new classmates in August. We will use the training to support our Reef Assessment project described in this proposal.

Dry Tortugas Research Cruise: We proposed that we would have 12 students conduct reef assessments, fish counts and shoot underwater video. We did have 12 students go on the trip. They conducted twelve reef assessments, 20 fish counts and shot more than 2 hours of video. We will return to the Dry Tortugas as part of our Reef Assessment project described in this proposal.

Artificial Reef Monitoring: We proposed to have at least 6 students conduct 2 artificial reef monitoring events, one at each of our 2 sites, in the fall and 2 in the spring. Due to delays in the funding and poor weather we did not conduct the fall monitoring events. We have 2 monitoring events scheduled in early May. To achieve our goal of conducting 2 events in one school year this project will have to carry over until next year. We are including it as part of this proposal.

Depleted Species Aquaculture Project: We proposed to have students maintain a Queen Conch aquaculture facility on our aquaculture patio next to our marine science classroom. Due to delays in the completion of our new school construction the resulting and problems setting up our aquaculture facility the focus of this project was changed to the design and set-up of the facility. With considerable effort from our students we now have all of our tanks and support equipment and all the necessary permits. We have added the Diadema sea urchin for our 2004-5 project.

Web Based Video Documentaries: We proposed to have 6 students produce one video product per month and have it posted on our school web site. Due to the delay in funding the project did not start until January. We have produced 4 video products including a DVD that was shown at the National Service Learning Conference. We are still working with our District web master to get our videos on our web site. Building on our successes and learning from our shortfalls we are planning an improved Video Documentary project for our 2004-5 project.

3

Activities, Elements, Scale and Timeline: Our 2004-5 FL L & S project will involve the 5 sub-projects briefly described in the *Community Needs* section. The science curricular links for each of the 5 student-projects are too numerous to identify so I will refer to the Marine Science Learner Outcome Rubric *(see attachment 1)* for the science curricular links. Other curricular links, including Mathematics and Language Arts, are identified on pages 1 and 2 of this proposal.

Seagrass Restoration: For this **new project** we will assess, restore and monitor at least 100 square meters of prop scars in the nearshore waters of the Upper Keys. We will also host a seagrass awareness event. The event will help make visitors and locals more aware of the importance of seagrass as while serving as a fundraiser for our project. For the seagrass restoration process we will: 1). Select, assess and measure a prop scar site. 2.) Construct a "bird stake" must for every 2 meters of prop scar length. 3.) The bird stakes, 4" 2X4 tops on 1" PVC pipe, will then be deployed. 4.) Birds roost on the stakes and provide natural "fertilizer." 5.) Fast growing Shoal grass is then planted in the spaces between the stakes. 6.) The site is monitored quarterly for 18 months. If the shoal grass has stabilized the damaged area then the stakes are removed. There are at least 14 learner outcomes *(attachment 1)* that are addressed by this project.

Reef Assessment: Using an Ocean Conservancy protocol called RECON or REef CONdition our students will assess the health and biodiversity of our coral reefs. The data becomes part of the Ocean Conservancy international data base on coral reefs. We plan to conduct at least 30 reef assessments in the Upper Keys and the Dry Tortugas. Our current Florida Learn and Serve project enabled three of our returning students to become RECON Instructors. They will train their incoming classmates in the RECON protocol. Derived from our Tortugas and RECON sub-projects of 2003-4 this project addresses at least 16 learner outcomes *(attachment 1)*.

Artificial Reef Habitat Monitoring: For this project, carried over from 2003-4, we plan to conduct 2 monitoring visits per year at each of the 2 artificial reef sites we deployed in 1999-2001 to provide data for the FKNMS on the efficacy of this method of habitat enhancement. We were unable to conduct a monitoring event in the fall because of a delay in funding and bad weather. FKNMS feels the data is more valid if all the monitoring events are conducted by the same groups of students. We will use funds from our current project, assuming we get an extension, for 2 September monitoring events and funds from this proposal for 2 more events in April or May. There are at least 16 learner outcomes *(attachment 1)* that are addressed by this project.

Depleted Species Aquaculture: For this project, an expansion of our 2003-4 project in partnership with Keys Marine Conservancy, we plan to maintain Queen Conch and Diadema sea urchin grow-out tanks on our "aquaculture patio" adjacent to the Marine Science room at Coral Shores. We used funds from our 2003-4 project to design and construct our aquaculture facility. We will care for the conch and urchins until they are large enough to release in breeding colonies at specific locations on the reef. There are at least 8 learner outcomes *(attachment 1)* that are addressed by this project.

Video Documentaries: For this project, a continuation of collaboration with the TV Production program, we plan to use our underwater digital video systems and editing computer to produce at least 8 video documentaries for our local cable network, our school and for presentations. Some of the videos will document the activities of the Marine Studies Program while others will be used to educate other students and community members about our marine environment. It is possible for every learner outcome *(attachment 1)* to be addressed by this project.

Reflection and recognition: Oral and written reflection will occur continuously throughout every project. A directed reflective writing assignment is done at the end of each semester. Recognition will occur through the newspaper articles and the videos that are shown locally and at conferences or posted to the web and through web-based portfolios for each student. The student web-based portfolios will also serve as a reflection.

Frequency and total service hours: For the 5 sub-projects we estimate **2090** hours of service for an average of **83.6 hours per student** will be provided.

Seagrass Restoration: 25 students X 2 hours X 6 restoration events =	300 hours
Reef Assessment: 30 assessments X 5 hours =	150 hours
Artificial Reef Monitoring: 10 students X 4 monitoring events X 8 hours =	320 hours
Aquaculture: 3 students X 260 days (5 per week for calendar year) X 1 hour =	780 hours
Web Based Video: 6 students X 90 days X 1 hour =	540 hours
Total:	**2090 hours**

Timeline:

Project/ Month	Seagrass Restoration	Reef Assessments	Artificial Reef Monitoring	Depleted Species Aquaculture	Video Documentaries
Aug.	Select site(s)	Training	Training	Training/set-up	Training
Sept.	Assess site(s)	6 assessments	2 mon. events	Maintain tanks	Planning
Oct.	Restore site(s)	6 assessments		Maintain tanks	1 Product
Nov.		6 assessments		Maintain tanks	1 Product
Dec.				Maintain tanks	1 Product
Jan.	Monitor			Maintain tanks	1 Product
Feb.				Maintain tanks	1 Product
Mar.				Maintain tanks	1 Product
April	Monitor	6 assessments	2 mon. events	Maintain tanks	1 Product
May		6 assessments		Maintain tanks	1 Product
June				Maintain tanks	
July	Monitor			Maintain tanks	

Partnerships: For the 5 sub-projects in this proposal we have 7 community partners. We also are collaborating with the Television Production teacher, Jill Stevens. Here are our partners and their roles:

Ocean Conservancy: Through the efforts of local Ocean Conservancy representative Loretta Lawrence, our students will be provided with survey equipment, a training CD and training and supervision as they receive their RECON training and conduct reef assessments and artificial reef monitoring. Mrs. Lawrence will be compensated at 25% of her usual fee for RECON training and research supervision. She will also serve on the **Marine Studies Program Advisory Committee.** This is a continuation and expansion of our current partnership.

Florida Keys National Marine Sanctuary (FKNMS): FKNMS staff will provide support and feedback for the development and refinement of monitoring protocols for our Artificial Reef Habitat sites. Sanctuary staff will also provide support and training for our Seagrass Restoration project. This is a continuation and expansion of our current partnership.

Keys Marine Conservancy: Keys Marine Conservancy will provide 500 juvenile Queen Conch and 100 juvenile Diadema specimens as well as training for the set-up and maintenance of an aquaculture hatchery and grow-out facility at Coral Shores High School. Jack Sievers, from Keys Marine Conservancy, will serve on the **Marine Studies Program Advisory Committee.** This is an expansion of our existing partnership. In the future, when Keys Marine Conservancy completes their aquaculture facility, we plan additional collaboration including possible internships.

Village of Islamorada: The village will provide input and possible funding for our Seagrass Restoration Project. Zully Williams, Village Public Works Director, will serve on the **Marine Studies Program Advisory Committee.** This represents an expansion of a successful partnership.

5

Tavernier Dive Center: One of our dive shop partners, Tavernier Dive Center, will provide up to 50 complimentary individual dive trips. They will provide 2 RECON training trips at no charge and 5 additional trips will cost half of the usual $600 charter rate for the 25 passenger vessel. Mike Ho Sing Loy, the owner of Tavernier Dive Center, will also serve on our **Marine Studies Program Advisory Committee.** This represents a continuation and expansion of a successful partnership.

NOAA Damage Assessment team: Sean Meehan and at least one colleague from the NOAA Damage Assessment team will provide training and supervision for our Seagrass Restoration project. He will also secure all our permits. This represents a new partnership.

Advisory Committee: The Advisory Committee is drawn from our partners and includes: Loretta Lawrence from Ocean Conservancy, Jack Sievers from Keys Marine Conservancy, Zully Williams from the Village of Islamorada and Mike Ho Sing Loy from Tavernier Diver Center. The members of the Advisory Committee will provide assistance in fund raising efforts, act as a resource for students and participate in long range planning for the program. Other members may be added.

Evaluation Plan: The program will be managed so the items required for the annual progress report will be generated on a continual basis. Most if not all of the data and information will be produced by the students as part of their documentation requirements.

Description of Project Activities: The description of project activities will be taken from the narrative descriptions of each project that every student is required to provide as part of their electronic portfolio.

Outputs: In the final directed reflective writing each student will be asked to provide the number of hours served, projects completed, credits earned and trainings completed. The Learner Outcome Rubric *(attachment1)* is already correlated to the Sunshine State Standards in Science. Data for Sunshine State Standards in Language Arts and Mathematics are recorded electronically in our electronic grade book for other accountability purposes. This data is easily transcribed for the annual progress report.

Academic Outcome: All student activities are recorded by the corresponding learner outcome on the Learner Outcome Rubric *(attachment 1)*. The academic progress in science for each student is assessed through the web portfolios and the Learner Outcome Rubric. The TV Production students will have a similar rubric. Academic progress of the program will be evaluated by compiling the data from all the student rubrics.

Affective Outcomes: Attitude related questions will be provided on the directed reflective writing assignments that are given throughout the year.

Service Outcomes: Service outcomes for each project will be evaluated by the following criteria:

> *Seagrass Restoration:* **At least 100 square meters of seagrass** will be restored.
>
> *Reef Assessment:* **At least 30 RECON assessments** will be completed.
>
> *Artificial Reef Habitat Monitoring Project:* Monitoring **trips to each of our artificial reef sites** will be done in the **fall** and again in the **spring**. The reports of those trips will be delivered to the Florida Keys National Marine Sanctuary office.
>
> *Depleted Species Aquaculture Project:* The **aquaculture tanks** at Coral Shores High School will be **successfully stocked and maintained** by Marine Studies students.
>
> *Web Based Video Documentaries:* Production of **at least 8 video products** during the school year.

Service Learning Dissemination Activities: Even though this is not a dissemination grant one of the goals of this project is to promote service learning throughout our District and beyond. We will do so by **posting our projects and portfolios on our web page**. We will also **make a presentation** about our program to: the **Monroe County School Board**, at least **two community organizations** and a minimum of **one state or national conference**. We will **solicit newspaper articles** and attempt to get some of our **video products** on our **local cable** channel.

Marine Science Learner Outcomes

We are only including pages 1 and 4 of the learner outcome rubric because of 6 page limitation on attachments

1 of 4

Marine Science Learner Outcomes	Documentation of mastery:	Points:			
		1	2	3	4
1. History: The learner will: 1.1 identify significant advances in ocean exploration.					
2. Physical / Chemical Oceanography: The learner will: 2.1 determine the temperature of a water sample.					
2.2 determine the salinity of a water sample.					
2.3 determine the dissolved oxygen level of a water sample.					
2.4 determine the nutrient concentration of a water sample.					
2.5 measure the turbidity of a body of water.					
2.5 determine the location of a thermocline in a body of water.					
2.6 compile and analyze water quality data.					
2.7 describe the relationship to the health of the ecosystem: a. dissolved oxygen					
b. salinity					
c. temperature					
e. nutrient concentration					
Comments:		Page Total:			
		1	2	3	4

Documentation of mastery:	Points:			
	1	2	3	4
8. Humans and the marine environment: The learner will:				
8.1 identify the natural and human threats to the survival of the mangrove community in the Keys.				
8.2 identify the natural and human threats to the survival of the seagrass communities in the Keys				
8.3 identify the natural and human threats to the survival of the Coral Reefs.				
8.4 identify examples of local endangered species.				
8.5 describe the importance of good water quality in the Keys marine environment.				
8.6 describe the relationship between submerged cultural resources and the marine environment.				
8.7 describe the role of artificial reefs in the coral reef ecosystem				
9. Marine Resource Management: The learner will:				
9.1 identify the relationship in the Keys between a healthy marine environment and the economy.				
10. Marine Related Careers: The learner will:				
10.1 investigate career opportunities related to the marine environment.				
10.2 investigate and apply aquaculture sciences				
Comments:				
	Page Total:			
	Semester Total:			
	1	2	3	4

April 13, 2004

David Makepeace
Coral Shores High School
89901 Old Highway
Tavernier, FL 33070

Dear Mr. Makepeace,

I welcome the opportunity to write this letter of support for the Coral Shores High School Marine Studies Program and its Florida Learn and Serve funding proposal. Keys Marine Conservancy has been a partner for the Marine Studies Program for more than two years. We are committed to a continued and expanded role next year and in future years.

Keys Marine Conservancy will provide 500 juvenile Queen Conch and 100 Diadema specimens for the grow-out facility at Coral Shores High School. The estimated value of the juvenile specimens is at least $3.00. We will also provide training for the set-up and maintenance of the aquaculture tanks. As President of Keys Marine Conservancy, I will serve on the Marine Studies Program Advisory Committee.

Please feel free to forward this letter to any and all appropriate agencies. They may contact me at 305-393-3561 if they have any questions.

Sincerely,

Jack Sievers
President, Keys Marine Conservancy

April 9, 2004

David Makepeace
Coral Shores High School
89901 Old Highway
Tavernier, FL 33070

Dear Mr. Makepeace,

I have been a partner and supporter of the Coral Shores High School Marine Studies Program for more than three years. I am writing this letter of support for the program and their Florida Learn and Serve funding proposal.

As a RECON trainer for Ocean Conservancy and longtime steward of the Keys marine resources I will provide:

- Survey Equipment
- Training CD
- Training and Supervision
- RECON Assessment
- Artificial Reef Monitoring

The training and monitoring supervision will be provided at a 75% discount off my normal rate so that I may cover my expenses. I will also serve on the Marine Studies Program Advisory Committee.

Please feel free to forward this letter to any and all appropriate agencies. They may contact me at 305-664-9204 or 305-924-1384 if they have any questions.

Sincerely,

Loretta Lawrence
LorettaLawrence@aol.com

MAYOR CHRIS SANTE
VICE MAYOR MARK GREGG
COUNCILMAN MIKE FORSTER

COUNCILMAN ROBERT JOHNSON
COUNCILMAN MICHAEL RECKWERDT

April 13, 2003

David Makepeace
Coral Shores High School
89901 Old Hwy
Islamorada, FL 33070

RE: *Funding Request*

Dear Mr. Makepeace:

It is with great pleasure that Islamorada, Village of Islands writes a letter of support for the funding request by the Marine Studies Program at Coral Shores High School.

As a member of the Marine Studies Program Service Learning Advisory Committee I will represent the Village's desire to support the program as it truly enhances the educational experience of the students. I will provide support for and work toward finding long term funding for the Seagrass Restoration project. I will also assist in other fundraising efforts.

Please feel free to forward this letter to the appropriate agency considering funding the grant application submitted by the Marine Studies Program at Coral Shores High School.

Please feel free to contact me at (305) 664-2345, if you have any questions.

Sincerely,

Zully Williams
Public Works Director

c: Bernie LaPira, Village Manager

P.O. Box 568, Islamorada, FL 33036
305.664.2345 FAX 305.853.5357 www.islamorada.fl.us

TAVERNIER DIVE CENTER

April 9, 2004

David Makepeace
Coral Shores High School
89901 Old Highway
Tavernier, FL 33070

Dear Mr. Makepeace,

It is with great enthusiasm that I write this letter of support for the Coral Shores High School Marine Studies Program and its Florida Learn and Serve funding proposal. Tavernier Dive Center has been a long time supporter of the Marine Studies Program and we look forward to our expanded role next year.

As part of that expanded role Tavernier Dive Center will provide space for not more than 4 individual divers on any dive trip on which there is room. We will provide up to 50 complimentary individual dive trips. We will also take 2 RECON training trips at no charge. Any additional trips will cost half of the usual $600 charter rate for our 25 passenger vessel. Mike Ho Sing Loy, the owner and president of Tavernier Dive Center, will also serve on the Marine Studies Program Advisory Committee.

Please feel free to forward this letter to any and all appropriate agencies. They may contact me at 305-852-4007 if they have any questions.

Sincerely,

Mike Ho Sing Loy
President, Tavernier Dive Center

P.O. Box 465 • Mile Marker 90.7 • Tavernier, FL 33070
305-852-4007 • 800-787-9797 • FAX 305-852-0869

APPLICANT CHECKLIST

PLEASE COMPLETE AND RETURN WITH PROPOSAL

☑ DOE 100A – Project Application Form
☑ DOE 101 – Budget Narrative Form
☑ Budget Justification and Match Section (up to 2 single-spaced pages)
☑ Proposal Narrative (up to 6 single-spaced numbered pages, including required timeline)
☑ Attachments (up to 6 pages)
☑ Applicant Checklist

Please check the appropriate box to indicate the type of project proposed:
    ☒ School-Based Service-Learning Project
    ☐ District Infrastructure-Building Project

A. School Contact Information (if applicable)
    1. Name of School: CORAL SHORES HIGH SCHOOL
    2. Project Coordinator at the School: DAVID MAKEPEACE
    3. E-mail Address: makepeaced@monroe.K12.fl.us
    4. Phone Number: 365-853-3222 x 327
    5. Fax Number: 365-853-3228
    6. Mailing Address: 89901 OLD HIGHWAY
        TAVERNIER, FL 33070

B. District Contact Information
    1. Project Title: MARINE STUDIES PROGRAM
    2. Project Contact at the District Level: MIKE HENRIQUEZ
    3. E-mail Address: henriquezm@monroe.K12.fl.us
    4. Phone Number: 305-293-1400 x 389
    5. Fax Number: 365 293 1485
    6. Mailing Address: 241 TRUMBO ROAD
        KEY WEST, FL 33040

C. Project Information
Please check the box(es) that best describe(s) the type of project proposed:
    ☐ Reading
    ☐ Civics/History
    ☐ Drug/Violence Prevention
    ☐ Intergenerational Interaction
    ☒ Environmental

DISCLOSURE OF LOBBYING ACTIVITIES
Complete this form to disclose lobbying activities pursuant to 31 U.S.C. 1352
(See reverse for public burden disclosure.)

Approved by OMB
0348-0046

1. Type of Federal Action:	2. Status of Federal Action:	3. Report Type:
☐ a. contract b. grant c. cooperative agreement d. loan e. loan guarantee f. loan insurance	☐ a. bid/offer/application b. initial award c. post-award	☐ a. initial filing b. material change **For Material Change Only:** year _____ quarter _____ date of last report _

4. Name and Address of Reporting Entity: ☐ Prime ☐ Subawardee Tier _____, *if known*: Congressional District, *if known*: 4c	5. If Reporting Entity in No. 4 is a Subawardee, Enter Name and Address of Prime: Congressional District, *if known*:
6. Federal Department/Agency:	7. Federal Program Name/Description: CFDA Number, *if applicable*: _____
8. Federal Action Number, *if known*:	9. Award Amount, *if known*: $
10. a. Name and Address of Lobbying Registrant (*if individual, last name, first name, MI*):	b. Individuals Performing Services (*including address if different from No. 10a*) (*last name, first name, MI*):

11. Information requested through this form is authorized by title 31 U.S.C. section 1352. This disclosure of lobbying activities is a material representation of fact upon which reliance was placed by the tier above when this transaction was made or entered into. This disclosure is required pursuant to 31 U.S.C. 1352. This information will be available for public inspection. Any person who fails to file the required disclosure shall be subject to a civil penalty of not less than $10,000 and not more than $100,000 for each such failure.	Signature: _____ Print Name: _____ Title: _____ Telephone No.: _____ Date: _____
Federal Use Only:	Authorized for Local Reproduction Standard Form LLL (Rev. 7-97)

PROPOSAL #5

Investor Relations
Environmental
Subsidiaries
Press Room
About Us

NiSource

What's Happening   EH&S Policy   Climate Change Policy   Our Organization   Environmental Challenge Fund   Metrics   Progress Report   Press Releases
Contact Us

Contact Us
Site Map
Search

Environmental

Back to Environmental Challenge Fund

**Environmental Challenge Fund
Guidelines and Application Form**

WHO IS ELIGIBLE?

- 501 (c) (3) organizations or other non-profit organizations as determined by the Internal Revenue Service whose projects enhance, protect or preserve the environment, produce a tangible result, and have a direct impact in the markets served by NiSource companies.
- Organizations who serve the community without discrimination based on race, color, sex, age, religion, national or ethnic origin or physical disability.

PROJECT CRITERIA

The Fund seeks to support restoration, natural resource enhancement, and wildlife habitat improvement projects, that are concrete in nature and for which the planning has already been completed. In other words, the applicant should have already identified the actual restoration/enhancement work they want to do and simply be seeking funding for that work. Educational initiatives are supported only when they involve students/volunteers actively performing environmental work. Project must be completed within 3 years of award date. Failure to complete project could result in forfeiture of award balance due.

Along those lines, the ECF is not designed to support the following:

- Trails
- Landscaping or beautification projects
- Surveys/Studies/Monitoring/Retention of Consultants
- Infrastructure items - e.g. benches, signage, etc.
- Salaries/compensation for those involved in the project
- Printed eductional materials such as flyers
- Land aquisition

EVALUATING GRANT REQUESTS

- Awards may be granted up to 80 percent of the total cost of the project. Broad-based support and multiple partners, especially on larger projects, will be looked upon favorably in the review process.
- Awards are made on the basis of direct environmental benefits; certain educational aspects and recreational features that are essential to the overall success of the project may also be considered for funding. If the proposed project will spawn new ideas/approaches or lead to additional activities or projects this information should also be reflected in your responses.
- The Environmental Challenge Fund Advisory Committee uses a consistent method to evaluate requests focusing on the following areas: quality, strategic potential, community impact/public benefit and management.

FUNDING

- This is a small grants program. Partial project funding is possible. It is anticipated that project awards will be between $500 and $5,000. Occasionally, for exceptional projects, the Fund may grant requests of up to $10,000. An initial payment of 75% of the grant is funded with the remaining 25% paid upon proof of project completion.

REPORTING

- The Environmental Challenge Fund Advisory Committee may request interim reports on the status of the project. A final report is required with documentation of results (including pictures and accounting of all grant monies) at the completion of the project. Please note that you may receive a site visit from representatives of the ECF to evaluate the progress of your project at any point during the award period.

SUBMITTAL GUIDELINES

1. The form form below is to be used for project submittal.

2. Incomplete applications will not be considered. If a section does not apply, type "not applicable."

3. Applications will be accepted from November 1 through February 28, with awards being announced on Earth Day in April.

4. **Submit online** using the Online Grant Proposal Form below.

5. If you have any questions, please call 219-647-5246 or 219-647-5253.

    IMPORTANT - All future correspondence must reference the exact project name and award period.

Grant Proposal Form - Columbia Gas of Pennsylvania & Columbia Gas of Maryland

Date	
Project Name	
Organization	
Tax Exempt ID Number 501(c)(3) & State Registered In	
Address	
City, State, ZIP	
Email Address	
Phone	Fax
Contact Person	Title
County	
Project Location	
Project Location (Line 2)	
Requested Amt	
Total Project Budget	

Project Overview

1. Please provide a project description. Be as specific as possible concerning the type of project you are proposing including a timetable for its completion and the procedures and personnel you will utilize to complete it.

- Estimated completion date (maximum 3 years from date of award):

2. Why is your project important to the environment and your community? Be specific about the goals and objectives of your project and how you will achieve them. How is this project consistent with your organization's mission and long range plans?

3. What criteria will you use to evaluate the success of your project upon its completion?

05.11.05 13.35

4. What permits/access agreements, if any, are necessary? Have they been obtained?

5. Is any NiSource employee involved/volunteering in your organization? If so, please provide information.

Project Evaluation & Sustainability

6. How will you ensure that the project continues to meet the goals outlined in Question 2 including maintenance activities required to sustain the project?

Budget

7. Total Project Budget

8. This Grant Request (This can be no more than 80% of the project total)

9. Itemize all cash and in-kind contribution and list their sources. (You must list required additional support of at least 20% of the project total.)

NiSource Inc.

10. Describe in detail, how would this grant money be allocated?

[Submit Grant Proposal Application] [Reset]

Source: Reprinted with permission of NiSource Inc. © 2005.

Tayamentasachta – Wetland Improvement and Alternate Energy Demonstration Project

Date: 15 January 2004
Project Name: Tayamentasachta – Wetland Improvement and Alternate Energy Demonstration Project
Organization: Greencastle-Antrim SD Education Foundation
Tax Exempt ID # & State Registered In: 36-4491930; Pennsylvania
Address: 500 East Leitersburg Street, Greencastle, PA 17225
E-mail Address: taces@innernet.net
Phone: (717) 597-6458
Contact Person: Charles White, Director
County: Franklin
Project Location: Tayamentasachta, A Center for Environmental Studies
    500 E. Leitersburg Street, Greencastle, PA 17225
Requested Amount: $4,700
Total Project Budget: $7,205

PROJECT OVERVIEW

Project Description

Tayamentasachta, a Center for Environmental Studies, is a part of the Greencastle-Antrim School District. It is located in rural Franklin County in south-central Pennsylvania, along the Mason-Dixon line. Tayamentasachta was established in 1966 after the school district purchased a 35-acre farm adjacent to its campus. The district and community is so committed to environmental studies that Tayamentasachta has employed a full-time director since its inception. Tayamentasachta hosts programs for all 2,500 students in the district as well a wide assortment of activities and programs for the wider community. With over 14,000 visitors each year, Tayamentasachta plays an important role in teaching ecological responsibility and how to live in harmony with the earth.

In the mid-1970s, a high school environmental science class designed a wetland in a former erosion sedimentation basin for the elementary school that was located between the elementary building and Tayamentasachta. Students planted over 35 species of plants native to wetlands in Pennsylvania. In addition, a bridge was designed and installed over the wetland to facilitate observation of plant and animal life.

This project is two-pronged. First, the high school environmental science class, working in conjunction with Tayamentasachta's Director and a NiSource Columbia Gas technician, will research solar energy, design and install a solar water pump on the Center's windmill to move water from a spring-fed pond at the Center to the student-made wetland, approximately 300 feet away. The installation of the solar pumping system will allow the area to stay wet year-round. To compliment this effort, two signs will be installed: one - a lexan sign describing the importance of wetlands to the environment and two - an interpretive sign explaining the importance of using alternate sources of energy (solar and wind).

Second, the environmental studies class will research hydroelectric power, design and install a low headwater turbine in the spillway of the Center's pond. The electricity generated will be used to run a 12 or 24-volt pump to irrigate flower and vegetable gardens at Tayamentasachta and aerate pond water to reduce nitrate levels. An interpretive sign will also be designed and installed.

Timetable:

Fall 2004: High School Environmental Studies students, with assistance from Tayamentasachta's Director and a NiSource Columbia Gas technician, will research solar energy, design a pumping system that helps to maintain the wetland at the Center.

Spring 2005: (1) High School Environmental Studies students will design and install a sign that explains the importance of wetlands to the environment. (2)The solar energy system will be installed onto an existing windmill and students will design and install a sign explaining solar and wind energy and its benefits to the environment.

Fall 2005: High School Environmental Studies students, with assistance from Tayamentasachta's Director and a NiSource Columbia Gas technician, will research hydroelectric power and design a pumping system that will be used to irrigate vegetable and flower gardens at the Center. This pumping system will also be used to aerate the pond water to reduce a high nitrate problem.

Spring 2006: High School Environmental Studies students, with assistance from Tayamentasachta's Director and a NiSource Columbia Gas technician, will install the hydroelectric system into the pond's spillway. Students will design and install a sign explaining hydroelectric energy and its benefits to the environment.

Estimated project completion date: June 2006

Why is the project important?

The primary goal of Tayamentasachta, A Center for Environmental Studies, is to educate students and community members in aspects of ecological responsibility through environmental education and interpretive programming. With its inception 38 years ago, Tayamentasachta has become a living laboratory for environmental investigation and demonstration projects.

The goal of this project is to enhance the living laboratory at Tayamentasachta by using alternate energies to (1) sustain the wetland and (2) provide irrigation to student and community gardens at the center and reducing the nitrate level in the pond while teaching students and community members the value and uses of alternative energy sources.

The outcomes expected as a result of this project include:
    (1) Improved species diversity in wetland area (plant, bird, wildlife)
    (2) Reduced nitrate level in Tayamentasachta's pond
    (3) Improved garden access to water through pumping system
    (4) Increased understanding of the importance of wetlands and alternate energy
       sources by students and community members

Evaluation of project success?

The primary measure of success for this project will be the installation of the solar and hydroelectric systems at Tayamentasachta to accomplish the outcomes listed above. The Project Director will keep baseline data documenting the wetland area and pond nitrate level prior to the project and document changes as expected through the installation of the systems outlined.

A secondary measure of success will include an increase in public use for bird and nature watching because of increased species diversity.

No permits are needed to implement this project.

NiSource employee involvement with project/organization:

Columbia Gas and Tayamentasachta Environmental Center have had a successful partnership in the past. A gas line and pumping station bisected the school and environmental center campus. When the line was relocated across the environmental center, Columbia Gas provided Tayamentasachta with funds to plant the borders of the gas line with shrubs native to Pennsylvania. High school students successfully implemented this project as a hands-on interdisciplinary effort.

For this project, Todd Barkdoll, a NiSource utility inspector for the Hagerstown, MD/Greencastle, PA region has agreed to volunteer his assistance for this project. Mr. Barkdoll has been a volunteer at Tayamentasachta on a number of occasions in the past.

Sustainability:

Since 1966, Tayamentasachta has been maintained and staffed by the Greencastle-Antrim School District. The school district and community have a deep commitment to the ongoing efforts of the environmental center. Tayamentasachta is the home for environmental programming for more than 2,500 students and hosts more than 14,000 community visitors annually. A community-based advisory board works with the district to raise funds to sustain programs and initiatives of the Center.

Total Budget: $7,205

Grant Request: $4,700

Cash & In-kind contributions:

$ 125   for 500' of 1" plastic water line (Zarger Plumbing Supply)
$1,030   200 student hours of work @ $5.15/hr

$ 620	20 hours of prep/project time @ $26/hr (HS Environmental Ed teacher & Environmental Center director)
$ 250	3 hours from Vertus Bream solar energy consultant
$ 200	10 hours @ $20/hr from school district plumber & electrician
$ 280	Tayamentasachta Community Advisory Board contribution; mounting brackets for solar panels
$2,505	**TOTAL Cash/in-kind contribution**

Use of Grant Funds

$1,100	2 – 12 or 24 volt DC centrifugal pump
$ 700	100 watt solar panels
$ 400	electrical and plumbing hardware
$1,300	low headwater turbine
$1,200	3 – 2ft x 3ft interpretive signs (wetland, alternative energy, hydroelectric)
$4,700	**TOTAL GRANT REQUEST**

PROPOSAL #6

Application Requirements
For
A.L.L.M.F. Funds Distribution

The Abigail L. Longenecker Memorial Foundation accepts applications from nonprofit organizations in Lancaster County wishing to apply for the foundation's annually distributed funds.

Funding decisions should be made in early March with the funds distributed at the annual skating event on March 13, 2005.

Applicants must be nonprofit organizations in Lancaster County, and the funds requested must be used for specific projects that benefit children.

Applications must be postmarked no later than January 25, 2005 and include the following information:

1. The non profit organization's name, address & phone number and person submitting the application.
2. The organization's mission statement.
3. Detailed description of the project (500 words or less).
4. Total amount of funds requested, showing specific use/breakdown of funds, up to $1000 (one thousand dollars).
5. Approximate number of children affected and the length of time the project will be in place.
6. Names and phone numbers of at least two additional contact persons.

In addition to the application, Please provide:

- Most recent financial statements including sources of funding.
- Copy of organization's 501(c)3 designation from the IRS.

Mail applications to:

The Abigail L. Longenecker Memorial Foundation
P. O. Box 4692
Lancaster Pennsylvania 17604-4692

Questions may be sent to info@abbysfoundation.com

Current applications must include the above information for consideration.

Back to Home Page

ABIGAIL L. LONGENECKER MEMORIAL FOUNDATION
GRANT APPLICATION 2004

1. NAME OF ORGANIZATION <u>Lancaster Emergency Medical Services</u>
<u>Association (LEMSA)</u>

ADDRESS <u>P.O. Box 4652, Lancaster, PA 17604-4652</u>

TELEPHONE <u>481-4841</u>

PERSON SUBMITTING PROPOSAL <u>C. Robert May</u> **TITLE** <u>Exec. Director</u>

CONTACT PERSON <u>same</u> **TITLE** <u>same</u>

TELEPHONE <u>481-4841</u> **FAX** <u>481-4845</u>

2. MISSION STATEMENT

The mission of Lancaster Emergency Medical Services Association (LEMSA) is
to provide comprehensive, proficient, cost efficient pre-hospital care services to
the Lancaster Community. We achieve our mission by providing: primary
emergency health care services to nine municipalities including Basic and
Advanced Life Support Services; an Emergency Medical Services bicycle team
that responds to emergencies in situations where there are large crowds and
vehicles have trouble getting through; education programs for local school
children about how to recognize and respond in an emergency; and CPR
training for adults.

3. AMOUNT REQUESTED FROM FOUNDATION $900.00

4. DETAILED DESCRIPTION OF THE PROJECT AND SPECIFIC USE OF FUNDS

Each year, LEMSA transports approximately 2,000-3,000 children to the
hospital who range in age from infants to age eight. These numbers include
both children who require transport to the hospital for medical attention, and
those whose parent requires transport, however, no one is immediately
available to care for them at the site. In this type of situation, we allow the child
to accompany their parent to the hospital. We would like to request $900 from
the Abigail L. Longenecker Memorial Foundation in order to replace 15 car
seat/booster seats to be placed in 15 of our ambulances. (Our current seats are
over 8 years old and need to be replaced.)

5. NUMBER OF CHILDREN AFFECTED AND LENGTH OF PROJECT

This project will benefit between 2,000-3,000 children ages 6 months to eight years old each year. We will purchase and install the seats as soon as we receive funding notification and expect that the seats will last approximately 5 years.

6. SOURCES OF FUNDING AND MOST RECENT FINANCIAL STATEMENTS

LEMSA receives funding from: local government, individual donors, memberships, businesses, grants, and insurance reimbursement.

Most recent financial statements are enclosed.

7. COPY OF 501(c)3 DESIGNATION FROM IRS

See enclosed.

8. ADDITIONAL CONTACT PERSONS

Mrs. Gladdie McMurtrie, Chair, Board of Directors
Mr. Doug Rinehart, Treasurer

~

APPENDIX A

Federal and Private Websites

~

FEDERAL WEBSITES

Cabinet Departments

Agriculture Department
http://www.usda.gov/

Commerce Department
http://www.osec.doc.gov

Defense Department
http://dtic.dla.mil/

Education Department
http//www.ed.gov/

Energy Department
http://www.doe.gov/

Health and Human Services Department
http:www.hhs.gov

Homeland Security Department
http://www.dhs.gov

Housing and Urban Development
http://www.hud.gov/

Interior Department
http://www.doi.gov/

Justice Department
http://www.usdoj.gov/

Labor Department
http://www.dol.gov/

State Department
http://www.state.gov/

Transportation Department
http://www.dot.gov/

Treasury Department
http://www.ustreas.gov

Veterans Attairs Department
http://www.va.gov

FEDERAL AGENCIES

Corporation for National and Community Service
http://www.nationalservice.org or *http://www.cns.gov*

Environmental Protection Agency
http://www.epa.gov

Institute of Museum and Library Services
http://www.imls.gov

National Aeronautics and Space Administration
http://www.nasa.gov

National Endowment for the Arts
http://www.nea.gov

National Endowment for the Humanities
http://www.neh.gov or *http://www.neh.fed.us*

National Institutes of Health
http://www.nih.gov

National Science Foundation
http://www.nsf.gov or *http://nsf.gov/*

PRIVATE WEBSITES

The *American Philanthropy Review's* site provides information on fundraising. The Review also hosts two popular discussion lists, Talk-AmPhil Rev (a "Big Tent" list covering just about any topic of interest to professionals in the nonprofit sector) and PG-AmPhil Rev (a planned giving discussion list).
http://www.amphilrev.com/

The Association for Fund Raining Professionals (formerly NSFRE) website provides information about education, training, and advocacy for the philanthropic sector.
http://www.afpnet.org

Charity Channel has forum discussion lists, e-newsletters, updated news links, book reviews, interviews, job listings, consultants listings and product/services listings.
http://www.charitychannel.com

Charity Village, a Canadian-based organization, has a site that provides "news, information resources and discussion for the nonprofit community."
http://www.charityvillage.com

Conference Management Enterprises: free meeting planning services for nonprofits.
http://www.qpage.com/host/meetings.shtml

The *Contact Center's* site contains a variety of resources for nonprofits, including a searchable directory and a list of directories available on the Web.
http://www.contact.org

Council on Foundations' site provides a wealth of information for grantseekers.
http://www.cof.org

The *Foundation Center's* site provides information on its five libraries, its publications, seminars, funding trends, and other valuable information.
http://fdncenter.org

Foundations.org provides a directory of foundations and grantmakers.
http://www.foundations.org/index.html

The *Green Book Grants Management* web site is a resource for charter and other public schools looking for grants funding opportunities.
http://www.gbgm.info

Handsnet provides information and training services for nonprofits.
http://www.handnet.org

Hoover's is a subscription-based service that provides in-depth information on thousands of corporations worldwide. The site has a great links page for corporate Web sites.
http://www.hoovers.com

The *Independent Sector's* site provides information on government actions that affect the industry, as well as other organizational information.
http://www.indepsec.org

The *Internet Prospector* website has a reference desk and prospect research sources related to corporations, foundations/grants, people, and tools.
http://www.internet-prospector.org

The *Internet Resources for Nonprofit Public Service Organizations'* site houses links and information for nonprofits.
http://www.sils.umich.edu/~nesbeitt/nonprofits/nonprofits.html

The *Nonprofit Times'* website provides weekly electronic articles on nonprofit management.
http://www.nptimes.com

The *Office of Development Research at Northwestern University's* site contains a valuable links list of prospect and fundraising sites.
http://pubweb.nwu.edu/~sne380/bookmark.html

The *Philanthropy Journal* website has news, resources, and links related to the world and policy information specific to North Carolina.
http://philanthropyjournal.org/

School Grants offers pre-Kindergarten – 12 school grant opportunities and sample proposals.
http://www.schoolgrants.org/

The *SRA International* website has a listing of public, private, and Government grants, and a comprehensive list of public and private funding assistance resources.
http://www.srainternational.org

APPENDIX B

Resources

Books, Directories and Guides

How to Get Grants and Gifts For the Public Schools has helpful ideas and techniques to help make schools competitive in the search for grants, how to set up an education foundation, and how to solicit individuals in the community. This paperback is available from Allyn and Bacon Publishing, 75 Arlington Street, Boston, MA, 02116; http://www.ablongman.com.

The Only Grant-Writing Book You'll Ever Need shows winning strategies for developing grant proposals, including how to identify a compelling need, how to develop programs that will have an impact, and how to build coalitions. This 288-page paperback is available from Carroll and Graf Publishers, Publishing Group West, 1700 Fourth Street, Berkeley, CA, 94710, 1-800-788-3123; http://www.pgw.com.

The following resources are available from Corwin Press, 2455 Teller Road, Thousand Oaks, CA, 91320, 1-805-499-0721: http://www.corwinpress.com:

Finding Funding, Fourth Edition, is for educators interested in winning government, foundation, and private grants for research, programs or special projects. This 392-page paperback costs $49.95.

The First-Time Grantwriter's Guide to Success includes an in-depth review of the application package, expert writing tips, specific techniques for an efficient plan of operation, and advice about budget development. This 152-page paperback costs $24.95.

The Grantwriter's Internet Companion is for educators who want to learn how to use the Internet to find funding and grants. This 128-page paperback costs $24.95.

Simplified Grantwriting is a step-by-step guidebook that will give educators the practical tools that they need to create and write well-constructed and effective grant proposals. This 144-page paperback costs $24.95.

School Technology Funding Directory contains more than 500 grants and funding sources for K–12 technology and expert advice from grantseekers. This 298-page paperback is $20 from eSchool News Communications Group, 7920 Norfolk Avenue, Suite 900, Bethesda, MD, 20814, 301-913-0115; http://www.eschoolnews.com.

The following resources are available from The Foundation Center, 79 Fifth Avenue, New York, NY, 10013, 1-800-424-9836; http://www.fdncenter.org:

The Foundation Directory, 2004 Edition, Parts One and Two, features key facts on the nation's top 20,000 foundations by total giving with over 51,000 descriptions of selected grants. The cost is $215. Also available on CD-ROM, includes links to foundation websites, search tutorials, and 12 search fields. Cost is $495 for single user version and $795 for network version..

The Foundation Grants Index on CD-ROM covers grants of over 1,000 of the largest independent, corporate, and community foundations in the United States and features approximately 125,000 grant descriptions. Cost is $165 for single user version; call for information regarding network version.

Grants Guides are specialized subject directories in the categories of: Arts and Culture, Children and Youth Services, Education, Environmental and Animal Welfare, Health, International, Libraries and Information Services, Religion, and Social Services. Cost is $75 per guide.

The Grantsmanship Center offers CD-ROMs of top-ranked grant proposals in specific subject areas, or you can design a custom-made CD-ROM and select from the proposals that are available. The CD-ROMs for specific subject areas cost $99 each and the custom-made CD-ROMs vary depending on the number of proposals you include. To order, contact The Grantsmanship Center, P.O. Box 17220, Los Angles, CA, 90017; http://www.tgci.com.

The following resources are available from the Greenwood Publishing Group, 88 Post Road West, Westport, CT, 1-800-225-5800; http://www.greenwood.com:

How to Evaluate and Improve Your Grants Efforts offers a dynamic, flexible, and adaptable system for the efficient procurement and administration of external funds and contains helpful worksheets and checklists. This 336-page hardcover costs $44.95.

The "How To" Grants Manual, Fifth Edition, for novice and seasoned grantseekers, provides a historical prospective of grants. It discusses technology, collaboration, and future trends. A CD-ROM accompanies the book. This 304-page hardcover costs $42.50.

Proposal Planning and Writing, Third Edition, assists with developing ideas, identifying funding sources, budget forecasting, submission procedures, and follow-up techniques. This 216-page hardcover costs $39.95.

The following resource is available from Jones and Bartlett Publishers, 40 Tall Pine Drive, Sudbury, MA, 01776, 1-800-832-0034, http://www.jbpub.com.

Grant Application Writers Handbook, Fourth Edition, shows how to plan and develop a good proposal, explains what reviewers look for in an application and discusses changes at the National Institutes of Health and the National Science Foundation. This 416-page paperback costs $44.95.

The following resources are available from Jossey-Bass Publishers, 10475 Crosspoint, Boulevard, Indianapolis, IN, 46256, 1-877-762-2974; http://www.josseybass.com/WileyCDA/:

Approaching Foundations: Suggestions and Insights for Fundraisers provides information about preparing and submitting applications, and emphasizes preparations and tasks to complete before approaching foundations. The 100-page paperback costs $29.

Demystifying Grant Seeking: What You REALLY Need to Do to Get Grants is an inspirational and instructional guide to grantseeking and provides a systematic and logical way of searching for grants. The 272-page hardcover costs $26.95.

Grant Seeker's Budget Toolkit provides step-by-step guidance, insider tips, and all the tools you need to create budgets and financial plans that win grants. This 288-page paperback costs $39.95.

Grant Winner's Toolkit: Project Management and Evaluation provides expert advice and guidance on managing every aspect of a funded project. Includes forms, checklists, timesheets, practice exercises, and other valuable tools. This 392-page paperback costs $39.95.

Grantwriting for Dummies is a reference guide containing information about searching for government grants, how to convey your need, presenting the budget, multiple grant requests, and numerous other topics. This 336-page paperback costs $21.99.

Grassroots Grants: An Activist's Guide to Grantseeking, Second Edition, covers the challenges of incorporating grants into a complete fundraising program, using grant proposals as organizing plans, and fostering effective communication with funders who support the activist community. This 288-page paperback costs $29.

How to Write a Grant Proposal concentrates on all the behind-the-scenes, pre-writing work that makes the difference between successful proposals and those that funders consider "unresponsive." A companion CD-ROM contains guidesheets and templates. This 360-page paperback costs $39.

The Insider's Guide to Grantmaking: How Foundations Find, Fund, and Manage Effective Programs covers the history, structure, and function of foundations and the complex role that program officers play in their day-to-day activities. This 320-page hardcover costs $37.

Storytelling for Grantseekers: The Guide to Creative Nonprofit Fundraising contains the resources needed to help you craft a persuasive synopsis, package a compelling story, create a short-story approach to inquiry, and compose cover letters to support the larger proposal. This 144-page paperback costs $26.

Webster's New World Grant Writing Handbook is a comprehensive, step-by-step guide to grant writing that provides guidance and information needed to succeed. This 336-page paperback costs $16.99.

Winning Grants: Step by Step, Second Edition provides information on how to create a proposal that fulfills important criteria grantmakers demand from a successful request. This 188-page paperback costs $29.

These resources are available from LRP Publications, 1-800-341-7874; http://www.lrpdartnell.com:

Giving By Industry, 2003 Edition is an analytical directory of the philanthropic activity of the nation's largest corporations. This paperback costs $84.95 plus shipping and handling.

Grants for At-Risk Youth, 2004 Edition, contains information about federal and private funders who support at-risk youth and students whop are in danger of dropping out of school. The paperback costs $93 plus shipping and handling.

Sources of Operating Grants, Sixth Edition, helps you quickly locate hard-to-find funding for personnel, administrative, and other non-program related operating expenses. The paperback costs $79.95 plus shipping and handling.

The following resources are available from The Taft Group, Thomson Gale, 27500 Drake Road, Farmington Hills, MI, 48331, 1-800-877-GALE; http://www.gale.com/taft.htm:

Corporate Giving Directory, 27th Edition, contains information on the 1,000 largest corporate giving programs. Features include recent grants; application information; and biographical data on directors, officers and trustees. The directory costs $595.

Foundation Reporter, 38th Edition, provides all the important contact, financial, and grants information on the top 1,000 private foundations in the United States. The directory costs $560.

For a list of general fundraising and grantseeking resources, go to Amazon. Com's listing of books on "Fund Raising And Grants (General)" at:
http://www.amazon.com/exec/obidos/subject-combination/0568-5163501-951535

PERIODICALS

Business Publishers, Inc.

The following resources are available from Business Publishers, Inc., 8737 Colesville Road, 10th Floor, Silver Spring, MD, 20910, 1-800-274-6737; http://www.bpinews.com:

Education Technology News provides the latest information on new technologies and applications, innovative school programs, research studies, funding and grants. Twelve monthly issues cost $127 per year.

Economic Opportunity Report provides information about social service programs, job training, employment iniatives welfare reform, and grants. Twenty-five bi-weekly issues for $337 for one year.

Legislative Network for Nurses covers health care shortages, Medicare issues, working conditions, and public and private sources of funding. Twenty-five bi-weekly issues for $297 for one year.

Report on Literacy Programs includes information about programs, conferences, grants, contracts and allotments. Twenty-five bi-weekly issues for $317 for one year.

Report on Preschool Programs is a central source of funding and program information on child development programs. Twenty-five bi-weekly issues for $357 for one year.

The following newsletters are available from Capitol City Publishers, 1525-B 29th Street NW, Washington, DC, 20007, 1-800-637-9915; http://www.capitolcitypublishers.com:

Arts and Culture Funding Report covers federal, state, private and nonprofit sector funding and financial assistance to arts and cultural organization. 12 issues per year for $198.

Criminal Justice Funding Report provides federal and private-sector funding information for law enforcement, courts and correctional institutions. 24 issues per year for $278.

The Welfare Reporter covers welfare, welfare reform and welfare-to-work for state and local governments. It includes funding trends and priorities and private funding initiatives. 12 issues per year for $279.

The following newsletters are available from CD Publications, 8204 Fenton Street, Silver Spring, MD, 20910, 1-800-666-6380; http://www.cdpublications.org;

Aid for Education provides funding information for preschool, K-12, community colleges and universities. 24 issues per year, online subscription available for $369.

Children and Youth Funding Report includes public and private grant opportunities in programs including: youth development, education, health care, juvenile justice, mental health, nutrition, and child welfare. 24 issues per year, online subscription available for $369.

Community Health Funding Report provides detailed information about federal, regional, and private funding sources to help community health centers, safety-net hospitals, rural health agencies, and state and county health departments. 24 issues per year, online subscription available for $369.

Disability Funding Week provides information about public and private funding opportunities for programs in areas such as emotional disabilities, physical handicaps, learning disabilities, and autism. 48 issues per year, online subscription available for $369.

Federal Assistance Monitor is a comprehensive review of federal funding announcements, private grants, and legislative action affecting community programs. 24 issues per year, online subscription available for $369.

Homeland Security Funding Report contains funding opportunities available for public safety programs. 24 issues per year, online subscription available for $369.

Substance Abuse Funding Week focuses on public and private funding opportunities for substance abuse prevention and treatment programs, including tobacco cessation. 48 issues per year, online subscription available for $369.

Chronicle of Philanthropy. The Newspaper of the Non-Profit World keeps you up-to-date on the latest news, fundraising techniques, IRS regulations and recent foundation and corporate grants. Bi-weekly; $72 for 24 issues from The Chronicle of Philanthropy, P.O. Box 1989, Marion, OH 43306, (800) 728-2819; http://www.philanthropy.com.

Grants and Funding Alert, an email newsletter, includes public and private funding opportunities to support technology in education. The subscription for 24 issues costs $35 and is available from eSchool News Communications Group, 7920 Norfolk Avenue, Suite 900, Bethesda, MD, 20814, 301-913-0015; http://www.eschoolnews.com.

The following newsletters are available from LRP Publications, 1-800-341-7874; http://www.irpdartnell.com:

Corporate Philanthropy Report covers trends in corporate philanthropy, philanthropic programs that cover a variety of fields, sponsorship opportunities and donations. 12 issues per year cost $316 plus shipping and handling.

Education Grants Alert provides comprehensive information about K–12 funding opportunities and inside advice and expert strategies to maximize your chances of being funded. 52 issues per year cost $292 plus shipping and handling.

Federal Grants and Contracts Weekly contains tips and inside information about how to find and win federal funds for a wide variety of areas. 50 issues per years cost $489 plus shipping and handling.

Foundation and Corporate Grants Alert provides information about foundation, corporate and regional funders. Includes foundation profiles and interviews with program officers. 12 issues per year cost $383 plus shipping and handling.

Health Grants and Contracts Weekly provides information about federal funds available in every health-related area including: AIDS, maternal health, family violence, nutrition research, biomedical research and training. 50 issues per year cost $459 plus shipping and handling.

The following newsletters are available from Quinlan Publishing Company, 23 Drydock Avenue, Boston, MA 02210, 1-800-229-2084; http://www.quinlan.com:

Funding Private Schools includes articles, helpful tips and foundation profiles geared toward the funding needs of individual private schools. Published monthly, a one-year subscription costs $187.

Grants and Funding for Higher Education is a resource for federal, corporate, and foundation grants and funding programs for colleges and universities. Published monthly, a one-year subscription costs $187.

Grants for Cities and Towns Hotline includes funding opportunities for roads, bridges, sewer projects, public housing, capital improvements, and community development. Published biweekly, a one-year subscription costs $187.

Grants for K–12 Hotline provides information about K–12 education grants and funding opportunities. Published twice a month, a one-year subscription costs $187.

Grants for Libraries includes information about grants and funding opportunities, technology updates, and professional development opportunities for libraries. Published monthly, a one-year subscription costs $187.

Online Databases

The Chronicle of Philanthropy's Guide to Grants is a database of all corporate and foundation grants listed in the Chronicle of Philanthropy since 1995. Cost is $295 per year; to subscribe go to http://www.philanthropy/com/grants.

GrantSearch is a database designed for Grants Resource Center institutions (members of the American Association of State Colleges and Universities), and profiles more than 2,000 federal and private funding programs that focus on higher education. For more information go to http://www.aascu.org.

Grants Office is a database of government, foundation, and corporate sources for municipalities, nonprofits, and industry. Cost ranges from $39.95 (single user) to $3,500 (single industry account) per year. To subscribe go to http://www.grantsoffice.com/GOJoin.asp.

GrantSelect is a database of 10,000 funding opportunities, which includes sponsored research. Cost ranges from $750 to $1,500 per year. To subscribe go to http://www.grantselect.com.

GrantStation is a database that also includes a Grantseeker's Toolkit and Proposal Building assistance. Cost is $399 per year for basic membership; to subscribe go to http://www.grantstation.com/Public/Meminfopx/joingrantstationpx.asp.

GuideStar Grant Explorer is a database containing more than 42,000 foundations and over 1 million grants of $5,000 or greater. Cost is $499 per year; to subscribe go to http://www.guidestar.org/services/ge.jsp.

Prospect Research Online (Pro 2.0) is a database that provides detailed information on individuals, foundations, and corporations. For more information go to http://www.iwave.com.

Grant Domain is a website of three databases that provide information on government, foundation, and corporate funding sources. Cost for one year is $495. To subscribe go to http://www.grantdomain.com.

APPENDIX C

State Single Points of Contact

Intergovernmental Review (SPOC List)

It is estimated that in 2004 the Federal Government will outlay $400 billion in grants to State and local governments. Executive Order 12372, "Intergovernmental Review of Federal Programs," was issued with the desire to foster the intergovernmental partnership and strengthen federalism by relying on State and local processes for the coordination and review of proposed Federal financial assistance and direct Federal development. The Order allows each State to designate an entity to perform this function. Below is the official list of those entities. For those States that have a home page for their designated entity, a direct link has been provided below.

States that are not listed on this page have chosen not to participate in the intergovernmental review process, and therefore do not have a SPOC. If you are located within a State that does not have a SPOC, you may send application materials directly to a Federal awarding agency

Contact information for Federal agencies that award grants can be found in Appendix IV of the Catalog of Federal Domestic Assistance.

ARKANSAS Tracy L. C Copeland Manager, State Clearinghouse Office of Intergovernmental Services Department of Finance and Administration 1515 W. 7th St., Room 412 Little Rock, Arkansas 72203 Telephone: (501) 682-1074 Fax: (501) 682-5206 tracy.copeland@dfa.state.ar.us	**CALIFORNIA** Grants Coordination State Clearinghouse Office of Planning and Research P.O. Box 3044, Room 222 Sacramento, California 95812-3044 Telephone: (916) 445-0613 Fax: (916) 323-3018 state.clearinghouse@opr.ca.gov
DELAWARE Sandra R. Stump Executive Department Office of the Budget 540 S. Dupont Highway, 3rd Floor Dover, Delaware 19901 Telephone: (302) 739-3323 Fax: (302) 739-5661 sandy.stump@state.de.us	**DISTRICT OF COLUMBIA** Marlene Jefferson DC Government Office of Partnerships and Grants Development 441 4th Street, NW Washington, DC 20001 Telephone: (202) 727-6515 Fax: (202) 727-1652 marlene.jefferson@dc.gov

FLORIDA Lauren P. Milligan Florida State Clearinghouse Florida Dept. of Environmental Protection 3900 Commonwealth Blvd., Mail Station 47 Tallahassee, Florida 32399-3000 Telephone: (850) 245-2161 Fax: (850) 245-2190 Lauren.Milligan@dep.state.fl.us	**GEORGIA** Barbara Jackson Georgia State Clearinghouse 270 Washington Street, SW, 8th Floor Atlanta, Georgia 30334 Telephone: (404) 656-3855 Fax: (404) 656-7916 gach@mail.opb.state.ga.us
ILLINOIS Roukaya McCaffrey Department of Commerce and Economic Opportunities 620 East Adams, 6th Floor Springfield, Illinois 62701 Telephone: (217) 524-0188 Fax: (217) 558-0473 roukaya_mccaffrey@illinoisbiz.biz	**IOWA** Kathy Mabie Iowa Department of Management State Capitol Building Room G12 1007 E Grand Avenue Des Moines, Iowa 50319 Telephone: (515) 281-8834 Fax: (515) 242-5897 Kathy.Mabie@iowa.gov
KENTUCKY Ron Cook The Governor's Office for Local Development 1024 Capital Center Drive, Suite 340 Frankfort, Kentucky 40601 Telephone: (502) 573-2382 / (800) 346-5606 Fax: (502) 573-2512 Ron.Cook@Ky.Gov	**MAINE** Joyce Benson State Planning Office 184 State Street 38 State House Station Augusta, Maine 04333 Telephone: (207) 287-3261 (direct) (207) 287-1461 Fax: (207) 287-6489 joyce.benson@state.me.us
MARYLAND Linda C. Janey, J.D. Director, Maryland State Clearinghouse For Intergovernmental Assistance 301 West Preston Street, Room 1104 Baltimore, Maryland 21201-2305 Telephone: (410) 767-4490 Fax: (410) 767-4480 ljaney@mdp.state.md.us	**MICHIGAN** Richard Pfaff Southeast Michigan Council of Governments 535 Griswold, Suite 300 Detroit, Michigan 48226 Telephone: (313) 961-4266 Fax: (313) 961-4869 pfaff@semcog.org

MISSISSIPPI	**MISSOURI**
Mildred Tharpe	Laurie Morris
Clearinghouse Officer	Federal Assistance Clearinghouse
Department of Finance and Administration	Office of Administration
1301 Woolfolk Building, Suite E	Capitol Building, Room 125
501 North West Street	Jefferson City, Missouri 65102
Jackson, Mississippi 39201	Telephone: (573) 751-0337
Telephone: (601) 359-6762	Fax: (573) 751-1212
Fax: (601) 359-6758	igr@oa.mo.gov
NEVADA	**NEW HAMPSHIRE**
Michael Stafford	MaryAnn Manoogian
Department of Administration	Director, New Hampshire Office of
State Clearinghouse	Energy and Planning
209 E. Musser Street, Room 200	Attn: Intergovernmental Review Process
Carson City, Nevada 89701	Benjamin Frost
Telephone: (775) 684-0209	57 Regional Drive
Fax: (775) 684-0260	Concord, New Hampshire 03301-8519
mstafford@budget.state.nv.us	Telephone: (603) 271-2155
	Fax: (603) 271-2615
	irp@nh.gov
NEW YORK	**NORTH DAKOTA**
Linda Shkreli	Jim Boyd
Office of Public Security	ND Department of Commerce
Homeland Security Grants Coordination	1600 East Century Avenue, Suite 2
633 3rd Avenue	P.O. Box 2057
New York, NY 10017	Bismarck, North Dakota 58502-2057
Telephone: (212) 867-1289	Telephone: (701) 328-2676
Fax: (212) 867-1725	Fax: (701) 328-2308
	jboyd@state.nd.us
RHODE ISLAND	**SOUTH CAROLINA**
Joyce Karger	SC Clearinghouse
Department of Administration	Budget and Control Board
One Capitol Hill	Office of State Budget
Providence, Rhode Island 02908-5870	1201 Main Street, Suite 950
Telephone: (401) 222-6181	Columbia, South Carolina 29201
Fax: (401) 222-2083	Telephone: (803) 734-0494
jkarger@doa.state.ri.us	Fax: (803) 734-0645
	clearinghouse@budget.state.sc.us

TEXAS Denise S. Francis Director, State Grants Team Governor's Office of Budget and Planning P.O. Box 12428 Austin, Texas 78711 Telephone: (512) 305-9415 Fax: (512) 936-2681 dfrancis@governor.state.tx.us	**UTAH** Sophia DiCaro Utah State Clearinghouse Governor's Office of Planning and Budget Utah State Capitol Complex Suite E210, PO Box 142210 Salt Lake City, Utah 84114-2210 Telephone: (801) 538-1027 Fax: (801) 538-1547 sdicaro@utah.gov
WEST VIRGINIA Fred Cutlip Director, Community Development Division West Virginia Development Office Building #6, Room 553 Charleston, West Virginia 25305 Telephone: (304) 558-4010 Fax: (304) 558-3248 fcutlip@wvdo.org	**WISCONSIN** Jeff Smith Section Chief, Federal/State Relations Wisconsin Department of Administration 101 East Wilson Street, 6th Floor P.O. Box 7868 Madison, Wisconsin 53707 Telephone: (608) 266-0267 Fax: (608) 267-6931 jeffrey.smith@doa.state.wi.us
AMERICAN SAMOA Pat M. Galea'i Federal Grants/Programs Coordinator Office of Federal Programs/Office of the Governor Department of Commerce American Samoa Government Pago Pago, American Samoa 96799 Telephone: (684) 633-5155 Fax: (684) 633-4195 pmgaleai@samoatelco.com	**GUAM** Director Bureau of Budget and Management Research Office of the Governor P.O. Box 2950 Agana, Guam 96910 Telephone: 011-671-472-2285 Fax: 011-472-2825 jer@ns.gov.gu

NORTH MARIANA ISLANDS Ms. Jacoba T. Seman Federal Programs Coordinator Office of Management and Budget Office of the Governor Saipan, MP 96950 Telephone: (670) 664-2289 Fax: (670) 664-2272 omb.jseman@saipan.com	**PUERTO RICO** Jose Caballero / Mayra Silva Puerto Rico Planning Board Federal Proposals Review Office Minillas Government Center P.O. Box 41119 San Juan, Puerto Rico 00940-1119 Telephone: (787) 723-6190 Fax: (787) 722-6783
VIRGIN ISLANDS Ira Mills Director, Office of Management and Budget #41 Norre Gade Emancipation Garden Station Second Floor Saint Thomas, Virgin Islands 00802 Telephone: (340) 774-0750 Fax: (340) 776-0069 lrmills@usvi.org	

Changes to this list can be made only after OMB is notified by a State's officially designated representative. E-mail messages can be sent to ephillips@omb.eop.gov. If you prefer, you may send correspondence to the following postal address:

> Attn: Grants Management
> Office of Management and Budget
> New Executive Office Building, Suite 6025
> 725 17th Street, NW
> Washington, DC 20503

Please note: Inquiries about obtaining a Federal grant should not be sent to the OMB e-mail or postal address shown above. The best source for this information is the *Catalog of Federal Domestic Assistance* or CFDA (http://www.cfda.gov) and the Grants.gov website (http://www.grants.gov).

For the most current listing, please go to www.whitehouse.gov/omb/grants/spoc.html.

APPENDIX D

Sample Budget Forms and Narratives
and
Federal Application Forms

PROJECT BUDGET

Use this format as a guide for presenting your budget. Lay out your columns and categories as illustrated below.

KEY TERMS:

➤➤ **Requested funds (up to $1,000)** are direct cash awards requested from the initiative to support your project.

➤➤ **Cash contributions** are moneys raised for the project. These moneys come from outside sources. Mini–Project grant applicants do not need to provide a cash contribution but are encouraged to contribute funds as a confirmation of their community's interest and support.

Categories	Requested Funds	Cash Contributions
A. Your Staff (Indicate names, positions, and rates.)		
B. Advisors (Indicate names and rates.)		
C. Program Personnel (Indicate names, positions, and rates for presenters, workshop leaders, panelists, etc.)		
D. Travel and Expenses (Specify items and rates. Mileage should not exceed $.34 per mile.)		
E. Production Expenses		
F. Supplies or Materials		
G. Promotion		
H. Printing		
I. Postage		
J. Telephone		
K. Space Rental		
L. Other		
TOTALS		

(From the Pennsylvania Humanities Council and Pennsylvania Council on the Arts Humanities-and-the-Arts Mini-Project grant.)

SAMPLE BUDGET NARRATIVE: YEAR ONE

Personnel
Project Director (1.0 FTE) $50,000

The project director will have oversight of the program and provide supervision, recruitment and training of the program liaisons. At a minimum, this position requires a Masters Degree with an emphasis in social work or other related field.

Program Liaisons (2 @ 1.0 FTE)   (2 x $35,000) = $70,000

Two program liaisons will be responsible for day-to-day school/community outreach activities. At a minimum, staff will hold a Bachelors Degree (or equivalent) in the social services field. It is anticipated that each liaison will be responsible for 25 annual events.

Staff Assistant (1.0 FTE) $25,000

The staff assistant will perform all clerical duties for the project staff. This position requires a high school diploma or equivalent.

Total $145,000

Fringe Benefits
Happy Days pays 100% medical, dental, vision, life and disability for full-time employees, and is calculated at .25% of annual salary. The calculations are as follows:

Program Director ($50,000 x .25)	$12,500
(2) Program Liaisons ($70,000 x .25)	$17,500
Staff Assistant ($25,000 x .25)	$6,250
Total	$36,250

Travel
Funds are requested for travel for 2 staff members to attend 3 local conferences (Happy Days reimburses staff at a rate of 50 cents per mile). Funds are also allocated for one staff member to travel to 2 conferences in Washington DC - including air travel, per diem, and hotel room. Anticipated expenses are:

Mileage reimbursement for travel to local conferences

Estimated 200 miles x .50/mile	$100
(2) Washington, DC meetings	$900
Hotel ($75/night x 4 nights)	$300
Airfare ($150/ticket x 2)	$300
Per Diem ($75 x 4 days)	$300
Total	$1,000

Supplies

(4) Apple iMac computers @ $1,250 each	$5,000

Each staff member will be assigned a computer for all work-related tasks. Proprietary software for program implementation will be donated by Happy Days School District.

(1) Fax Machine	$500
General office supplies	$1,500

General office supplies include paper, pens, pencils and other desk supplies.

Total	$7,000

Contractual

External Evaluator	$20,000

An external evaluator will oversee all program evaluation activities including developing appropriate instruments, conducting focus groups and interviews with students, staff, and agencies, and preparing the required evaluation reports.

The evaluation team will also work extensively with project staff to develop a relational database to ensure accurate data collection for program monitoring and reporting purposes.

Audit	$10,000

An independent auditor will be contracted to conduct a yearly audit of program finances. The auditor will be selected using standard Happy Days fiscal/administrative management procedures.

Total	$30,000

Other

Equipment lease	$10,000

This item includes charges for leased telephones, photocopier. All leased equipment is for use by program staff at the main office.

Facilities rent, utilities, and maintenance	$15,000

Rental costs cover direct service staff at the main office. It is anticipated that the program will require 500 square feet of space at $1.00/square foot. Utilities are estimated to be $400 and the building maintenance fee is $100.

Total	$25,000
Total Cost Project Year One	**$244,250**

(From the Grant Application Technical Assistance Resources of the U.S. Department of Education, Office of Safe Schools)

Budget Detail Worksheet

Purpose: The Budget Detail Worksheet may be used as a guide to assist you in the preparation of the budget and budget narrative. You may submit the budget and budget narrative using this form or in the format of your choice (plain sheets, your own form, or a variation of this form). However, all required information (including the budget narrative) must be provided. Any category of expense not applicable to your budget may be deleted.

A. Personnel - List each position by title and name of employee, if available. Show the annual salary rate and the percentage of time to be devoted to the project. Compensation paid for employees engaged in grant activities must be consistent with that paid for similar work within the applicant organization.

Name/Position	Computation	Cost
		TOTAL_____

B. Fringe Benefits - Fringe benefits should be based on actual known costs or an established formula. Fringe benefits are for the personnel listed in budget category (A) and only for the percentage of time devoted to the project. Fringe benefits on overtime hours are limited to FICA, Workman's Compensation, and Unemployment Compensation.

Name/Position	Computation	Cost
		TOTAL_____
	Total Personnel & Fringe Benefits_____	

C. Travel - Itemize travel expenses of project personnel by purpose (e.g., staff to training, field interviews, advisory group meeting, etc.). Show the basis of computation (e.g., six people to 3-day training at $X airfare, $X lodging, $X subsistence). In training projects, travel and meals for trainees should be listed separately. Show the number of trainees and the unit costs involved. Identify the location of travel, if known. Indicate source of Travel Policies applied, Applicant or Federal Travel Regulations.

Purpose of Travel	Location	Item	Computation	Cost

TOTAL_____

D. Equipment - List non-expendable items that are to be purchased. Non-expendable equipment is tangible property having a useful life of more than two years and an acquisition cost of $5,000 or more per unit. (Note: Organization's own capitalization policy may be used for items costing less than $5,000). Expendable items should be included either in the "supplies" category or in the "Other" category. Applicants should analyze the cost benefits of purchasing versus leasing equipment, especially high cost items and those subject to rapid technical advances. Rented or leased equipment costs should be listed in the "Contractual" category. Explain how the equipment is necessary for the success of the project. Attach a narrative describing the procurement method to be used.

Item	Computation	Cost

TOTAL_____

E. Supplies - List items by type (office supplies, postage, training materials, copying paper, and expendable equipment items costing less than $5,000, such as books, hand held tape recorders) and show the basis for computation. (Note: Organization's own capitalization policy may be used for items costing less than $5,000). Generally, supplies include any materials that are expendable or consumed during the course of the project.

Supply Items	Computation	Cost

TOTAL_____

F. Construction - As a rule, construction costs are not allowable. In some cases, minor repairs or renovations may be allowable. Check with the program office before budgeting funds in this category.

Purpose	Description of Work	Cost

TOTAL_____

G. Consultants/Contracts - Indicate whether applicant's formal, written Procurement Policy or the Federal Acquisition Regulations are followed.

Consultant Fees: For each consultant enter the name, if known, service to be provided, hourly or daily fee (8-hour day), and estimated time on the project. Consultant fees in excess of $450 per day require additional justification and prior approval from OJP.

Name of Consultant	Service Provided	Computation	Cost

Subtotal_____

Consultant Expenses: List all expenses to be paid from the grant to the individual consultants in addition to their fees (i.e., travel, meals, lodging, etc.)

Item	Location	Computation	Cost

Subtotal_____

Contracts: Provide a description of the product or service to be procured by contract and an estimate of the cost. Applicants are encouraged to promote free and open competition in awarding contracts. A separate justification must be provided for sole source contracts in excess of $100,000.

Item	Cost

Subtotal_____

TOTAL_____

H. Other Costs - List items (e.g., rent, reproduction, telephone, janitorial or security services, and investigative or confidential funds) by major type and the basis of the computation. For example, provide the square footage and the cost per square foot for rent, or provide a monthly rental cost and how many months to rent.

Description	Computation	Cost

TOTAL_____

I. Indirect Costs - Indirect costs are allowed only if the applicant has a Federally approved indirect cost rate. A copy of the rate approval, (a fully executed, negotiated agreement), must be attached. If the applicant does not have an approved rate, one can be requested by contacting the applicant's cognizant Federal agency, which will review all documentation and approve a rate for the applicant organization, or if the applicant's accounting system permits, costs may be allocated in the direct costs categories.

Description	Computation	Cost

TOTAL_____

Budget Summary- When you have completed the budget worksheet, transfer the totals for each category to the spaces below. Compute the total direct costs and the total project costs. Indicate the amount of Federal requested and the amount of non-Federal funds that will support the project.

Budget Category	Amount
A. Personnel	_____
B. Fringe Benefits	_____
C. Travel	_____
D. Equipment	_____
E. Supplies	_____
F. Construction	_____
G. Consultants/Contracts	_____
H. Other	_____
Total Direct Costs	_____
I. Indirect Costs	
TOTAL PROJECT COSTS	_____

Federal Request   _____

Non-Federal Amount   _____

OMB APPROVAL NO. 1121-0188
EXPIRES 5-98 (Rev. 12/97)

Budget Detail Worksheet

Purpose: The Budget Detail Worksheet may be used as a guide to assist you in the preparation of the budget and budget narrative. You may submit the budget and budget narrative using this form or in the format of your choice (plain sheets, your own form, or a variation of this form). However, all required information (including the budget narrative) must be provided. Any category of expense not applicable to your budget may be deleted.

A. Personnel - List each position by title and name of employee, if available. Show the annual salary rate and the percentage of time to be devoted to the project. Compensation paid for employees engaged in grant activities must be consistent with that paid for similar work within the applicant organization.

Name/Position	Computation	Cost
John Smith, Investigator	*($50,000 x 100%)*	*$50,000*
2 Investigators	*($50,000 x 100% x 2)*	*$100,000*
Secretary	*($30,000 x 50%)*	*$15,000*
Cost of living increase	*($165,000 x 2% x .5 yr.)*	*$1,650*
Overtime per investigator	*($37.50/hr. x 100 hrs. x 3)*	*$11,250*

The three investigators will be assigned exclusively to homicide investigations. A 2% cost of living adjustment is scheduled for all full-time personnel 6 months prior to the end of the grant. Overtime will be needed during some investigations. A half-time secretary will prepare reports and provide other support to the unit.

TOTAL $177,900

B. Fringe Benefits - Fringe benefits should be based on actual known costs or an established formula. Fringe benefits are for the personnel listed in budget category (A) and only for the percentage of time devoted to the project. Fringe benefits on overtime hours are limited to FICA, Workman's Compensation, and Unemployment Compensation.

Name/Position	Computation	Cost
Employer's FICA	*($177,900 x 7.65%)*	*$13,609*
Retirement	**($166,650 x 6%)*	*$9,999*
Uniform Allowance	*($50/mo. x 12 mo. x 3)*	*$1,800*
Health Insurance	**($166,650 x 12%)*	*$19,998*
Workman's Compensation	*($177,900 x 1%)*	*$1,779*
Unemployment Compensation	*($177,900 x 1%)*	*$1,779*
*($177,900 less $11,250)		

TOTAL $48,964

Total Personnel & Fringe Benefits $226,864

C. Travel - Itemize travel expenses of project personnel by purpose (e.g., staff to training, field interviews, advisory group meeting, etc.). Show the basis of computation (e.g., six people to 3-day training at $X airfare, $X lodging, $X subsistence). In training projects, travel and meals for trainees should be listed separately. Show the number of trainees and the unit costs involved. Identify the location of travel, if known. Indicate source of Travel Policies applied, Applicant or Federal Travel Regulations.

Purpose of Travel	Location	Item	Computation	Cost
Training	*Boston*	*Airfare*	*($150 x 2 people x 2 trips)*	*$600*
		Hotel	*($75/night x 2 x 2 people*	
			x 2 trips)	*$600*
		Meals	*($35/day x 3 days x 2 people*	
			x 2 trips)	*$420*
Investigations	*New York City*	*Airfare*	*($600 average x 7)*	*$4,200*
		Hotel and Meals	*($100/day average*	
			x 7 x 3 days)	*$2,100*

Two of the investigators will attend training on forensic evidence gathering in Boston in October and January. The investigators may take up to seven trips to New York City to follow up investigative leads. Travel estimates are based on applicant's formal written travel policy.

TOTAL $7,920

D. Equipment - List non-expendable items that are to be purchased. Non-expendable equipment is tangible property having a useful life of more than two years and an acquisition cost of $5,000 or more per unit. (Note: Organization's own capitalization policy may be used for items costing less than $5,000). Expendable items should be included either in the "supplies" category or in the "Other" category. Applicants should analyze the cost benefits of purchasing versus leasing equipment, especially high cost items and those subject to rapid technical advances. Rented or leased equipment costs should be listed in the "Contractual" category. Explain how the equipment is necessary for the success of the project. Attach a narrative describing the procurement method to be used.

Item	Computation	Cost
3 - 486 Computer w/CD ROM	*($2,000 x 3)*	*$6,000*
Video Camera	*$1,000*	*$1,000*

The computers will be used by the investigators to analyze case and intelligence information. The camera will be used for investigative and crime scene work.

TOTAL $7,000

E. Supplies - List items by type (office supplies, postage, training materials, copying paper, and expendable equipment items costing less than $5,000, such as books, hand held tape recorders) and show the basis for computation. (Note: Organization's own capitalization policy may be used for items costing less than $5,000). Generally, supplies include any materials that are expendable or consumed during the course of the project.

Supply Items	Computation	Cost
Office Supplies	*($50/mo. x 12 mo.)*	*$600*
Postage	*($20/mo. x 12 mo.)*	*$240*
Training Materials	*($2/set x 500 sets)*	*$1,000*

Office supplies and postage are needed for general operation of the program. Training materials will be developed and used by the investigators to train patrol officers how to preserve crime scene evidence.

TOTAL $1,840

F. Construction - As a rule, construction costs are not allowable. In some cases, minor repairs or renovations may be allowable. Check with the program office before budgeting funds in this category.

Purpose	Description of Work	Cost
Renovation	*Add walls*	*$5,000*
	Build work tables	*$3,000*
	Build evidence storage units	*$2,000*

The renovations are needed to upgrade the forensic lab used to analyze evidence for homicide cases.

TOTAL $10,000

G. Consultants/Contracts - Indicate whether applicant's formal, written Procurement Policy or the Federal Acquisition Regulations are followed.

Consultant Fees: For each consultant enter the name, if known, service to be provided, hourly or daily fee (8-hour day), and estimated time on the project. Consultant fees in excess of $450 per day require additional justification and prior approval from OJP.

Name of Consultant	Service Provided	Computation	Cost
John Doe	Forensic Specialist	($150/day x 30 days)	$4,500

John Doe, Forensic Specialist, will be hired, as needed, to assist with the analysis of evidence in homicide cases.

Subtotal $4,500

Consultant Expenses: List all expenses to be paid from the grant to the individual consultants in addition to their fees (i.e., travel, meals, lodging, etc.)

Item	Location	Computation	Cost
Airfare	Miami	($400 x 6 trips)	$2,400
Hotel and Meals		($100/day x 30 days)	$3,000

John Doe is expected to make up to 6 trips to Miami to consult on homicide cases.

Subtotal $5,400

Contracts: Provide a description of the product or service to be procured by contract and an estimate of the cost. Applicants are encouraged to promote free and open competition in awarding contracts. A separate justification must be provided for sole source contracts in excess of $100,000.

Item	Cost
Intelligence System Development	$102,000

The State University will design an intelligence system to be used in homicide investigations. A sole source justification is attached. Procurement Policy is based on the Federal Acquisition Regulation.

Subtotal $102,000

TOTAL $111,900

H. Other Costs - List items (e.g., rent, reproduction, telephone, janitorial or security services, and investigative or confidential funds) by major type and the basis of the computation. For example, provide the square footage and the cost per square foot for rent, or provide a monthly rental cost and how many months to rent.

Description	Computation	Cost
Rent	*(700 sq. ft. x $15/sq. ft.)*	
	($875/mo. x 12 mo.)	*$10,500*

This rent will pay for space for the new homicide unit. No space is currently available in city-owned buildings.

Telephone	*($100/mo. x 12 mo.)*	*$1,200*
Printing/Reproduction	*($150/mo. x 12 mo.)*	*$1,800*

TOTAL $13,500

I. Indirect Costs - Indirect costs are allowed only if the applicant has a Federally approved indirect cost rate. A copy of the rate approval, (a fully executed, negotiated agreement), must be attached. If the applicant does not have an approved rate, one can be requested by contacting the applicant's cognizant Federal agency, which will review all documentation and approve a rate for the applicant organization, or if the applicant's accounting system permits, costs may be allocated in the direct costs categories.

Description	Computation	Cost
10% of personnel and fringe benefits	*($226,864 x 10%)*	*$22,686*

The indirect cost rate was approved by the Department of Transportation, the applicant's cognizant Federal agency, on January 1, 1994. (A copy of the fully executed, negotiated agreement is attached.)

TOTAL $22,686

Budget Summary- When you have completed the budget worksheet, transfer the totals for each category to the spaces below. Compute the total direct costs and the total project costs. Indicate the amount of Federal requested and the amount of non-Federal funds that will support the project.

Budget Category	Amount
A. Personnel	$177,900
B. Fringe Benefits	$48,964
C. Travel	$7,920
D. Equipment	$7,000
E. Supplies	$1,840
F. Construction	$10,000
G. Consultants/Contracts	$111,900
H. Other	$13,500
Total Direct Costs	$379,024
I. Indirect Costs	$22,686
TOTAL PROJECT COSTS	$401,710
Federal Request	$301,283
Non-Federal Amount	$100,427

OMB Approval No. 0348-0044

BUDGET INFORMATION - Non-Construction Programs

SECTION A - BUDGET SUMMARY

Grant Program Function or Activity (a)	Catalog of Federal Domestic Assistance Number (b)	Estimated Unobligated Funds		New or Revised Budget		
		Federal (c)	Non-Federal (d)	Federal (e)	Non-Federal (f)	Total (g)
1.		$	$	$	$	$ 0.00
2.						0.00
3.						0.00
4.						0.00
5. Totals		$ 0.00	$ 0.00	$ 0.00	$ 0.00	$ 0.00

SECTION B - BUDGET CATEGORIES

6. Object Class Categories	GRANT PROGRAM, FUNCTION OR ACTIVITY				Total
	(1)	(2)	(3)	(4)	(5)
a. Personnel	$	$	$	$	$ 0.00
b. Fringe Benefits					0.00
c. Travel					0.00
d. Equipment					0.00
e. Supplies					0.00
f. Contractual					0.00
g. Construction					0.00
h. Other					0.00
i. Total Direct Charges (sum of 6a-6h)	0.00	0.00	0.00	0.00	0.00
j. Indirect Charges					0.00
k. TOTALS (sum of 6i and 6j)	$ 0.00	$ 0.00	$ 0.00	$ 0.00	$ 0.00
7. Program Income	$	$	$	$	$ 0.00

Authorized for Local Reproduction

Previous Edition Usable

Standard Form 424A (Rev. 7-97)
Prescribed by OMB Circular A-102

SECTION C - NON-FEDERAL RESOURCES

(a) Grant Program	(b) Applicant	(c) State	(d) Other Sources	(e) TOTALS
8.	$	$	$	$ 0.00
9.				0.00
10.				0.00
11.				0.00
12. TOTAL (sum of lines 8-11)	$ 0.00	$ 0.00	$ 0.00	$ 0.00

SECTION D - FORECASTED CASH NEEDS

	Total for 1st Year	1st Quarter	2nd Quarter	3rd Quarter	4th Quarter
13. Federal	$ 0.00	$	$	$	$
14. Non-Federal	0.00				
15. TOTAL (sum of lines 13 and 14)	$ 0.00	$ 0.00	$ 0.00	$ 0.00	$ 0.00

SECTION E - BUDGET ESTIMATES OF FEDERAL FUNDS NEEDED FOR BALANCE OF THE PROJECT

(a) Grant Program	FUTURE FUNDING PERIODS (Years)			
	(b) First	(c) Second	(d) Third	(e) Fourth
16.	$	$	$	$
17.				
18.				
19.				
20. TOTAL (sum of lines 16-19)	$ 0.00	$ 0.00	$ 0.00	$ 0.00

SECTION F - OTHER BUDGET INFORMATION

21. Direct Charges:	22. Indirect Charges:

23. Remarks:

Authorized for Local Reproduction

INSTRUCTIONS FOR THE SF-424A

Public reporting burden for this collection of information is estimated to average 180 minutes per response, including time for reviewing instructions, searching existing data sources, gathering and maintaining the data needed, and completing and reviewing the collection of information. Send comments regarding the burden estimate or any other aspect of this collection of information, including suggestions for reducing this burden, to the Office of Management and Budget, Paperwork Reduction Project (0348-0044), Washington, DC 20503.

PLEASE DO NOT RETURN YOUR COMPLETED FORM TO THE OFFICE OF MANAGEMENT AND BUDGET. SEND IT TO THE ADDRESS PROVIDED BY THE SPONSORING AGENCY.

General Instructions

This form is designed so that application can be made for funds from one or more grant programs. In preparing the budget, adhere to any existing Federal grantor agency guidelines which prescribe how and whether budgeted amounts should be separately shown for different functions or activities within the program. For some programs, grantor agencies may require budgets to be separately shown by function or activity. For other programs, grantor agencies may require a breakdown by function or activity. Sections A, B, C, and D should include budget estimates for the whole project except when applying for assistance which requires Federal authorization in annual or other funding period increments. In the latter case, Sections A, B, C, and D should provide the budget for the first budget period (usually a year) and Section E should present the need for Federal assistance in the subsequent budget periods. All applications should contain a breakdown by the object class categories shown in Lines a-k of Section B.

Section A. Budget Summary Lines 1-4 Columns (a) and (b)

For applications pertaining to a *single* Federal grant program (Federal Domestic Assistance Catalog number) and *not requiring* a functional or activity breakdown, enter on Line 1 under Column (a) the Catalog program title and the Catalog number in Column (b).

For applications pertaining to a *single* program *requiring* budget amounts by multiple functions or activities, enter the name of each activity or function on each line in Column (a), and enter the Catalog number in Column (b). For applications pertaining to multiple programs where none of the programs require a breakdown by function or activity, enter the Catalog program title on each line in *Column* (a) and the respective Catalog number on each line in Column (b).

For applications pertaining to *multiple* programs where one or more programs *require* a breakdown by function or activity, prepare a separate sheet for each program requiring the breakdown. Additional sheets should be used when one form does not provide adequate space for all breakdown of data required. However, when more than one sheet is used, the first page should provide the summary totals by programs.

Lines 1-4, Columns (c) through (g)

For new applications, leave Column (c) and (d) blank. For each line entry in Columns (a) and (b), enter in Columns (e), (f), and (g) the appropriate amounts of funds needed to support the project for the first funding period (usually a year).

For continuing grant program applications, submit these forms before the end of each funding period as required by the grantor agency. Enter in Columns (c) and (d) the estimated amounts of funds which will remain unobligated at the end of the grant funding period only if the Federal grantor agency instructions provide for this. Otherwise, leave these columns blank. Enter in columns (e) and (f) the amounts of funds needed for the upcoming period. The amount(s) in Column (g) should be the sum of amounts in Columns (e) and (f).

For supplemental grants and changes to existing grants, do not use Columns (c) and (d). Enter in Column (e) the amount of the increase or decrease of Federal funds and enter in Column (f) the amount of the increase or decrease of non-Federal funds. In Column (g) enter the new total budgeted amount (Federal and non-Federal) which includes the total previous authorized budgeted amounts plus or minus, as appropriate, the amounts shown in Columns (e) and (f). The amount(s) in Column (g) should not equal the sum of amounts in Columns (e) and (f).

Line 5 - Show the totals for all columns used.

Section B Budget Categories

In the column headings (1) through (4), enter the titles of the same programs, functions, and activities shown on Lines 1-4, Column (a), Section A. When additional sheets are prepared for Section A, provide similar column headings on each sheet. For each program, function or activity, fill in the total requirements for funds (both Federal and non-Federal) by object class categories.

Line 6a-i - Show the totals of Lines 6a to 6h in each column.

Line 6j - Show the amount of indirect cost.

Line 6k - Enter the total of amounts on Lines 6i and 6j. For all applications for new grants and continuation grants the total amount in column (5), Line 6k, should be the same as the total amount shown in Section A, Column (g), Line 5. For supplemental grants and changes to grants, the total amount of the increase or decrease as shown in Columns (1)-(4), Line 6k should be the same as the sum of the amounts in Section A, Columns (e) and (f) on Line 5.

Line 7 - Enter the estimated amount of income, if any, expected to be generated from this project. Do not add or subtract this amount from the total project amount, Show under the program

INSTRUCTIONS FOR THE SF-424A (continued)

narrative statement the nature and source of income. The estimated amount of program income may be considered by the Federal grantor agency in determining the total amount of the grant.

Section C. Non-Federal Resources

Lines 8-11 Enter amounts of non-Federal resources that will be used on the grant. If in-kind contributions are included, provide a brief explanation on a separate sheet.

> **Column (a)** - Enter the program titles identical to Column (a), Section A. A breakdown by function or activity is not necessary.
>
> **Column (b)** - Enter the contribution to be made by the applicant.
>
> **Column (c)** - Enter the amount of the State's cash and in-kind contribution if the applicant is not a State or State agency. Applicants which are a State or State agencies should leave this column blank.
>
> **Column (d)** - Enter the amount of cash and in-kind contributions to be made from all other sources.
>
> **Column (e)** - Enter totals of Columns (b), (c), and (d).

Line 12 - Enter the total for each of Columns (b)-(e). The amount in Column (e) should be equal to the amount on Line 5, Column (f), Section A.

Section D. Forecasted Cash Needs

Line 13 - Enter the amount of cash needed by quarter from the grantor agency during the first year.

Line 14 - Enter the amount of cash from all other sources needed by quarter during the first year.

Line 15 - Enter the totals of amounts on Lines 13 and 14.

Section E. Budget Estimates of Federal Funds Needed for Balance of the Project

Lines 16-19 - Enter in Column (a) the same grant program titles shown in Column (a), Section A. A breakdown by function or activity is not necessary. For new applications and continuation grant applications, enter in the proper columns amounts of Federal funds which will be needed to complete the program or project over the succeeding funding periods (usually in years). This section need not be completed for revisions (amendments, changes, or supplements) to funds for the current year of existing grants.

If more than four lines are needed to list the program titles, submit additional schedules as necessary.

Line 20 - Enter the total for each of the Columns (b)-(e). When additional schedules are prepared for this Section, annotate accordingly and show the overall totals on this line.

Section F. Other Budget Information

Line 21 - Use this space to explain amounts for individual direct object class cost categories that may appear to be out of the ordinary or to explain the details as required by the Federal grantor agency.

Line 22 - Enter the type of indirect rate (provisional, predetermined, final or fixed) that will be in effect during the funding period, the estimated amount of the base to which the rate is applied, and the total indirect expense.

Line 23 - Provide any other explanations or comments deemed necessary.

OMB Approval No. 0348-0040

ASSURANCES - NON-CONSTRUCTION PROGRAMS

Public reporting burden for this collection of information is estimated to average 15 minutes per response, including time for reviewing instructions, searching existing data sources, gathering and maintaining the data needed, and completing and reviewing the collection of information. Send comments regarding the burden estimate or any other aspect of this collection of information, including suggestions for reducing this burden, to the Office of Management and Budget, Paperwork Reduction Project (0348-0040), Washington, DC 20503.

PLEASE DO NOT RETURN YOUR COMPLETED FORM TO THE OFFICE OF MANAGEMENT AND BUDGET. SEND IT TO THE ADDRESS PROVIDED BY THE SPONSORING AGENCY.

NOTE: Certain of these assurances may not be applicable to your project or program. If you have questions, please contact the awarding agency. Further, certain Federal awarding agencies may require applicants to certify to additional assurances. If such is the case, you will be notified.

As the duly authorized representative of the applicant, I certify that the applicant:

1. Has the legal authority to apply for Federal assistance and the institutional, managerial and financial capability (including funds sufficient to pay the non-Federal share of project cost) to ensure proper planning, management and completion of the project described in this application.

2. Will give the awarding agency, the Comptroller General of the United States and, if appropriate, the State, through any authorized representative, access to and the right to examine all records, books, papers, or documents related to the award; and will establish a proper accounting system in accordance with generally accepted accounting standards or agency directives.

3. Will establish safeguards to prohibit employees from using their positions for a purpose that constitutes or presents the appearance of personal or organizational conflict of interest, or personal gain.

4. Will initiate and complete the work within the applicable time frame after receipt of approval of the awarding agency.

5. Will comply with the Intergovernmental Personnel Act of 1970 (42 U.S.C. §§4728-4763) relating to prescribed standards for merit systems for programs funded under one of the 19 statutes or regulations specified in Appendix A of OPM's Standards for a Merit System of Personnel Administration (5 C.F.R. 900, Subpart F).

6. Will comply with all Federal statutes relating to nondiscrimination. These include but are not limited to: (a) Title VI of the Civil Rights Act of 1964 (P.L. 88-352) which prohibits discrimination on the basis of race, color or national origin; (b) Title IX of the Education Amendments of 1972, as amended (20 U.S.C. §§1681-1683, and 1685-1686), which prohibits discrimination on the basis of sex; (c) Section 504 of the Rehabilitation Act of 1973, as amended (29 U.S.C. §794), which prohibits discrimination on the basis of handicaps; (d) the Age Discrimination Act of 1975, as amended (42 U.S.C. §§6101-6107), which prohibits discrimination on the basis of age; (e) the Drug Abuse Office and Treatment Act of 1972 (P.L. 92-255), as amended, relating to nondiscrimination on the basis of drug abuse; (f) the Comprehensive Alcohol Abuse and Alcoholism Prevention, Treatment and Rehabilitation Act of 1970 (P.L. 91-616), as amended, relating to nondiscrimination on the basis of alcohol abuse or alcoholism; (g) §§523 and 527 of the Public Health Service Act of 1912 (42 U.S.C. §§290 dd-3 and 290 ee 3), as amended, relating to confidentiality of alcohol and drug abuse patient records; (h) Title VIII of the Civil Rights Act of 1968 (42 U.S.C. §§3601 et seq.), as amended, relating to nondiscrimination in the sale, rental or financing of housing; (i) any other nondiscrimination provisions in the specific statute(s) under which application for Federal assistance is being made; and, (j) the requirements of any other nondiscrimination statute(s) which may apply to the application.

7. Will comply, or has already complied, with the requirements of Titles II and III of the Uniform Relocation Assistance and Real Property Acquisition Policies Act of 1970 (P.L. 91-646) which provide for fair and equitable treatment of persons displaced or whose property is acquired as a result of Federal or federally-assisted programs. These requirements apply to all interests in real property acquired for project purposes regardless of Federal participation in purchases.

8. Will comply, as applicable, with provisions of the Hatch Act (5 U.S.C. §§1501-1508 and 7324-7328) which limit the political activities of employees whose principal employment activities are funded in whole or in part with Federal funds.

9. Will comply, as applicable, with the provisions of the Davis-Bacon Act (40 U.S.C. §§276a to 276a-7), the Copeland Act (40 U.S.C. §276c and 18 U.S.C. §874), and the Contract Work Hours and Safety Standards Act (40 U.S.C. §§327-333), regarding labor standards for federally-assisted construction subagreements.

10. Will comply, if applicable, with flood insurance purchase requirements of Section 102(a) of the Flood Disaster Protection Act of 1973 (P.L. 93-234) which requires recipients in a special flood hazard area to participate in the program and to purchase flood insurance if the total cost of insurable construction and acquisition is $10,000 or more.

11. Will comply with environmental standards which may be prescribed pursuant to the following: (a) institution of environmental quality control measures under the National Environmental Policy Act of 1969 (P.L. 91-190) and Executive Order (EO) 11514; (b) notification of violating facilities pursuant to EO 11738; (c) protection of wetlands pursuant to EO 11990; (d) evaluation of flood hazards in floodplains in accordance with EO 11988; (e) assurance of project consistency with the approved State management program developed under the Coastal Zone Management Act of 1972 (16 U.S.C. §§1451 et seq.); (f) conformity of Federal actions to State (Clean Air) Implementation Plans under Section 176(c) of the Clean Air Act of 1955, as amended (42 U.S.C. §§7401 et seq.); (g) protection of underground sources of drinking water under the Safe Drinking Water Act of 1974, as amended (P.L. 93-523); and, (h) protection of endangered species under the Endangered Species Act of 1973, as amended (P.L. 93-205).

12. Will comply with the Wild and Scenic Rivers Act of 1968 (16 U.S.C. §§1271 et seq.) related to protecting components or potential components of the national wild and scenic rivers system.

13. Will assist the awarding agency in assuring compliance with Section 106 of the National Historic Preservation Act of 1966, as amended (16 U.S.C. §470), EO 11593 (identification and protection of historic properties), and the Archaeological and Historic Preservation Act of 1974 (16 U.S.C. §§469a-1 et seq.).

14. Will comply with P.L. 93-348 regarding the protection of human subjects involved in research, development, and related activities supported by this award of assistance.

15. Will comply with the Laboratory Animal Welfare Act of 1966 (P.L. 89-544, as amended, 7 U.S.C. §§2131 et seq.) pertaining to the care, handling, and treatment of warm blooded animals held for research, teaching, or other activities supported by this award of assistance.

16. Will comply with the Lead-Based Paint Poisoning Prevention Act (42 U.S.C. §§4801 et seq.) which prohibits the use of lead-based paint in construction or rehabilitation of residence structures.

17. Will cause to be performed the required financial and compliance audits in accordance with the Single Audit Act Amendments of 1996 and OMB Circular No. A-133, "Audits of States, Local Governments, and Non-Profit Organizations."

18. Will comply with all applicable requirements of all other Federal laws, executive orders, regulations, and policies governing this program.

SIGNATURE OF AUTHORIZED CERTIFYING OFFICIAL	TITLE
	SUPERINTENDENT
APPLICANT ORGANIZATION	DATE SUBMITTED
GREENCASTLE-ANTRIM SD.	7-3-03

Standard Form 424B (Rev. 7-97) Back

DISCLOSURE OF LOBBYING ACTIVITIES

Complete this form to disclose lobbying activities pursuant to 31 U.S.C. 1352

(See reverse for public burden disclosure.)

Approved by OMB

0348-0046

1. Type of Federal Action:	2. Status of Federal Action:	3. Report Type:
☐ a. contract b. grant c. cooperative agreement d. loan e. loan guarantee f. loan insurance	☐ a. bid/offer/application b. initial award c. post-award	☐ a. initial filing b. material change **For Material Change Only:** year _____ quarter _____ date of last report _____

4. Name and Address of Reporting Entity: ☐ Prime ☐ Subawardee Tier _____, *if known*: **Congressional District**, *if known*: 4c	5. If Reporting Entity in No. 4 is a Subawardee, Enter Name and Address of Prime: **Congressional District**, *if known*:
6. Federal Department/Agency:	7. Federal Program Name/Description: CFDA Number, *if applicable*: _____
8. Federal Action Number, *if known*:	9. Award Amount, *if known*: $
10. a. Name and Address of Lobbying Registrant (*if individual, last name, first name, MI*):	b. Individuals Performing Services (*including address if different from No. 10a*) (*last name, first name, MI*):

11. Information requested through this form is authorized by title 31 U.S.C. section 1352. This disclosure of lobbying activities is a material representation of fact upon which reliance was placed by the tier above when this transaction was made or entered into. This disclosure is required pursuant to 31 U.S.C. 1352. This information will be available for public inspection. Any person who fails to file the required disclosure shall be subject to a civil penalty of not less than $10,000 and not more than $100,000 for each such failure.	Signature: _____ Print Name: _____ Title: _____ Telephone No.: _____ Date: _____
Federal Use Only:	Authorized for Local Reproduction Standard Form LLL (Rev. 7-97)

INSTRUCTIONS FOR COMPLETION OF SF-LLL, DISCLOSURE OF LOBBYING ACTIVITIES

This disclosure form shall be completed by the reporting entity, whether subawardee or prime Federal recipient, at the initiation or receipt of a covered Federal action, or a material change to a previous filing, pursuant to title 31 U.S.C. section 1352. The filing of a form is required for each payment or agreement to make payment to any lobbying entity for influencing or attempting to influence an officer or employee of any agency, a Member of Congress, an officer or employee of Congress, or an employee of a Member of Congress in connection with a covered Federal action. Complete all items that apply for both the initial filing and material change report. Refer to the implementing guidance published by the Office of Management and Budget for additional information.

1. Identify the type of covered Federal action for which lobbying activity is and/or has been secured to influence the outcome of a covered Federal action.

2. Identify the status of the covered Federal action.

3. Identify the appropriate classification of this report. If this is a followup report caused by a material change to the information previously reported, enter the year and quarter in which the change occurred. Enter the date of the last previously submitted report by this reporting entity for this covered Federal action.

4. Enter the full name, address, city, State and zip code of the reporting entity. Include Congressional District, if known. Check the appropriate classification of the reporting entity that designates if it is, or expects to be, a prime or subaward recipient. Identify the tier of the subawardee, e.g., the first subawardee of the prime is the 1st tier. Subawards include but are not limited to subcontracts, subgrants and contract awards under grants.

5. If the organization filing the report in item 4 checks "Subawardee," then enter the full name, address, city, State and zip code of the prime Federal recipient. Include Congressional District, if known.

6. Enter the name of the Federal agency making the award or loan commitment. Include at least one organizational level below agency name, if known. For example, Department of Transportation, United States Coast Guard.

7. Enter the Federal program name or description for the covered Federal action (item 1). If known, enter the full Catalog of Federal Domestic Assistance (CFDA) number for grants, cooperative agreements, loans, and loan commitments.

8. Enter the most appropriate Federal identifying number available for the Federal action identified in item 1 (e.g., Request for Proposal (RFP) number; Invitation for Bid (IFB) number; grant announcement number; the contract, grant, or loan award number; the application/proposal control number assigned by the Federal agency). Include prefixes, e.g., "RFP-DE-90-001."

9. For a covered Federal action where there has been an award or loan commitment by the Federal agency, enter the Federal amount of the award/loan commitment for the prime entity identified in item 4 or 5.

10. (a) Enter the full name, address, city, State and zip code of the lobbying registrant under the Lobbying Disclosure Act of 1995 engaged by the reporting entity identified in item 4 to influence the covered Federal action.

    (b) Enter the full names of the individual(s) performing services, and include full address if different from 10 (a). Enter Last Name, First Name, and Middle Initial (MI).

11. The certifying official shall sign and date the form, print his/her name, title, and telephone number.

APPLICATION FOR FEDERAL ASSISTANCE		**2. DATE SUBMITTED**		Applicant Identifier	Version 7/03

1. TYPE OF SUBMISSION:

Application	Pre-application
☐ Construction	☐ Construction
☑ Non-Construction	☐ Non-Construction

3. DATE RECEIVED BY STATE	State Application Identifier
4. DATE RECEIVED BY FEDERAL AGENCY	Federal Identifier

5. APPLICANT INFORMATION

Legal Name:	**Organizational Unit:**
	Department:
Organizational DUNS:	Division:

Address:	**Name and telephone number of person to be contacted on matters involving this application (give area code)**
Street:	Prefix: First Name:
City:	Middle Name
County:	Last Name
State: Zip Code	Suffix:
Country:	Email:

6. EMPLOYER IDENTIFICATION NUMBER *(EIN):* ☐☐-☐☐☐☐☐☐☐	Phone Number (give area code) Fax Number (give area code)

8. TYPE OF APPLICATION:

☐ New   ☐ Continuation   ☐ Revision

If Revision, enter appropriate letter(s) in box(es)
(See back of form for description of letters.)   ☐   ☐

Other (specify)

7. TYPE OF APPLICANT: (See back of form for Application Types)

Other (specify)

9. NAME OF FEDERAL AGENCY:

10. CATALOG OF FEDERAL DOMESTIC ASSISTANCE NUMBER: ☐☐-☐☐☐ TITLE (Name of Program):	**11. DESCRIPTIVE TITLE OF APPLICANT'S PROJECT:**

12. AREAS AFFECTED BY PROJECT *(Cities, Counties, States, etc.):*

13. PROPOSED PROJECT		**14. CONGRESSIONAL DISTRICTS OF:**	
Start Date:	Ending Date:	a. Applicant	b. Project

15. ESTIMATED FUNDING:

a. Federal	$	.00
b. Applicant	$	.00
c. State	$	.00
d. Local	$	.00
e. Other	$	.00
f. Program Income	$	.00
g. TOTAL	$	.00

16. IS APPLICATION SUBJECT TO REVIEW BY STATE EXECUTIVE ORDER 12372 PROCESS?

a. Yes. ☐ THIS PREAPPLICATION/APPLICATION WAS MADE AVAILABLE TO THE STATE EXECUTIVE ORDER 12372 PROCESS FOR REVIEW ON

DATE:

b. No. ☐ PROGRAM IS NOT COVERED BY E. O. 12372

☐ OR PROGRAM HAS NOT BEEN SELECTED BY STATE FOR REVIEW

17. IS THE APPLICANT DELINQUENT ON ANY FEDERAL DEBT?

☐ Yes If "Yes" attach an explanation.   ☐ No

18. TO THE BEST OF MY KNOWLEDGE AND BELIEF, ALL DATA IN THIS APPLICATION/PREAPPLICATION ARE TRUE AND CORRECT. THE DOCUMENT HAS BEEN DULY AUTHORIZED BY THE GOVERNING BODY OF THE APPLICANT AND THE APPLICANT WILL COMPLY WITH THE ATTACHED ASSURANCES IF THE ASSISTANCE IS AWARDED.

a. Authorized Representative

Prefix	First Name	Middle Name
Last Name		Suffix
b. Title		c. Telephone Number (give area code)
d. Signature of Authorized Representative		e. Date Signed

Previous Edition Usable
Authorized for Local Reproduction

Standard Form 424 (Rev.9-2003)
Prescribed by OMB Circular A-102

Form Approved Through 09/30/2007

OMB No. 0925-0001

Department of Health and Human Services Public Health Services **Grant Application** *Do not exceed character length restrictions indicated.*	LEAVE BLANK—FOR PHS USE ONLY.		
	Type	Activity	Number
	Review Group		Formerly
	Council/Board (Month, Year)		Date Received

1. TITLE OF PROJECT *(Do not exceed 81 characters, including spaces and punctuation.)*

2. RESPONSE TO SPECIFIC REQUEST FOR APPLICATIONS OR PROGRAM ANNOUNCEMENT OR SOLICITATION ☐ NO ☐ YES
(If "Yes," state number and title)
Number: Title:

3. PRINCIPAL INVESTIGATOR/PROGRAM DIRECTOR	New Investigator ☐ No ☐ Yes	
3a. NAME (Last, first, middle)	3b. DEGREE(S)	3h. eRA Commons User Name
3c. POSITION TITLE	3d. MAILING ADDRESS *(Street. citv. state. zip code)*	
3e. DEPARTMENT, SERVICE, LABORATORY, OR EQUIVALENT		
3f. MAJOR SUBDIVISION		
3g. TELEPHONE AND FAX *(Area code, number and extension)* TEL: FAX:	E-MAIL ADDRESS:	

4. HUMAN SUBJECTS RESEARCH No ☐ Yes ☐	4b. Human Subjects Assurance No.	5. VERTEBRATE ANIMALS ☐ No ☐ Yes	
	4c. Clinical Trial ☐ No ☐ Yes	4d. NIH-defined Phase III Clinical Trial ☐ No ☐ Yes	5a. If "Yes," IACUC approval Date	5b. Animal welfare assurance no.
4a. Research Exempt No ☐ Yes ☐	If "Yes," Exemption No.		

6. DATES OF PROPOSED PERIOD OF SUPPORT *(month, day, year—MM/DD/YY)*		7. COSTS REQUESTED FOR INITIAL BUDGET PERIOD		8. COSTS REQUESTED FOR PROPOSED PERIOD OF SUPPORT	
From	Through	7a. Direct Costs ($)	7b. Total Costs ($)	8a. Direct Costs ($)	8b. Total Costs ($)

9. APPLICANT ORGANIZATION	10. TYPE OF ORGANIZATION
Name Address	Public: → ☐ Federal ☐ State ☐ Local Private: → ☐ Private Nonprofit For-profit: → ☐ General ☐ Small Business ☐ Woman-owned ☐ Socially and Economically Disadvantaged
	11. ENTITY IDENTIFICATION NUMBER DUNS NO. Cong. District

12. ADMINISTRATIVE OFFICIAL TO BE NOTIFIED IF AWARD IS MADE	13. OFFICIAL SIGNING FOR APPLICANT ORGANIZATION
Name	Name
Title	Title
Address	Address
Tel: FAX:	Tel: FAX:
E-Mail:	E-Mail:

14. PRINCIPAL INVESTIGATOR/PROGRAM DIRECTOR ASSURANCE: I certify that the statements herein are true, complete and accurate to the best of my knowledge. I am aware that any false, fictitious, or fraudulent statements or claims may subject me to criminal, civil, or administrative penalties. I agree to accept responsibility for the scientific conduct of the project and to provide the required progress reports if a grant is awarded as a result of this application.	SIGNATURE OF PI/PD NAMED IN 3a. *(In ink. "Per" signature not acceptable.)*	DATE
15. APPLICANT ORGANIZATION CERTIFICATION AND ACCEPTANCE: I certify that the statements herein are true, complete and accurate to the best of my knowledge, and accept the obligation to comply with Public Health Services terms and conditions if a grant is awarded as a result of this application. I am aware that any false, fictitious, or fraudulent statements or claims may subject me to criminal, civil, or administrative penalties.	SIGNATURE OF OFFICIAL NAMED IN 13. *(In ink. "Per" signature not acceptable.)*	DATE

PHS 398 (Rev. 09/04)   Face Page   **Form Page 1**

DOE F 4650.2
(10-99)
(All Other Editions Are Obsolete)

Department of Energy
Office of Science (SC)

Face Page

OMB Control No.
1910-1400
(OMB Burden Disclosure
Statement on Back)

TITLE OF PROPOSED RESEARCH: _____

1. CATALOG OF FEDERAL DOMESTIC ASSISTANCE #:
   81.049

2. CONGRESSIONAL DISTRICT:
   Applicant Organization's District: _____
   Project Site's District: _____

3. I.R.S. ENTITY IDENTIFICATION OR SSN:

4. AREA OF RESEARCH OR ANNOUNCEMENT TITLE/#:

5. HAS THIS RESEARCH PROPOSAL BEEN SUBMITTED
   TO ANY OTHER FEDERAL AGENCY?
   Yes ____   No ____
   PLEASE LIST: _____

6. DOE/OER PROGRAM STAFF CONTACT (if known):

7. TYPE OF APPLICATION:
   New ____   Renewal ____
   Continuation ____   Revision ____
   Supplement ____

8. ORGANIZATION TYPE:
   Local Govt. ____   State Govt. ____
   Non-Profit ✔   Hospital ____
   Indian Tribal Govt. ____   Individual ____
   Other ____   Inst. of Higher Educ. ____
   For-Profit ____
   Small Business ____   Disadvan. Business ____
   Women-Owned ____   8(a) ____

9. CURRENT DOE AWARD # (IF APPLICABLE):

10. WILL THIS RESEARCH INVOLVE:
    10A Human Subjects No ____   If yes, ____
        Exemption No. _____ **or**
        IRB Approval Date _____
        Assurance of Compliance No: _____
    10B Vertebrate Animals No ____   If yes, ____
        IACUC Approval Date _____
        Animal Welfare Assurance No: _____

11. AMOUNT REQUESTED FROM DOE FOR ENTIRE
    PROJECT PERIOD $ _____

12. DURATION OF ENTIRE PROJECT PERIOD:
    _____ **to** _____
    Mo/day/yr.   Mo/day/yr.

13. REQUESTED AWARD START DATE
    _____ (Mo/day/yr.)

14. IS APPLICANT DELINQUENT ON ANY FEDERAL DEBT?
    Yes (attach an explanation) ____   No ✔

15. PRINCIPAL INVESTIGATOR/PROGRAM DIRECTOR
    NAME, TITLE, ADDRESS, AND PHONE NUMBER

16. ORGANIZATION'S NAME, ADDRESS AND CERTIFYING
    REPRESENTATIVE'S NAME, TITLE, AND PHONE NUMBER

SIGNATURE OF PRINCIPAL INVESTIGATOR/
PROGRAM DIRECTOR
_____ Date

PI/PD ASSURANCE: I agree to accept responsibility for the scientific conduct of the project and to
provide the required progress reports if an award is made as a result of this submission. Willful
provision of false information is a criminal offense. (U.S. Code, Title 18, Section 1001).

SIGNATURE OF ORGANIZATION'S CERTIFYING
REPRESENTATIVE
_____ Date

CERTIFICATION & ACCEPTANCE: I certify that the statements herein are true and complete to the
best of my knowledge, and accept the obligation to comply with DOE terms and conditions if an
award is made as the result of this submission. A willfully false certification is a criminal offense.
(U.S. Code, Title 18, Section 1001).

NOTICE FOR HANDLING PROPOSALS
This submission is to be used only for DOE evaluation purposes and this notice shall be affixed to any reproduction or abstract thereof. All Government and non-Government personnel handling this submission shall
exercise extreme care to ensure that the information contained herein is not duplicated, used, or disclosed in whole or in part for any purpose other than evaluation without written permission except that if an
award is made based on this submission, the terms of the award shall control disclosure and use. This notice does not limit the Government's right to use information contained in the submission if it is obtainable
from another source without restriction. This is a Government notice, and shall not itself be construed to impose any liability upon the Government or Government personnel for any disclosure or use of data
contained in this submission.
PRIVACY ACT STATEMENT
If applicable, you are requested, in accordance with 5 U.S.C., Sec. 562A, to voluntarily provide your Social Security Number (SSN). However, you will not be denied any right, benefit, or privilege provided by
law because of a refusal to disclose your SSN. We request your SSN to aid in accurate identification, referral and review of applications for research/training support for efficient management of Office of Science
grant/contract programs.

Application for Federal Education Assistance (ED 424)

U.S. Department of Education
Form Approved
OMB No. 1890-0017
Exp. OMB Approved

Applicant Information

1. Name and Address

Legal Name: _____

Address: _____

City _____

Organizational Unit

_____

State _____ County _____ ZIP Code + 4 _____ - ___

2. Applicant's D-U-N-S Number ☐☐☐☐☐☐☐☐☐

3. Applicant's T-I-N ☐☐ - ☐☐☐☐☐☐☐

4. Catalog of Federal Domestic Assistance #: **8 4** ☐☐☐

Title: _____

5. Project Director: _____

Address: _____

City _____ State _____ ZIP Code + 4 _____ - ___

Tel. #: _____ Fax #: _____

E-Mail Address: _____

6. Novice Applicant ☐ Yes ☐ No

7. Is the applicant delinquent on any Federal debt? ☐ Yes ☐ No
(If "Yes," attach an explanation.)

8. Type of Applicant *(Enter appropriate letter in the box.)* ☐

  A State   G Public College or University
  B Local   H Private, Non-Profit College or University
  C Special District   I Non-Profit Organization
  D Indian Tribe   J Private, Profit-Making Organization
  E Individual   K Other *(Specify):*_____
  F Independent School
     District   _____

9. State Application Identifier: _____

Application Information

10. Type of Submission:

—*PreApplication*   —*Application*

☐ Construction   ☐ Construction

☐ Non-Construction   ☐ Non-Construction

11. Is application subject to review by Executive Order 12372 process?

☐ Yes *(Date made available to the Executive Order 12372 process for review):* _____

☐ No *(If "No," check appropriate box below.)*

  ☐ Program is not covered by E.O. 12372.

  ☐ Program has not been selected by State for review.

            Start Date: **End Date:**

12. Proposed Project Dates: _____ _____

13. Are any research activities involving human subjects planned at any time during the proposed project period?

☐ Yes (Go to 13a.)   ☐ No (Go to item 14.)

13a. Are **all** the research activities proposed designated to be exempt from the regulations?

☐ Yes (Provide Exemption(s) #): _____

☐ No (Provide Assurance #): _____

14. Descriptive Title of Applicant's Project:

Estimated Funding

15a. Federal	$	.00
b. Applicant	$	.00
c. State	$	.00
d. Local	$	.00
e. Other	$	.00
f. Program Income	$	.00
g. TOTAL	$	.00

Authorized Representative Information

16. To the best of my knowledge and belief, all data in this preapplication/application are true and correct. The document has been duly authorized by the governing body of the applicant and the applicant will comply with the attached assurances if the assistance is awarded.

a. Authorized Representative *(Please type or print name clearly.)*

b. Title

c. Tel. #: _____ Fax #: _____

d. E-Mail Address:

e. Signature of Authorized Representative   Date: _____

APPLICATION COVER SHEET FOR NEH GRANT PROGRAMS

1. PROJECT DIRECTOR OR INDIVIDUAL APPLICANT

❏ Mr. ❏ Mrs. ❏ Ms. ❏ Dr. ❏ Prof.   Major Field of Study: _____

Name (last, first, middle): _____

Address: _____

_____

City:_____ State: _____ Zip Code: _____

E-mail: _____

Telephone (work): _____ (home): _____ Fax: _____

2. INSTITUTION INFORMATION

Name: _____

Address: _____

_____

City: _____ State: _____ Zip Code: _____

DUNS Number: _____ Employer ID Number: _____

3. TYPE OF APPLICANT

		Fellowships, Stipends, &
❏ Institution	❏ Individual	*Faculty Research Awards*

Type: _____   Citizenship: ❏ US ❏ Other   ❏ University ❏ College Teacher /

Status: ❏ Private Nonprofit   Country:_____   Teacher   Ind. Scholar

❏ Unit of State/Local Gov't   Month/Year:_____   ❏ Jr. Scholar ❏ Sr. Scholar

4. CONGRESSIONAL DISTRICT: _____

5. GRANT PROGRAM: _____

6. TYPE OF APPLICATION: ❏ New   ❏ Supplement   Current Grant Number(s): _____

7. PROJECT FIELD CODE: _____

8. PROJECT TITLE: _____

9. PROJECT DESCRIPTION (use only space provided):

10. REQUESTED GRANT PERIOD: From: _____ To: _____

OMB No. 3136-0134 ~ Expires 6/30/06

Applicant Name: _____

Project Title: _____

11. PROJECT FUNDING FOR INSTITUTIONS

Programs other than Challenge Grants

a. Outright Funds $_____

b. Federal Match $_____

c. Total from NEH $_____

d. Cost Sharing $_____

e. Total Project Costs $_____

Challenge Grants applicants only

a. Fiscal Year #1 $_____

b. Fiscal Year #2 $_____

c. Fiscal Year #3 $_____

d. Total from NEH $_____

e. Non-Federal Match $_____

f. Total $_____

12. ADDITIONAL FUNDING

Will this proposal be submitted to another NEH division, government agency, or private entity for funding?

❑ Yes   ❑ No   If yes, indicate where and when: _____

_____

13. GRANT ADMINISTRATOR INFORMATION FOR INSTITUTIONS

❑ Mr. ❑ Mrs. ❑ Ms. ❑ Dr. ❑ Prof.   Title: _____

Name (last, first, middle): _____

Institution: _____

Address: _____

_____

City: _____ State:_____ Zip: _____

Telephone: _____ Fax: _____

E-mail: _____

14. FELLOWSHIPS AND SUMMER STIPENDS APPLICANTS

List the name, department, and institutional affiliation of your referees.

a. _____

b. _____

Summer Stipends applicants only: Provide the name, title, and signature of your nominating official.

Printed name: _____ Title: _____

Signature: _____ Date: _____

15. CERTIFICATION

By signing and submitting this application, the individual applicant or authorizing official certifies that all statements contained herein are true and correct to the best of their knowledge and belief, and, if applying for more than $100,000, is providing the certification on lobbying activities as set forth in these guidelines.

Printed name of individual applicant / authorizing official: _____

Title of individual applicant / authorizing official: _____

Signature: _____ Date: _____

For NEH use only: date received: application #:   initials: